Praise for *Managing AI Projects*

Packed with practical insights, proven frameworks, and real world examples, *Managing AI Projects* demystifies the complexity of delivering a successful AI implementation. It shows you how to align teams, manage risk, and translate technical innovation into measurable impact. In an era of rapid technological evolution, *Managing AI Projects* is your roadmap to keeping strategy, people, and technology moving in sync. It's become my new reference guide for implementing AI projects.

—*Jason Nitz, mining technical and operations consultant*

This book is an excellent resource treating AI project management as a serious discipline. It combines technical realism, delivery pragmatism, and organizational insight in a way that most other AI books avoid. A must-read for any project manager responsible for turning AI ambition into real world outcomes.

—*Sheldon Rodrigues, senior applied scientist, Microsoft*

Managing AI Projects

*Drive Innovation and Successfully Navigate
the Full AI Project Lifecycle*

Malini Jain Runtasewee and
Adrián González Sánchez

Managing AI Projects

by Malini Jain Runtasewee and Adrián González Sánchez

Published by O'Reilly Media, Inc., 141 Stony Circle, Suite 195, Santa Rosa, CA 95401.

O'Reilly books may be purchased for educational, business, or sales promotional use. Online editions are also available for most titles (*https://oreilly.com*). For more information, contact our corporate/institutional sales department: 800-998-9938 or *corporate@oreilly.com*.

Acquisitions Editor: David Michelson	**Indexer:** BIM Creatives, LLC
Development Editor: Angela Rufino	**Cover Designer:** Susan Thompson
Production Editor: Christopher Faucher	**Cover Illustrator:** Susan Thompson
Copyeditor: Paula L. Fleming	**Interior Designer:** Monica Kamsvaag
Proofreader: J.M. Olejarz	**Interior Illustrator:** Kate Dullea

May 2026:   First Edition

Revision History for the First Edition

2026-05-19:   First Release

See *https://oreilly.com/catalog/errata.csp?isbn=9798341641013* for release details.

979-8-341-64101-3

[LSI]

Contents

Preface: Our AI Project Management Dream

Here we are. The fourth O'Reilly book after my first three titles: *Kubernetes and Cloud Native Associate (KCNA) Study Guide, Azure OpenAI Service for Cloud Native Applications,* and *Generative AI on Microsoft Azure*. All of them focus heavily on cloud computing and artificial intelligence and are fairly technical. As an author, I like to think these books help people who are not necessarily hypertechnical understand complex topics and join the tech industry. Due to personal bias and writing style, I believe some of these books are great resources for software architects and technical product managers, who are part of that privileged cohort of hybrid professionals with mastery of both technical and business topics, especially in this era of artificial intelligence.

Also part of that group are traditional project managers (PMs)—or they can be, at least. Often misunderstood and confused with other roles that accompany Agile methodologies, like scrum masters and product owners, PMs are among the tactical professionals who manage and facilitate work at different levels, including projects, programs, and portfolios. Yet regardless of their role in the organization or their job title, PMs have taken longer than many others to join the wave of AI learning and upskilling.

Don't get me wrong: there are wonderful PMs working on data and AI projects who possess a relatively high level of technical knowledge and the ability to help all sorts of technical professionals perform several times better.

But it is also true that we see, for example, more product managers than project managers with appropriate levels of AI understanding, likely due to the fact that AI adoption has arisen mostly in product-led organizations. This is changing, though, with more kinds of organizations adopting AI and including it in their projects. The trend directly impacts the project management professionals who are leading and facilitating AI projects.

Nonetheless, the increasing number of AI projects hasn't yet resulted in a larger number of people who want to learn and apply AI project management. There are plenty of resources dedicated to "AI for project managers," when this is defined as a set of AI tools to help PMs increase their productivity and manage their projects more efficiently. However, there is very limited research and few resources (including books and courses) that focus on the details of how these professionals can manage and lead their projects to a successful end.

As part of my personal mission to alter this landscape, I started teaching AI project management topics in 2019 at multiple institutions in Canada (Concordia University and HEC Montréal) and Spain (IE University and the ethical AI observatory OdiseIA). I then expanded on the course content and decided to bring it to the O'Reilly online training platform, with recurrent sessions intended to demystify the specifics of managing AI projects. These sessions included live demonstrations of AI project roadmaps with definitions of tasks, estimates, and assignments to different team members. I regularly collected feedback from course attendees and started to observe a pattern of project management professionals having no or elementary knowledge of AI but a great interest in incorporating AI knowledge into their new AI projects.

And, of course, I paid special attention to neutral or negative feedback to understand my students' key concerns and needs. From those comments, I understood that once the AI project lifecycle terms were clear, a lot of project management topics related to Agile methodologies and operational concerns, such as planning, estimating, and delivering projects on time, were similar to those of any other project they were managing. I got very positive feedback from the live demonstrations, because the PMs could get solutions for challenges they had never faced before. I confirmed this point during other professional coaching and tutoring activities with the participants in the MIT Sloan/CSAIL GetSmarter course, in which we had to build and evaluate AI project plans for multiple industries and thousands of organizations.

My coauthor for this book, Malini Jain Runtasewee, complements this background by bringing a very rare skill set that includes not only the ability to manage complex projects for cloud, data, and AI implementations but also the capacity to get the best performance from varied different team members. I say "rare" because she is able to continue evolving her playbook project after project without being perceived by teammates as manipulative or bossy. She guides, coaches, and helps everyone understand their role and key expectations while connecting points, extracting dependencies, and anticipating risks that are highly specific to the data and AI roles and activities of the project.

That said, the challenge for this book was clear: how to strike a balance between the AI and project management fundamentals and the techniques and terms that an AI project manager needs to know. This book addresses exactly that. These chapters cover a mix of topics that will enable you, our dear reader, to leverage best practices with real and immediate value, as well as tools and templates for your project-planning activities. No matter what your exact project management background is, you will find this book not only easy to understand but also specific enough to develop your body of knowledge in AI project management.

In this book, you will learn our EMED (exploration, mobilization, execution, and delivery) methodology for AI project management. This approach, based on our combined experience and then tested and improved over the years, applies to both our extensive experience with managing technology projects and our experience with AI projects in companies around the world. And this book is only the core piece of a wider learning experience, which also includes new O'Reilly learning paths and live online trainings (*https://oreil.ly/6aCGb*), as well as other courses on LinkedIn Learning (*https://oreil.ly/CTTUo*), DeepLearning.ai (*https://oreil.ly/IXbM5*), and other platforms.

We hope you find this book informative. We also hope you enjoy it. This book is a very personal project, one that draws on many professionals' stories, ongoing discussions with friends and colleagues, and a vision of how project management best practices and practitioners need to evolve, upskill, and increase their level of specialization to bring tangible value to AI projects and teams. It is an obvious statement nowadays, but it took time for the project management field to understand and adopt AI and to embrace this new era of advanced, tactical AI management.

—Adrián González Sánchez

Who This Book Is For

This book is a practical guide to AI project management. Instead of simply combining AI and traditional project management concepts, it goes deep into project and technical lifecycles and the techniques required to successfully implement AI initiatives from initial ideation through final delivery. For that reason, this book is a great resource for:

- *Experienced project managers* who need practical frameworks to plan, scope, de-risk, and deliver AI projects in real-world environments

- *Scrum masters and product owners* who want to adapt Agile practices to the uncertainty, experimentation, and data dependency of AI work

- *Technical professionals* (e.g., data scientists, machine learning [ML] engineers, AI engineers, developers) who want to better understand governance, stakeholder management, delivery structures, and how their work fits into larger business outcomes

- *Other tactical managers* (e.g., product, operations, and IT managers; innovation and transformation leads) responsible for executing AI initiatives and coordinating cross-functional teams

- *Executives and managers* looking for guidance on hiring and needing clarity on processes, roles, team design, lifecycle governance, etc.

- *Coaches and consultants* who support organizations through AI transformations and need structured, field-tested delivery models to guide clients effectively

- *Entry-level professionals and career switchers* who seek a practical, structured introduction to how organizations' AI projects are actually run

How This Book Is Organized

This book presents an end-to-end approach to AI project management. Organized into seven chapters (see Figure P-1), it offers all the knowledge you will need to succeed in your job and, if desired, to land another position in today's competitive job market. It also provides plenty of notes, advice, and answers to questions like "Why is this relevant for AI project managers?" and "How is this different from regular project management?" Moreover, you'll appreciate the incremental approach we take, allowing you to build your knowledge step-by-step.

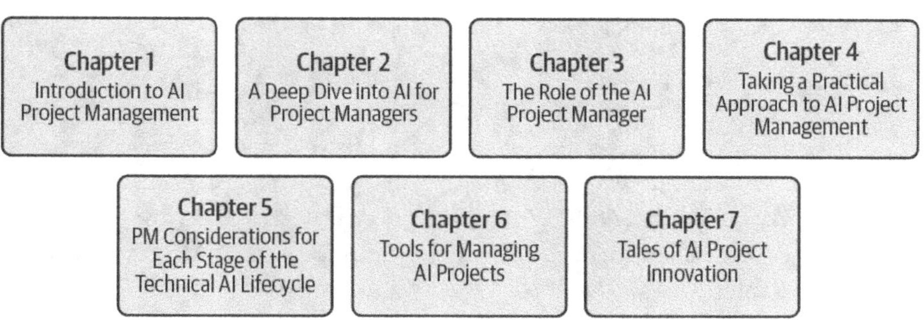

Figure P-1. This book's topics by chapter

Chapter 1, "Introduction to AI Project Management"
Offering far more than the usual primer, this chapter will go into the details of AI project management, including the reasons why it has become a new domain of work, the key considerations involved in its practice (especially compared to regular project management), and the main challenges and concerns PMs need to be aware of when dealing with AI projects. This chapter sets the stage for the rest of the book, establishing foundational knowledge of the topic, and will be a useful basis for moving forward regardless of your AI, project management, and AI project management experience.

Chapter 2, "A Deep Dive into AI for Project Managers"
Because we believe that no PM can manage AI projects without certain baseline AI knowledge, this chapter gets more technical, explaining key terms and technologies. It then connects this information to AI project management topics such as anticipating potential risks related to new and less mature technologies, the impact of technology stack choice on the pace

of implementation and total project duration, and how the feasibility of specific use cases depends on the type of AI technology used. In summary, Chapter 2 will contribute to your evolution toward being a "technical project manager."

Chapter 3, "The Role of the AI Project Manager"

The third chapter covers the role of the AI project manager and the relationship of the AI PM with every other stakeholder and role, including technical team members. It explores all the considerations involved in managing AI teams and discusses techniques specific to the context of data and AI teams, taking a PM-centric perspective on the topic.

Chapter 4, "Applied Approach to AI Project Management"

This chapter discusses our distinctive approach to AI project management, from the atypical AI project management lifecycle stages that we use in our day-to-day work to ways of combining project management methodologies you may be familiar with. With a focus on risk anticipation and mitigation, this chapter will prepare you for the technical aspects of AI lifecycles in the next chapter.

Chapter 5, "PM Considerations During the Technical AI Lifecycle"

This chapter brings the perspective of AI project management to each stage of the project implementation lifecycle. In fact, this is the second technical deep dive in this book, taking you through a series of stages and more-granular steps, while keeping in mind the role of the AI project manager and its importance to the progress of the entire team.

Chapter 6, "Tools for Managing AI Projects"

This chapter explains the technical toolkit for both managing and implementing AI projects. We discuss how to use the PM tools you may already be familiar with for AI projects, and we'll cover other technical tools you need to know how to use for your work with technical teams.

Chapter 7, "Tales of AI Project Innovation"

The last chapter contains a series of project experiences, illustrative examples, and applied recommendations that will help bring to life the situations you may face in the complex reality of AI projects.

In summary, the topics covered in these chapters address everything you need to upskill and shine as an AI project manager, positioning you to differentiate your skill set and the value you can add to data and AI teams.

O'Reilly Online Learning

For more than 40 years, *O'Reilly Media* has provided technology and business training, knowledge, and insight to help companies succeed.

Our unique network of experts and innovators share their knowledge and expertise through books, articles, and our online learning platform. O'Reilly's online learning platform gives you on-demand access to live training courses, in-depth learning paths, interactive coding environments, and a vast collection of text and video from O'Reilly and 200+ other publishers. For more information, visit *https://oreilly.com*.

How to Contact Us

Please address comments and questions concerning this book to the publisher:

O'Reilly Media, Inc.

141 Stony Circle, Suite 195

Santa Rosa, CA 95401

800-889-8969 (in the United States or Canada)

707-827-7019 (international or local)

707-829-0104 (fax)

support@oreilly.com

https://oreilly.com/about/contact.html

We have a web page for this book, where we list errata and any additional information. You can access this page at *https://oreil.ly/managing-AI-projects*.

For news and information about our books and courses, visit *https://oreilly.com*.

Find us on LinkedIn: *https://linkedin.com/company/oreilly*.

Watch us on YouTube: *https://youtube.com/oreillymedia*.

Acknowledgments

This book represents an extraordinary personal and collective effort to put together years of experience, customized frameworks and models, and a bunch of best practices and learnings from all kinds of mistakes and challenges in the field.

At a personal level, it is a very special project because we got the opportunity to work together. Married in real life, we are partners in crime for this writing adventure. So we have to thank each other for the passion, knowledge, and effort we each dedicated to make this book a reality. Even more important, we are very thankful for the continuous support and love of our family. Thank you all for everything—we are very lucky.

We must give a shout-out to the amazing work from the entire O'Reilly team. Thanks, David, for believing in this project. Thank you, Angela and Melissa, for your work during the entire writing process. Thanks to the production, design, and illustrations teams—you folks know how to convert raw text into an amazing-looking book. Thank you all, technical reviewers, for putting real effort into reading and analyzing every single detail of the final manuscript.

And finally, thank you, everyone, for all the kind notes, private messages, questions, and pieces of advice. Every time one person tells us that the book is making their AI projects a bit better and more successful, we feel the effort of creating this book was all worth it.

This is for you, Khun Mae Sukon Runtasewee. Thank you for everything. We miss you.

Introduction to AI Project Management

A few years ago, AI project management wasn't really a thing. There are several flavors of projects involving AI, machine learning, and related technologies, but managing AI projects didn't seem to be an area of study for project managers. Somehow, no one thought it would require new techniques or knowledge…until companies started to adopt AI and experience project failure. You probably heard the stories: unjustified return on investment (ROI), only 20% of projects succeeding (based on statistics from Gartner and others (*https://oreil.ly/SZMqn*)), eternal cycles of AI proof-of-conceptionitis (or being afraid to actually move to production and stop the experimentation phase). Implementing AI is not easy. It requires specialization at all levels, from technical roles to executive stakeholders, including all tactical roles at the project, product, program, and portfolio levels.

But still, you may be asking: Why focus on the project manager (PM)? Why is this role so important for the art of managing AI projects? This chapter will explain how PMs contribute to every aspect of AI projects. The following list previews how the role interacts with other project stakeholders:

Executive sponsors

Unlike other tactical managers, project-level professionals focus on the prioritization, planning, implementation, and completion of AI projects. That means that PMs are the point people for sharing relevant news with any executive who wants to understand the progress of their AI projects. As a team member who sits between the AI delivery team and the executive sponsors, an AI project manager can serve as a translator, or interface, between business and technical stakeholders.

Technical teams

Project managers and people in related Agile roles, such as scrum masters and product owners, spend a fair amount of time with the technical teams. There is a relational aspect to PM work that relies on having some empathy and emotional intelligence. The PM reads the day-to-day dynamics, coaches team members, understands potential blockers, finds a way to get additional resources, and adapts their leadership approach to the science, engineering, development, or design background of the technical team members.

Clients and partners

Due to the hybrid and multidisciplinary nature of their role, AI project managers are uniquely positioned to share project progress with relevant stakeholders, calibrating their reports to include an appropriate level of detail. This means sharing concrete information about project progress, for example, during and after project sprints. Key to success as a communicator is developing your hybrid profile by increasing your level of technical knowledge while optimizing your AI PM approach. (Good news—that is the goal of this book!)

Other tactical managers

While AI PMs focus on project details and progress, other professionals—such as product, program, and portfolio managers—work at different levels in the organization. They may handle AI products or a set of projects within a program/portfolio, but their type and scope of action is different. You, as an AI project manager, can bring concrete project insights, anticipate day-to-day roadblocks, spot needs for new resources, and so forth. While these tasks are not specific to AI (for example, check out this report from the Project Management Institute (*https://oreil.ly/VpRAR*) on collaboration between project and product professionals), this level of collaboration will be very relevant if your organization has these roles and you need to coordinate and collaborate with them.

These collaborative workstreams are closely tied to how we manage AI within organizations. Managing them requires a multilevel approach that combines top-down and bottom-up initiatives. Let's now explore the various levels of AI management.

Levels of AI Management

All the stakeholders that you'll interact with as an AI project manager are related to the trifecta of strategic, tactical, and technical/operational AI management within the company, as you can see in Figure 1-1.

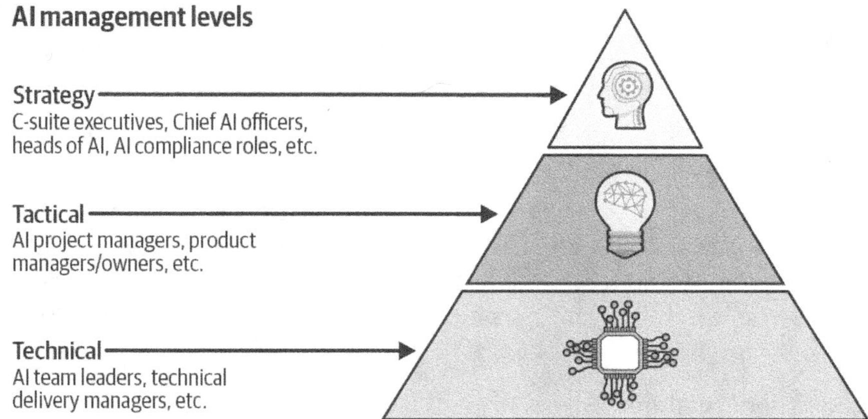

Figure 1-1. Levels of AI management

Let's discuss each level in more detail as a way to examine how your role contributes to the different levels of your company's AI management.

LEVEL 1: AI STRATEGY

The top level is top-down and strategic, aligning AI with the organization's overall business strategy. The AI strategy should lay the foundation for properly implementing AI technologies, based on a series of strategic pillars. Each of these AI maturity pillars establishes a top-down framework for embedding AI across the enterprise.

Business strategy

The business strategy defines how AI can align with organizational goals and create sustainable value. It emphasizes a long-term vision and objectives for AI adoption. Key objectives include improving operational efficiency, enhancing customer satisfaction, unlocking new revenue streams, and gaining a competitive edge.

Technology and data strategy

This area focuses on the infrastructure and data management strategies needed to enable effective AI solutions. It involves selecting the right technologies, managing data pipelines, and integrating systems. For example, it may be important to choose and deploy cloud platforms that are capable of handling large data volumes and training complex AI models; to build robust pipelines for data processing and analysis to ensure accessibility, cleanliness, and quality; or to leverage big data technologies and distributed storage to integrate AI into broader enterprise systems.

AI expertise and development strategy

This pillar involves the development and practical implementation of AI models within the organization. It emphasizes continuous experimentation, alignment with business objectives, technical feasibility, ROI, and impact on business processes. There are two main workstreams that contribute to the continuous increase of internal AI expertise.

Organizational culture

It is important to consider the cultural and organizational readiness to adopt AI, including the workforce's degree of technical and change management skills and openness to innovation and experimentation. Some potential actions include launching internal training programs to upskill employees in AI; fostering innovation and encouraging openness to technological change through hackathons, innovation labs, and incentives for new ideas; and leveraging multidisciplinary teams or pods in which AI experts work side by side with domain specialists to foster collaboration and knowledge sharing.

Internal AI governance

A good governance program ensures that AI is used ethically and responsibly within the organization. Some of the key elements of proper end-to-end AI governance are these:

Ethical AI principles

A good first step is to establish some AI principles that are aligned with the organization's values. These principles function as a declaration of intentions. The Principled Artificial Intelligence (*https://oreil.ly/Mk_88*) initiative, developed by the Berkman Klein Center for Internet & Society at Harvard University, includes a comprehensive collection of references to existing AI principles from various organizations around the world and highlights those that are most common. These include transparency, respect for privacy, and human control and oversight, among others.

Dedicated roles

AI governance is an important but time-consuming task. It shouldn't be handled as a solo mission but rather as a team sport, as it requires a combination of people and competencies to turn ethical ideation into action. Companies set up AI ethics committees to review and approve AI projects from an ethical perspective, and the work of those committees may converge with that of existing data ethics groups or corporate social responsibility (CSR) initiatives. Some companies also create a functional role known as the responsible AI champion, often taken on by an existing member of the organization as an additional responsibility. The role of an AI project manager can easily converge with that of the AI champion, as the PM can leverage their hybrid technical and project management skills to analyze the risks of AI initiatives in light of the organization's overall context and direction.

Alignment with external context

This is a never-ending exercise that depends on factors such as the organization's geographic location, business sector, and usage of AI as well as the role of sensitive and personal data in its business. Alignment requires following best practices as given shape by regulations and standards. For example, the European Union's Artificial Intelligence Act (AI Act), the National Institute of Standards and Technology's (NIST's) rules to support responsible AI use, and the ISO 42001:2023 framework for an AI management system define responsible AI deployment requirements at both the organizational and use case level. Alignment may include establishing internal AI usage policies to ensure compliance and the ethical use of AI and other technologies.

Though it's often seen as a "dry" topic, we believe that AI governance is a promising area, and understanding it is an important part of your AI upskilling journey. If you want to learn more about implementing AI governance in your organization, check out Adrián's other content for O'Reilly (*https://oreil.ly/adrian-gonzalez-sanchez*), which goes into more detail on how to operationalize responsible AI approaches.

These areas are interconnected and collectively contribute to *AI maturity*. To be successful, an AI strategy must be holistic, integrating technology, business alignment, organizational readiness, governance, and culture. Your role as an AI project manager is critical to connecting high-level strategy to tangible day-to-day AI activity.

LEVEL 2: TACTICAL MANAGEMENT

While the strategic level focuses on the medium to long term, Level 2 emphasizes short- to medium-term tactical management of AI-related initiatives. By convention, this is your playground as an AI project manager, but you'll come to understand that your influence within the organization goes beyond just this level. Here we will highlight one kind of initiative that supports and enables AI management at scale: establishing *AI Centers of Excellence (AI CoE)* and providing them with appropriate resources to translate the top-down strategy into tangible actions.

In general terms, creating AI CoEs is a common approach to standardizing best practices and accelerating AI maturity. Some typical responsibilities of the CoE include identifying priority use cases, defining measurable business and technical key performance indicators (KPIs), helping to develop AI project roadmaps, securing executive sponsorship, defining and evolving the company's technology stack based on both technical and financial planning, and promoting an AI culture via collaboration and new learning programs.

Obviously, CoEs are tightly linked to day-to-day project management activities, and depending on your company's internal structure, you may be in a position to either join an existing CoE or to contribute to—or even lead—the creation of a new one.

But none of this serves any purpose if the first two levels (strategic and tactical) are not backed by a solid operational and technical level of AI management, which is exactly what our third level is about.

LEVEL 3: TECHNICAL MANAGEMENT

This level focuses on the technical tasks that underpin effective AI design, implementation, maintenance, and performance. Though informed and fed by the first two levels, it also connects AI learnings to general organizational best practices. Let's go over some of the key workstreams.

Defining the technology stack

This includes not only defining the platforms and tooling required to use, develop, and maintain new AI developments but also designing the AI architectures that will connect all the elements. Defining the technology stack is an iterative exercise, as AI and data architectures span the enterprise but also adapt to specific projects and, in the process, add new pieces to the puzzle. For example, integrating AI into an existing data platform enhances both the project and the company's overall AI maturity, but you may need to add other tools (e.g., new databases, AI frameworks) for a second project. In Figure 1-2, you can see an illustrative example of data and AI architecture.

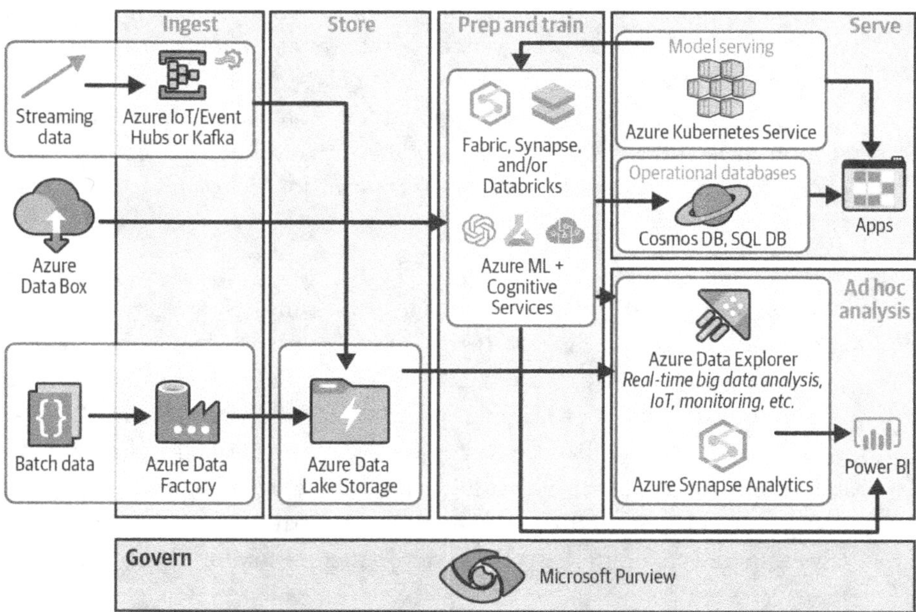

Figure 1-2. Illustrative AI architecture with Microsoft Azure

In Figure 1-2, the main elements are visualized as aggregated blocks of data and AI functionalities. Reading from left to right:

Data integration and ingestion
> This technology block handles periodic batch or real-time data ingestion, transformation, and distribution from diverse sources, including enterprise resource planning (ERP) systems, customer relationship management

(CRM) tools, and even Internet of Things (IoT) remote sensors. This block serves as the connection between those systems and your data and AI platform.

Data management and storage

The second layer includes relational (SQL) and NoSQL databases, data lakes, and distributed storage with encryption and access control. It is the foundation for model training, or fueling AI with specific knowledge bases. Data management and governance tools, including data catalogs and related metadata, may also live here.

Software development

This part of the architecture combines backend and frontend layers. Here you find business logic and system workflows along with microservices, containers, authentication, and scalability tools, plus the user-facing interfaces for web, mobile, and other applications. Software development can rely on tools such as GitHub and Jenkins for continuous integration and continuous deployment (CI/CD) or Terraform to deploy infrastructure as code (IaC) at scale.

AI platform

This piece hosts ML, natural language processing (NLP), generative AI, and other types of AI models. It includes the *inference layer*, which is the executive engine that processes data through trained models to generate output. It can be a purely technical platform based on APIs for developers, or it can have a user-friendly interface (e.g., visual AI playgrounds with simple testing capabilities, AI studios, model catalogs, drag-and-drop tools) that provides access to the models and other capabilities. These tools usually support operations at scale for deployment, monitoring, and lifecycle management.

Other infrastructure elements

All software-related projects, including those leveraging AI, require a series of elements that interconnect building blocks, data flows, security measures, and so forth. Examples include communication elements, APIs, messaging queues, and streaming services, as well as security tools for authentication, threat detection, access control, and even AI model protection and safety.

Managing and measuring technical AI performance

The notion of performance management is tied to the technical operations of AI applications. There are three key domains you need to understand when managing your AI projects.

DevOps (development operations)

DevOps is a collaborative approach uniting software development and IT operations with the primary goal of improving the speed, quality, and reliability of software delivery. This methodology emphasizes automation, CI/CD, infrastructure management, and real-time monitoring throughout the application lifecycle. One of the foundational principles in DevOps is IaC, which enables infrastructure components such as servers, networks, and configuration files to be defined and managed using code. This ensures consistency, scalability, and reproducibility across different environments (typically divided into development, staging, and production environments).

Moreover, DevOps encourages the implementation of robust monitoring and logging systems that provide early detection of issues and facilitate performance optimization. This visibility into system behavior allows for proactive incident response and system tuning. By fostering cross-functional collaboration and breaking down traditional silos between developers, system administrators, and other IT staff, DevOps leads to faster development cycles, shorter release times, and more stable system operations. Last but not least, DevOps not only accelerates the software development process but also improves scalability, system resilience, and customer satisfaction.

MLOps (machine learning operations)

MLOps is an extension of the DevOps philosophy tailored to the ML lifecycle. It addresses the unique challenges involved in developing, deploying, and maintaining machine learning models in production environments. The MLOps approach covers every stage of the ML lifecycle, including data collection, model training, experimentation, validation, deployment, and monitoring. It incorporates best practices such as version control for datasets and models, automated training pipelines, reproducible experiments, and robust governance mechanisms.

One of the core goals of MLOps is to ensure that ML models can be deployed consistently and reliably while maintaining performance over time. It is important, for example, to detect *data drift*, or changes to data over time due to a statistical shift in distribution between the training and production data. MLOps also involves managing model updates and scaling inference workloads efficiently, and it facilitates the continuous evaluation of model performance and helps teams roll back or update models quickly when necessary. Additionally, it supports compliance with business, legal, and ethical standards through traceability, auditability, and documentation. By integrating ML into CI/CD pipelines and enabling collaboration among data scientists, ML engineers, and IT teams, MLOps ensures that AI systems are not only accurate but also maintainable, secure, and aligned with evolving business goals.

GenAIOps and LLMOps (generative AI and large language model operations)
GenAIOps and LLMOps can be defined as a specialized subset of traditional MLOps that focuses on the operationalization of generative AI models. These models, due to their scale and complexity, introduce distinct challenges in terms of computational resources, latency, ethical considerations, and output control. GenAIOps/LLMOps encompasses strategies for optimizing model performance and cost-efficiency, such as model quantization, pruning, distillation, and workload distribution across edge and cloud environments. It also includes techniques for prompt optimization, continuous evaluation, and AI red teaming to secure and protect the models.

Another critical component is the continuous monitoring of model outputs to detect anomalies such as hallucinations (confident but false responses), biases, or toxic language. GenAIOps/LLMOps teams develop feedback loops and retraining mechanisms that adjust model parameters based on real-world usage. Security is also a central concern, as LLMs can inadvertently produce harmful or sensitive content. It is important to implement safety filters, access controls, and compliance checks to ensure responsible AI usage that aligns with privacy laws and ethical standards. Moreover, GenAIOps/LLMOps supports real-time usage scenarios—such as chatbots, virtual assistants, and enterprise-grade search tools—by ensuring low latency, high availability, and efficient scaling. These operational practices make it feasible to integrate large language and other generative AI models into mission-critical business systems where both performance and reliability are paramount.

While DevOps, MLOps, and GenAIOps/LLMOps are related in that they all promote automation, collaboration, and operational efficiency, each serves a distinct purpose, and they complement one another within your organization. As an AI project manager, you can explore and analyze the current level of maturity of these operations in your organization and facilitate technical discussions with your teams to determine the best practices and tooling to use when implementing them at scale. Your involvement will be critical to your AI projects' success, not only during the implementation phase but also during the productization and day-to-day usage of new AI applications. Moreover, these three topics will be relevant to AI project management due to the automation of certain traces and processes, such as the continuous release of new functionalities after you complete your backlog of tasks or the collection of performance metrics that will help you quantify AI model performance to validate implementations after the experimentation period ends.

Now that you understand the levels and types of AI management, let's turn our focus to your role and the importance of AI for your projects and your day-to-day activities. But remember, while your area of focus will be primarily on Level 2 (or what we call tactical AI management), you are an important resource for both general AI strategy and technical operations. Feel free to add your thoughts to the "Chapter 1 Notebook" on page 29 to capture your personal reflections on how you will bring value to the different levels of AI management within your organization.

Demystifying the AI Project Manager Role

While you will learn more about this in Chapter 3, there are a few topics that we want to bring to your attention up front so you can plan your AI project management journey with some clarity and peace of mind. This section intends to address the questions we get most often from the aspiring AI project managers out there.

FACT 1: THERE IS NO ONE WAY TO MANAGE AI PROJECTS

This book covers pretty much all the topics you need to keep in mind while managing AI projects, but unfortunately the business/technology environment doesn't have a clear and consistent idea of what managing an AI project means. Yes, the overall level of awareness of this specialty is growing as more organizations adopt AI, accompanied by a certain standardization of best practices, but there is still a long way to go.

That said, the profession is at an ideal point in its maturity for you to not only upskill (as you are doing by reading this book) but also shine by bringing your informed opinion and skills to your organization. In this way, you can expand your area of influence to each of the three AI management levels previously discussed. That means being an excellent AI project manager *and* a useful AI strategist *and* a team member who can make relevant contributions to technical discussions. The best AI project managers are valuable and necessary team members for their companies because they are an asset at all three levels.

FACT 2: "MANAGING AI PROJECTS" AND "AI FOR PROJECT MANAGERS" ARE NOT THE SAME

There is a misconception around the difference between managing AI projects and using AI for project management purposes. You may hear the term *AI project management* used to refer to either, but they are quite different. Using AI to do project management refers to your ability as a project management professional to leverage AI tools to perform better, do more, and simplify day-to-day operations. This AI-forward approach to work is a trend in many roles, especially in organizations that incentivize the use of AI to achieve productivity gains.

There are plenty of new resources from O'Reilly and elsewhere that are dedicated to using AI to be a more effective PM, but if you are looking for a few ideas to get started, here are some ways you can leverage AI for your activities, including AI projects.

Backlog enrichment

Regardless of the project management tool you use, you can leverage AI to help you and your team generate user and technical stories that accurately describe the tasks team members are planning to complete. For example, you might use the available information and commentary from your team along with a prompt like this:

```
> Generate a technical story for project management with the following
structure: Title, priority, points estimate, story description, acceptance
criteria. You can use the available information to generate a prefil-
led .json template. If you don't find information for a field, fill it with
"TO BE DEFINED."
[ ... INSERT RELEVANT DOC TEXT OR CALL TRANSCRIPTS ... ]
```

Optionally, you can specify which project management tool you're using in order to obtain output that matches up well with your tool's templates. You can then save the output as a file (e.g., *.csv*) and then use your tool's import function to automatically ingest the generated information. You might add a sentence like this to your prompt:

> I'm using *project management tool* [e.g., Jira]; please generate the user
> story based on this tool's data model.

And of course, if you use a typical user story (*https://oreil.ly/D-hwX*) structure to make your task descriptions more customer- or user-centric, you can add a sentence like this:

> For the description field, please use the following structure "As a [user
> type], I want [goal] so that [reason]."

You can adapt this prompt structure based on the content and structure you need to complete your backlog. Using AI output obviously doesn't replace holding regular discussions with your AI team, but it can be an accelerator for you (and them), saving you all valuable time.

Preassignment of user stories

Even if the framework of Agile sprint planning (*https://oreil.ly/mMEQK*) implies that you, as an AI project manager, may be leading or facilitating some of these Agile events, your technical AI team members will probably choose the stories they work on based on their own availability and skills. That said, you should have some sense of who can do what. This will help not only during the sprint planning meeting (it will save time for everyone) but also during the project progress analysis, as it will allow you to proactively spot roadblocks and even potential team skill gaps.

To leverage AI for this purpose, you could use a pre-build prompt that contains your team members' job titles and abilities, as well as the full list of tasks you created during the previous backlog enrichment activity:

> My team has different members with different skills and positions. Here
> is the list, giving their names, positions, and primary skills:
> I) [Paulo][AI engineer][LLM experimentations, RAG, fine-tuning, prompt engi-
> neering, Python]
> II) [Jane][data analyst][exploratory data analysis, pipelines, data aggrega-
> tion, BI, visualization]
> III) [name][profile][skills]
> ... (other team members)
> Here is the full list of tasks for the current sprint. Analyze the type
> of task and its point estimate to generate a fair distribution of work
> across the team members. If equal workloads are not possible, flag any risk
> of overwork or bottlenecks.

```
[Insert here your list of stories with title, priority, points estimate,
story description, and acceptance criteria.]
```

As usual, you shouldn't expect the AI to generate a perfect result, but its preliminary preassignment of tasks will give you a head start on organizing the workload for your team members and anticipating any potential risk related to a lack of available resources or unrealistic expectations.

Roadmap ideation

Based on the two previous uses of AI (i.e., for backlog enrichment and preassignment of user stories), you could generate a Gantt chart (*https://www.gantt.com*) in whatever format you need for your roadmap tool. You can provide all the available information and ask AI to generate the potential sequence of tasks, perform a roadblocks discovery, conduct a risk assessment, etc. For all technology projects, and especially for AI projects, the roadmap is a living document that serves as a baseline for ongoing discussion and adjustment, so use the AI output as your initial canvas. You can leverage the draft roadmap to give shape to the discussions and negotiations you facilitate with internal and external stakeholders. Remember that most of the folks out there don't have enough knowledge to outline the project at this level of detail, so anything you do here will be highly appreciated.

Here is an AI prompt you could use to ideate project roadmap options:

> Here is a mix of available information: *backlog stories with preassigned owners based on the backlog enrichment and preassignment steps.* Generate a potential roadmap using the x-axis for time by *X-week sprint duration* and the y-axis for task workstreams grouped by type of work. Keep the preassigned task owners, find potential roadblocks or capacity issues, and suggest a sequence of work to optimize the roadmap.
> [... INSERT RELEVANT INFO ...]
> Adapt the generated output to the data model format expected by *my roadmap tool* [e.g., Gantt, Jira, Trello, etc.].

Generation of additional documentation

Here is a way to use AI that will help you get even closer to true technical AI management. We will assume here that you don't have strong programming skills, since that's normal for most AI project managers. Besides exploring vibe coding (the ability to do development work by using natural language to interact with a coding tool) to create quick prototypes, you can leverage AI to analyze, collect, and generate new AI code documentation. This task, usually assigned to technical team members, is now very accessible to people in nontechnical roles, thanks to the use of development tools that leverage AI (e.g., GitHub Copilot, Cursor, Lovable).

If you want to be even more relevant as an AI project manager in your organization, being able to generate and consolidate code and project-level documentation is an effective and easy way for you to play a strong role on the team in the realm of technical management. Here is an example of the kind of prompt you might use (your prompt will obviously depend on the nature of the input information, such as code, other documentation, etc.).

```
> Here is the information [code, doc] related to my project. Generate a sum-
mary containing this information: project name, type of input, summary,
scope, any relevant project information.
[ ... INSERT RELEVANT INFO ... ]
```

If your input is just code, you could also leverage AI to find potential code optimizations that someone else can use to amend any technical debt:

```
> Comment every relevant line of this code with the role it plays within
the entire code, an explanation of how it works, and some potential opportu-
nities for improvement.
[ ... INSERT CODE ... ]
```

Creation of end-of-week or end-of-sprint email drafts

One obvious way for project managers to use AI is to save time on communication tasks such as internal and external emails. Of course, it's important to review any AI output and edit as needed before hitting send. While using AI in this way is helpful for any professional, it becomes especially critical for managers of AI projects. The uncertainty related to the nascent, complex, and evolving nature of AI is one of the reasons why AI projects get so much attention from stakeholders, and it is also a cause of nervousness during implementation. Therefore, regular and frequent communication to stakeholders is important. Here's a prompt idea for creating draft summary emails:

```
> Here is the trace of activities completed this week and summaries of live
discussions. Create a customer-facing summary with the main completed
actions, next steps, and potential risks and mitigations. Also include any
help requested to solve the issues.
[ ... INSERT BACKLOG TRACES ... ]
[ ... INSERT CALL SUMMARIES ... ]
```

Internal research for technical topics

As an AI project manager, you are free to get as technical as you want or can. Technical teams often rate the value of technical PMs higher, especially in the context of complex implementations like any AI project. In addition to the knowledge you'll get out of one-on-one discussions and knowledge sharing with your AI teams, you can get a wealth of knowledge from AI tools. The simplified explanations they can provide will accelerate your learning and increase your ability to participate in innovative projects. When exploring a new AI concept or technology, you can type this prompt:

```
> Explain complex AI topic to me in simple words. I'm not technical, but I
work as a project manager for work involving this topic. I need key con-
cepts and examples, and I need ideas for how I can adapt my project manage-
ment approach to this task to accelerate pace and reduce risk.
```

Creation of compliance documentation

As you will see in Chapters 2 and 3, regulations and compliance are increasingly important topics, not only at the level of the organization but also for your specific AI projects. This means that compliance requirements will involve more than the technical aspects of the AI implementation. For example, imagine you and your team are working on a new AI application that leverages an LLM from a specific provider. Regulations like the EU AI Act or industry standards like ISO 42001 may ask for additional documentation of the types of models and datasets being used. You can leverage code, backlog information, and any other technical documentation to map available information to specific data models for compliance. Your contribution to ensuring compliance will highlight your role as a responsible AI (RAI) champion—a role that we will explore in the coming chapters.

A prompt may look something like this:

```
> Based on the information provided below, map the following requirements
for transparency and compliance: type of AI system, industry, purpose, sys-
tem version, type of model, model provider, model API version, and any
other relevant information (under the heading "others") based on the EU AI
Act and ISO 42001 requirements.
```

A prompt like this will give you relatively complete information that you can then add to the project documentation and share with any relevant stakeholder. From an AI PM perspective, this is a way to increase your footprint and bring multidisciplinary value to your team, project, and organization.

These are just a few examples of how you can use AI as a productivity tool to support your AI project management activities. We recommend thinking through some prompt ideas of your own and adding them to the "Chapter 1 Notebook" on page 29. Next, get ready to understand what exactly AI-forward companies expect from AI project managers like you.

FACT 3: AI-FORWARD COMPANIES EXPECT CERTAIN SKILLS FROM YOU

There's no way to fully define what an organization will consider AI project management, because it will depend on the organization and its level of AI maturity. Nonetheless, you can anticipate that your employer will expect a certain mix of hard and soft skills. We've outlined some of these in Figure 1-3.

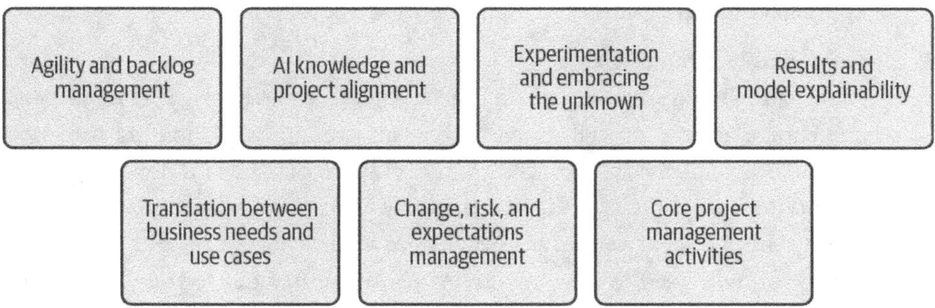

Figure 1-3. AI project management skills

Skills you will need to demonstrate

You should anticipate that at various points in your career, you'll need to have skills in these areas:

Agility and backlog management
> This means implementing hybrid and Agile project management methodologies (e.g., Scrum or Kanban) to ensure flexible planning, fast iteration, and adaptive responses to changing project needs. It is also about maintaining a prioritized product backlog that evolves with stakeholder input, model feedback, and changing business goals. We'll explore this further later in the book.

AI knowledge and project alignment
> You'll need enough baseline knowledge of AI to ensure proper alignment of AI techniques with the project objectives. This includes making sure the team has a timely discussion about the selection of suitable algorithms and

ensuring the project has access to quality datasets. You don't need to do this alone, but you are in charge of leading and facilitating the discussions with your technical teams.

Experimentation and embracing the unknown

This means adopting and encouraging a culture of hypothesis-driven development where failure is seen as a learning opportunity. There is a focus on scoping experimentation and supporting the design and testing of experimental models or features, and team members embrace the uncertainty inherent in the AI development discovery process. From the perspective of an AI project manager, promoting this approach will be especially important with your executive and client stakeholders, as not all of them will appreciate the uncertainty of the implementation phases.

Results and model explainability

A key skill is to be able to use technical knowledge to explain AI results to a client or a user. You will need to provide transparent insights into how models make decisions and ensure that the project stakeholders (especially the nontechnical ones) understand model behavior, especially in regulated or high-impact environments. Due to the technical nature of these discussions, you will need to rely on your AI team; your role is to translate technical and complex explanations into simple insights. This is another example of your added value as an AI project manager.

Translation between business needs and use cases

As noted in the previous point, your ability to act as a translator between the technical and business aspects of the project is critical. In this case, you can be the person who closes the gaps between executive stakeholders, domain experts, and technical teams by clearly defining AI use cases that help create business value. For example, you can convert high-level goals into specific, measurable AI tasks, ensuring relevance and ROI. You can rely on typical PM assets such as your project roadmaps to calculate the aggregated cost (human, infrastructure, data, etc.) and to explore the potential return on investment.

Change, risk, and expectations management

This one is critical: any project will benefit when you take the lead to proactively identify potential risks (e.g., data availability, model performance, ethical concerns) early and to define suitable mitigation strategies. You are also the team member who takes point on managing stakeholder expectations, grounding them in realistic outcomes, while dealing with the pervasive AI buzz. You will protect your AI team from any external pressure to produce remarkable results, particularly regarding the timeline, accuracy, and limits of AI systems.

Core project management

This is obvious, but besides the previous multidisciplinary tasks, you still need to do your regular PM job. This means coordinating cross-functional teams, allocating resources effectively, tracking progress against milestones, engaging stakeholders regularly, managing budgets, and ensuring on-time deliverables while maintaining quality and compliance. And all of this with the added complexity of AI projects.

Yes, this combination of tasks and skills is highly complex. You won't be strong in all areas from day one, but you can continue to steadily develop your competencies so that you improve in all these skills. Fortunately, the baseline project management skills and professional attitude you already have will guide your AI project management journey. Let's now explore a framework that will help you adjust your approach to become a best-in-class project manager.

Framework for AI project managers

To help you understand how to approach your AI project management journey (beyond the core upskilling activities), we created the *ADRIAN framework* (see Figure 1-4), which can serve as your guide to identify not only your priority areas for development but also the mix of soft skills that will differentiate you from other AI or regular project managers in the job market.

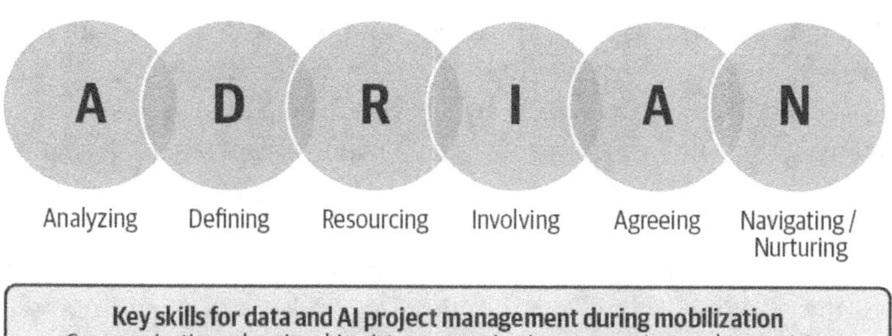

Figure 1-4. The ADRIAN framework for AI PMs

Let's walk through each part of the framework:

- *Analyzing* emphasizes the importance of thoroughly analyzing the project's requirements, data sources, potential challenges, and desired outcomes. In this stage, you must understand the business problem, assess the feasibility of AI solutions, and identify relevant metrics to evaluate success.

- *Defining* involves clearly articulating the project's scope, objectives, deliverables, and success criteria and gaining stakeholder agreement. Here you also define the roles and responsibilities within the project team.

- *Resourcing* focuses on identifying and securing the necessary human, technology, data, and financial resources required for the project's execution. In this stage, you allocate budgets, acquire specialized tools or platforms, and ensure the talent with the necessary AI and data expertise is onboarded.

- *Involving* highlights the crucial aspect of stakeholder engagement. This comes about through active communication and collaboration with all relevant parties, including business leaders, data scientists, engineers, end users, and legal/compliance teams. Effective involvement fosters shared ownership and reduces resistance.

- *Agreeing* emphasizes the need to gain consensus on and formal approval of key aspects of the project, such as technical approaches, timelines, and resource allocation. You need to negotiate potential conflicts, establish clear decision-making processes, and secure formal commitments from all parties to ensure smooth execution and avoid scope creep.

- *Navigating/Nurturing* encompasses the ongoing management of the project, including monitoring its progress, addressing challenges that arise, and adapting to change. By navigating, you guide the project through its lifecycle, while nurturing speaks to fostering team growth, maintaining motivation, and continuously improving processes.

As an AI project manager, you will want to gain a deep understanding of the stages of the ADRIAN framework and develop the key skills required to be successful at each stage. Critical to your development will be your willingness to embrace maturation in the following competencies:

Growth mindset

Essential for AI project managers, having a growth mindset means believing that your abilities and intelligence can be developed through dedication and hard work. For an AI project manager, this translates to embracing challenges as opportunities for learning, persisting in the face of the setbacks inherent in complex AI initiatives, seeking feedback to improve, and viewing the success of others as inspiration. It means continuously learning about new technologies, methodologies, and problem-solving approaches in the rapidly evolving AI landscape and fostering this same mindset within their team.

Communication

Effective communication is paramount for AI project managers, who need to be able to clearly articulate complex technical concepts to nontechnical stakeholders, actively listen to concerns, provide transparent updates, and facilitate productive discussions among diverse teams. To develop this competency, you will hone your active listening skills, develop persuasive presentation skills, and learn to adapt your communication style to different audiences.

Planning

Given the inherent uncertainties of AI projects, planning requires a meticulous approach. You need to know how to develop detailed project roadmaps, set realistic timelines, anticipate potential risks, and create contingency plans. Project managers with strong planning skills also embrace iterative planning, in which they are open to learning from past planning successes and failures and adjusting plans based on new insights.

Big picture

AI project managers need to maintain a big-picture perspective, understanding how a given AI initiative aligns with broader business objectives and will impact the organization. Project managers with strong big-picture thinking can connect the technical details to strategic goals and identify opportunities for long-term value creation. Growth in this area means continuously seeking to understand industry trends, business strategy, and the wider ecosystem in which the AI solution operates.

Organization

Strong organizational skills are crucial for managing the complex interplay of data, models, infrastructure, and diverse teams in AI projects. This includes structuring workflows, managing documentation, tracking progress, and ensuring efficient resource utilization. With strong organizational skills, you will be eager to adopt new organizational tools and methodologies, the continuous refinement of processes, and learning from project management best practices—and you will encourage others to be open to new approaches as well.

Persuasion

AI project managers often need to persuade stakeholders to adopt new technologies, allocate resources, or embrace novel approaches. With this skill, you will build compelling business cases for your projects, address concerns with data-driven arguments, and foster trust in your reasoning and capability. To develop your competency in persuasion, you will strengthen your negotiation skills, enhance your understanding of stakeholder motivations, and learn to articulate the value proposition of AI solutions effectively.

Proactivity

AI project managers must anticipate issues before they arise, take the initiative rather than wait to be told what to do, and drive projects forward. To take a proactive stance toward your projects, you must be able to identify potential risks, seek out opportunities for improvement, and foster a culture of continuous learning and adaptation within the team. You will actively seek feedback, learn from successes and mistakes, and continuously strive to improve processes and outcomes rather than simply reacting to events.

Summarizing, there is no magic formula that will allow you to be aligned with all organizations that might someday employ you (especially because most of them are still figuring out what they are looking for), but these are the fundamental activities and skills you want to keep in mind during your AI project management journey.

Last but not least, don't hesitate to search for examples of "AI project manager" job postings and take notes on the responsibilities and required experience and skills. For reference, you could list them in the "Chapter 1 Notebook" on page 29. You can reflect on the themes you see across different organizations and analyze any gap between your skills and what employers are seeking so you can plan your most important upskilling activities.

FACT 4: SUCCESS IS ALL ABOUT KNOWING THE DIFFERENCES BETWEEN "REGULAR" AND AI PROJECT MANAGEMENT

Now that you know what your role is as part of the AI management system of your organization, what AI project management is and isn't, and what most organizations will expect from you as an AI project manager, let us share a little secret with you. Especially if you are coming from a project management background, the reality is that learning AI project management is like learning a language that is very similar to your mother tongue. You don't need to learn everything from scratch but instead can focus on understanding and detecting the main differences.

We could list all the differences up front, but we want you to spot and note them as you read through the chapters. The final list will depend heavily on your current level of PM skills and on the approach you use to manage your projects. For example, you won't see anticipating AI security risks as a new activity if you already do that for your regular software projects. But you will notice a difference if your current PM approach doesn't go too far into the technical aspects of a project. For now, stay attentive and start spotting those differences.

Now that you understand the key factors in success as an AI project management professional, let's focus on the key challenges you will face.

Main Challenges for AI Project Management Professionals

As AI becomes a more integral part of business strategy, project managers stepping into this space must be prepared to face a set of challenges that differ significantly from those of traditional projects. From the lack of standardized frameworks and rapidly evolving technologies to the need to manage high uncertainty, inflated stakeholder expectations, and cross-functional collaboration, AI project management requires a blend of adaptability, technical fluency, and strategic thinking. This section outlines the key obstacles you're likely to encounter and offers a foundation for navigating the complexities ahead. By understanding these challenges early, you'll be better equipped to lead your AI initiatives with confidence, turning potential roadblocks into opportunities for growth and innovation.

Standardization and limitations of AI PM frameworks

AI project management still lacks widely adopted standards, and existing frameworks often fall short of encompassing the full lifecycle and unique characteristics of AI development. This can create inconsistencies in execution and make it difficult to benchmark progress or outcomes. As a result, AI project managers often customize or hybridize methodologies, drawing from the software, research, and product management domains, while dealing with gaps in guidance around specific technical topics. However, you can always explore AI materials published by international organizations such as the Project Management Institute (*https://oreil.ly/SbHF8*) and track newly created credentials, like the PMI Certified Professional in Managing AI (PMI-CPMAI) (*https://oreil.ly/q7swx*), that may complement your upskilling journey.

Dealing with uncertainty

As you already know, AI work is inherently experimental and highly iterative, introducing a significant level of uncertainty in outcomes and timelines. Unlike traditional software projects, where requirements and outputs are often more predictable, AI development involves exploratory data analysis, hyperparameter tuning, and model validation, all of which can yield unexpected results. Managing this uncertainty requires a mindset that embraces iteration, failure, and constant learning while still maintaining structure and accountability. It also calls for teaching executives and clients some agility concepts such as *spikes* (pre-research to "know what we don't know") and review sessions for feedback, as well as key AI topics such as model performance interpretation.

Managing expectations and buzz

You're already familiar with this challenge when considering how to grow your AI project manager skills to address it. There is a significant amount of hype around AI, which can lead stakeholders to expect fast, transformative results when they don't fully understand the technical and organizational prerequisites. One of the hardest challenges is to bridge the gap between what AI can realistically achieve and the overinflated expectations shaped by media narratives or vendor promises. As an AI project manager, you need to ground the conversation in realistic, measurable outcomes and foster a culture that values long-term value creation over flashy demos or promises.

Going technical enough

Here we have another example of both a key skill and a main challenge. Effective AI project leadership requires a baseline level of technical understanding: enough to ask the right questions, evaluate trade-offs, and guide decision making without necessarily being a machine learning expert. You need to understand concepts like model accuracy, data quality, and algorithmic bias to properly assess progress and risks. Without this foundation, there's a danger that you will miscommunicate requirements or misjudge a project's feasibility. Stay tuned—this book will help you here!

Understanding risks

AI introduces a unique set of risks, including ethical concerns, biased outputs, lack of interpretability, and unpredictable model behavior. Beyond technical performance, there are also regulatory, reputational, and operational risks to consider. AI project managers must identify, monitor, and mitigate these risks continuously, ideally with input from cross-functional teams that include legal, compliance, and other domain experts, to ensure responsible and sustainable deployment.

Guiding technology approaches

Decisions like choosing the right model architecture or technical approach are critical but not always straightforward. The right choice depends on multiple factors including data availability, computing resources, project goals, and integration needs. AI project managers facilitate informed discussions among data scientists, engineers, and business stakeholders, ensuring that model choices align with both technical constraints and desired business outcomes. This collaborative decision-making applies to any technical topic, such as infrastructure and cloud adoption, access to diverse sources of data, or embedded techniques to mitigate AI risks. The content of this book, along with a bit of field experience from your next AI projects, will help you build the foundational knowledge and skill set to facilitate these discussions.

Mapping resources and skills and closing the gap

AI initiatives often expose gaps in talent, tools, and infrastructure. Many organizations lack specialized roles such as data engineers, MLOps experts, or AI ethicists, all of which can be critical for success. Identifying these gaps early and addressing them (whether through hiring, training, or partnerships) is essential to avoid delays and ensure the project is not limited by internal capability shortfalls. With experience, you will develop an intuition that allows you to analyze and anticipate these kinds of issues with your projects and teams.

Estimating when new technologies are involved

With AI technologies evolving rapidly, it's difficult to estimate development timelines, required resources, or potential ROI with confidence. Tools, platforms, and methods are continuously changing, and what works well today may be obsolete tomorrow. You need to stay informed, leverage pilot programs, and structure initiatives with flexibility in mind, while still offering stakeholders credible forecasts and value assessments. You will get some interesting insights and assets to assist with estimation in the coming chapters.

Defining plans in detail

While AI projects require room for experimentation, they also benefit from clear and detailed planning, especially when moving from proof of concept to production. Balancing flexibility with structure means defining clear goals, success metrics, milestone checkpoints, and fallback plans. Overly rigid plans can stifle creativity, but overly vague ones can lead to scope creep and poor accountability.

Communicating among AI management levels

Translating strategic objectives into technical tasks and vice versa is a critical skill. You must be able to articulate how model outputs will drive business outcomes while also helping technical teams understand the broader context and priorities. This bidirectional communication helps align efforts, ensures shared understanding, and reduces friction between diverse stakeholders. The challenge comes from needing a certain skill set to enable that kind of communication and collaboration and the difficulty of aligning people with different perspectives and levels of oversight, often incentivized by different types of objectives and KPIs. For example, while a strategic partner will focus on the binary outcome of a project being completed or not, you need to make that project not only happen but happen on time.

Combining experimentation and delivery

Organizations must strike a balance between enabling innovation through experimentation and ensuring consistent, scalable delivery. Too much focus on experimentation can result in "proof-of-concept purgatory," while too much emphasis on delivery can stifle innovation. From one side, you and your organization need to create governance structures and roadmaps that allow for both discovery and execution, with clear criteria for when to transition between the two. On the other hand, you need to help your technical teams make progress and accomplish everything that you all planned, sprint by sprint.

Collaborating with other tactical roles

AI projects require close collaboration among various roles, for example, product managers, domain experts, data engineers, and software developers. These collaborators often speak different languages and prioritize different outcomes. Building strong communication channels, shared vocabularies, and mutual respect across functions is vital to creating coherent workflows and successful integrations. Depending on the organization, you could have the opportunity to facilitate cooperative operations and culture, even taking on several roles yourself, such as project manager, product owner, or scrum master.

Competing for resources

Unless your company has access to unlimited resources, your AI projects will often face intense competition for budget, infrastructure (like GPUs), and even talent. Since AI is usually not the only strategic initiative in an organization, you must clearly articulate the value of AI initiatives and be adept at influencing prioritization decisions. This involves not only justifying costs but also demonstrating progress and aligning with broader organizational goals.

Each project and team is different, yet learning from these and other challenges along the way will help you begin to generalize from your experiences, allowing you to anticipate risks and considerations that require your additional attention. Use each issue that arises as an opportunity to document the AI project challenges you experience and then to reflect on them, synthesizing broader insights and universal principles.

Conclusion

This first chapter is just the beginning of your AI project management upskilling journey. You now have a clear idea of the levels of management, as well as your role as both an enabler of the tactical day-to-day and a connector between different internal and external stakeholders. Awareness of this mix of activities, the challenges that accompany them, and the hard and soft skills you need to overcome those challenges will help you get ready for your next AI initiatives—or at the very least to know what you know and, even more importantly, what you don't know (yet). As you move forward, remember that successful AI project management is not about understanding every technical aspect of this work but about being an effective translator, orchestrator, and enabler of innovation. You are not expected to know everything on day one, but by embracing a growth mindset, building hybrid skills, and staying anchored in business value and delivery, you can guide your teams and stakeholders toward AI project success.

Next, Chapter 2 will be an applied deep dive into all relevant technical AI topics, adapted to the needs and level of understanding of an AI project manager.

Chapter 1 Notebook

A Deep Dive into AI for Project Managers

In the previous chapter, you started to understand and contextualize your role as an AI project manager in the organization, gaining some initial insights into the role itself and the typical challenges you may face in your work with both technical teams and general stakeholders.

This chapter will switch things up, covering the more technical aspects of artificial intelligence. As you already know, the only way to get closer to AI implementations and your technical team members is to continue increasing your level of AI literacy. What this looks like obviously depends on your existing knowledge of the topic, but we will make sure you learn all the information you need to, at the very least, understand the key aspects of your AI implementations.

Key AI Topics

There is no scarcity of technical resources about the many AI topics that exist today. There are hundreds of books, lectures, videos, technical articles, and Q&As with experts, and you can even access knowledge via AI tools. However, the main difficulty for most current and aspiring AI project managers is to find, curate, and prioritize their areas of technical learning. Given the practically infinite variety and quantity of resources, it can be easy to select the wrong areas of focus. Or you may inadvertently choose resources that are too general or too technical, which is often a path to disengagement and lack of progress.

This section discusses the evolution and history of AI technologies, offers an analysis of the main types of AI capabilities, and then does a technical deep dive into data, models, and other key AI topics—all adapted to your AI project management context.

Let's start with the chronological evolution of AI technologies. Please don't skip this section! This information is very relevant for you as an AI project manager, as it will contribute to your awareness of the overall context of AI development and prepare you for interactions with your technical team members.

EVOLUTION OF AI TECHNOLOGIES

The history of artificial intelligence is far more extensive than it might seem from the public's perspective, as many people have only recently become aware of AI thanks to the rapid rise of generative AI applications in recent years. But the road that led here is long and full of milestones marked by breakthroughs, setbacks, long periods of research, and key moments of success and adoption. Starting from the very beginning, these are the major phases of AI's historical development.

Prelude to AI (up to 1950)

Long before the term *artificial intelligence* was coined, both academia and science fiction were already exploring the idea of intelligent machines. The dream of creating robots and advanced machines was captured in cultural landmarks like Frank Baum's *The Wizard of Oz* and Isaac Asimov's *I, Robot*, shaping a collective image of what AI might one day become. Meanwhile, academic progress began to take shape, and Alan Turing published what would become the defining work of his career: "Computing Machinery and Intelligence" (1950). The paper famously opened with the provocative question "Can machines think?" While he was not the first to pose such a question, Turing's work introduced crucial ideas such as the imitation game and what we now call the Turing test, still a foundational benchmark in AI today. Even before that, Turing laid the groundwork with his concept of the Turing machine in 1936 and contributed to the Allied victory in World War II with the development of the Turing-Welchman Bombe machine, a device that helped decrypt Nazi communications.

The early days (the '50s)

The 1950s marked the academic birth of artificial intelligence. It was in this decade that the term artificial intelligence was coined and the field began to take shape. A pivotal moment came with the Dartmouth Summer Research Project in 1956 (*https://oreil.ly/VQ4Wd*), a workshop organized by John McCarthy, Marvin Minsky, Nathaniel Rochester, and Claude Shannon. This event brought together more than a dozen researchers to formalize a new area of study. Concretely, they proposed:

> *A 2-month, 10-man study of artificial intelligence to be carried out during the summer of 1956 at Dartmouth College. The study is to proceed on the basis of the conjecture that every aspect of learning or any other feature of intelligence can in principle be so precisely described that a machine can be made to simulate it.*

This vision of machines capable of language, abstraction, self-improvement, and problem-solving, which closely resembled many of today's capabilities, laid the foundation for the future of AI.

The rise of AI (up to 1974)

The 1960s and '70s saw growing academic interest and investment in AI. Institutions like the Defense Advanced Research Projects Agency (DARPA) in the United States played a central role in funding exploratory work. However, most efforts focused on narrow, rule-based systems for specific tasks, with limited flexibility. A key turning point came in 1969 with the publication of *Perceptrons* by Marvin Minsky and Seymour Papert (MIT Press), which highlighted critical limitations in early neural networks, particularly their inability to solve nonlinear problems. This critique had far-reaching consequences.

The first AI winter (1974 to 1980)

The so-called AI winters were periods of slowed progress and diminished funding due to unmet expectations. *Perceptrons* had already sparked debate, but the 1973 Lighthill Report, commissioned by the UK and led by Sir James Lighthill, sharply criticized the field's progress and practical applications. As a result, the UK drastically cut funding for AI research, triggering the first AI winter, a setback that would not be the last.

Rebound and second AI winter (1980s)

From 1980 to 1987, optimism returned with the rise of expert systems designed to solve problems in specific domains. Japan's Fifth Generation Computer Systems project and renewed interest in neural networks, especially with the reintroduction of multilayer networks and backpropagation by Geoffrey Hinton, David Rumelhart, and Ronald Williams in 1986, brought hope to the industry. But despite initial excitement, the commercial hype surrounding expert systems and Japan's initiative eventually faded. By 1987, AI faced its second winter, marked by skepticism and funding cuts once again.

The ML era (1990s and early 2000s)

The '90s marked a more grounded, practical phase in AI history. Research shifted toward machine learning, with models like support vector machines (SVMs) and random forests gaining traction in industries like finance and insurance. The explosion of data from the rise of the internet also accelerated progress, ushering in the era of big data. Some notable moments include the defeat of chess champion Garry Kasparov by IBM's Deep Blue in 1997, advances in computing power thanks to GPUs, and breakthroughs in language processing with long short-term memory (LSTM) networks and in computer vision with convolutional neural networks (CNNs). These developments set the stage for the deep learning revolution that would follow.

The deep learning comeback (2006 to the 2010s)

The resurgence of neural networks in the form of deep learning (DL) reshaped the field starting around 2006. Although previously set aside in favor of other algorithms, deep networks now benefited from vastly improved computing power (especially GPUs) and unprecedented amounts of training data.

In 2012, AlexNet, a deep CNN trained with GPUs, dramatically outperformed previous models in the ImageNet competition, signaling a new era. A few years later, in 2016, DeepMind's AlphaGo combined DL with reinforcement learning to master the game of Go, even learning by playing against itself. This marked the birth of deep reinforcement learning (DRL). Then in 2017, Google Brain published the now-legendary "Attention Is All You Need" paper (*https://arxiv.org/abs/1706.03762*), which introduced the transformer architecture and self-attention mechanisms, enabling parallel processing of sequences and opening the door to today's language models like Bidirectional Encoder

Representations from Transformers (BERT, 2018), Generative Pre-trained Transformer 1 (GPT-1, 2018), and GPT-2 (2019).

The generative AI explosion (2020 onward)

With solid technical foundations in place, the 2020s brought an era of exponential growth. AI entered the public consciousness like never before, expanding into scientific research, creative industries, and everyday applications. Among the most groundbreaking advances was Google DeepMind's AlphaFold, released as open source in 2021, which predicted protein structures with unprecedented accuracy using transformer-based models. And, of course, the arrival of ChatGPT in 2022, along with other major innovations in chat, vision, transcription, and reasoning from companies like OpenAI, Anthropic, Google (Gemini), DeepSeek, Mistral, and Meta (LLaMA), redefined what was possible.

This period has been characterized by intense competition, continuous model releases, infrastructure investments, and widespread AI adoption across sectors. What was once a niche research topic is now a central pillar of technological progress, with capabilities more accessible than ever before.

These are just some highlights from the long, complex journey of artificial intelligence, which has been marked by both moments of incredible excitement and times of disillusionment. But each stage paved the way for the technologies we now use every day and brought a new variety of techniques and applications that you and your team may leverage for your AI projects. Keep this timeline in mind as you seek to understand which technologies are relatively mature at this point and which have new, more advanced capabilities but less maturity, since they will bring more uncertainty and a steeper learning curve to your projects.

MAIN AI CAPABILITIES

Defining artificial intelligence is complex. While there is a set of technologies that clearly fall under the umbrella of AI, there are others that may or may not be considered part of the AI family but that are nonetheless relevant in the context of implementing AI-based solutions.

Among others, Québec's Institute for Data Valorisation (IVADO) has published a definition of digital intelligence that serves as both a reference point and a catch-all framework for data and AI technologies that can be adopted either jointly or independently. You can see a breakdown of this definition in Figure 2-1.

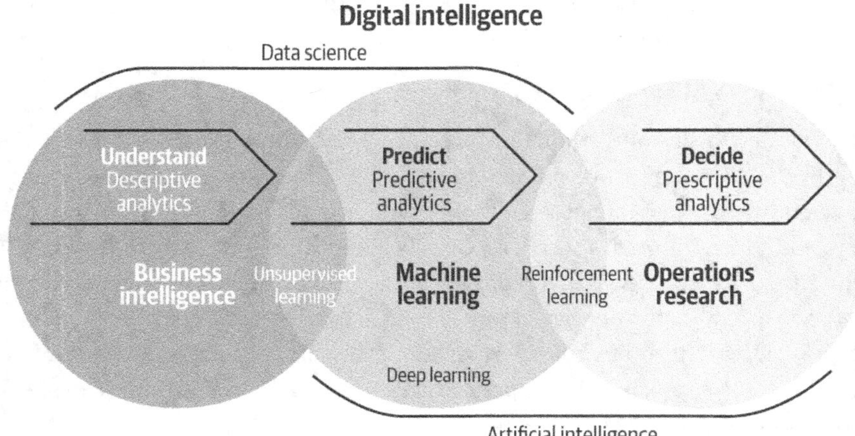

Figure 2-1. IVADO's definition of digital intelligence (https://oreil.ly/OrNbI)

The figure shows the different families of technologies that are part of digital intelligence broadly and of data science and artificial intelligence specifically:

- *Business intelligence (BI)* and *descriptive analytics*, in the field of data science, focus on delivering insights through dashboards and visualizations that illustrate numerical data and trends to support better business decision making. This analytical framework includes data science techniques we'll explore in this chapter, particularly in relation to data analysis and preparation.

- *Predictive analytics*, which sits at the intersection of data science and AI, uses past data to predict future outcomes using a wide variety of machine learning algorithms (many of which we'll cover in this chapter).

- *Prescriptive analytics* draws on a variety of AI technologies such as operations research (OR) and reinforcement learning. The concept of *prescription* or *recommendation* ties directly into one of the most important and complex areas of AI: dynamic recommendation systems. Other technologies, like natural language processing and generative AI, also are part of or converge with this broader notion of digital intelligence. Both are particularly relevant today for any AI professional, including you as an AI project manager.

From a functional point of view, as you can see in Figure 2-2, there are different core capabilities associated with these families of AI technologies.

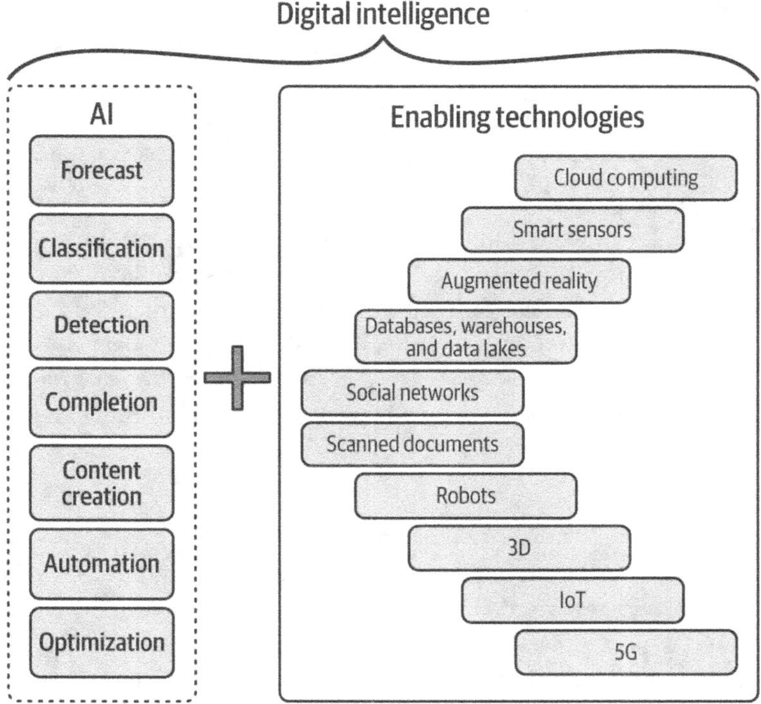

Figure 2-2. AI capabilities (adapted from IVADO)

The capabilities shown here include all types of AI outcomes and are supported by a series of enabling technologies that facilitate their adoption:

Forecasting

This is the ability of AI to analyze historical data and predict future values based on identified patterns and trends. Imagine you have historical sales data for your company, broken down by month, day of the week, and product. With AI, you can analyze that data to detect patterns. For instance, maybe a particular product consistently sees a sales spike on weekends in December. Based on that insight, you can forecast similar outcomes and better plan inventory and marketing strategies to maximize performance during those periods.

Classification

This is the ability of AI to group data into categories based on distinctive features learned during training. For example, say you have one thousand pictures of cats and one thousand of dogs. You can train an AI model to classify these into two groups, cats and dogs. The model learns to identify key differences like ear shape, body size, and fur patterns. Once trained, it can classify new images with high accuracy, which is useful for applications like organizing photo libraries or identifying animals in shelters.

Pattern and anomaly detection

This is the ability of AI to identify specific or unusual patterns in data and alert you to possible issues or irregularities. For example, if you're receiving continuous signals from telecom or power equipment and a normally steady signal suddenly fluctuates abnormally, the AI model can flag this as a potential issue, allowing you to take preventive action before a system failure occurs. This is key for maintaining service continuity and avoiding costly downtime.

Completion or autocompletion

This is the ability of AI to predict and complete phrases or words based on prior text or conversation. Picture this: in a chatbot interface, a text box suggests the next few words to complete your sentence naturally. If you start typing "What are your business hours…," the system might suggest "…for customer service?" This enhances communication efficiency and provides a smoother user experience.

Creation or generation

This is the ability of AI to create new content following the style and structure of previous examples. Say you have a knowledge base full of articles on specific topics. AI can generate new content in a similar format for different topics. For example, if you have articles on how to boost productivity at work, AI can generate one on how to manage your time effectively with a matching tone and organization. This helps maintain consistency in content production and reduces time spent writing.

Automation

This is the ability of AI to carry out repetitive digital tasks, boosting efficiency and reducing manual effort. In a human resources (HR) process, for instance, AI can automate sending welcome emails to new hires or reminders for upcoming document deadlines. This makes workflows more responsive to events and frees up HR teams to focus on more strategic tasks.

Optimization

This is the ability of AI to simulate scenarios and improve resource usage, reducing costs and improving operational efficiency. This is especially useful in physical space management. Say your factory has limited resources and storage space. AI can model different layouts and optimize the setup to get the most production out of the available space while minimizing energy consumption. This not only saves money but also reduces your operation's environmental footprint.

As you can see in Figure 2-2, these capabilities are enabled and complemented by other technologies, such as cloud computing from big technology companies or hyperscalers (e.g., Amazon Web Services [AWS], Microsoft Azure, Google Cloud Platform [GCP], Oracle, IBM, CoreWeave, Crusoe, OVHcloud), Internet of Things (IoT) and sensor-based systems, big data clusters, etc. Depending on your company's technology stack (a concept we will explore in Chapter 6) and ability to get additional resources for your new AI projects, the approach to implementation will vary, and you may have a chance to reduce unnecessary complexities.

TYPES OF AI LEARNING

There's one more essential concept we need to cover: how AI models actually learn. What is the underlying learning process? And how does this affect the way modern AI models are built? Here are the four main types of learning that power today's AI systems:

Unsupervised learning

In unsupervised learning, models are trained on unlabeled data, meaning there are no predefined outputs. The goal is to uncover hidden patterns, structures, or relationships within the data. This approach is commonly used in tasks like clustering (e.g., to segment a customer based on their purchasing behavior) and dimensionality reduction (i.e., reducing the number of input features while keeping the essential information for model training). Unsupervised learning is used with some models you will learn about later, like k-means clustering and principal component analysis (PCA).

Supervised learning

Supervised learning involves training a model on labeled data, where each input is paired with the correct output. The model learns to map inputs to their respective outputs, enabling it to make predictions based on new, as-yet-unseen data. This is widely used in tasks like classification, regression, and prediction. A classic example is image classification where, for example, you might train a model to recognize cats and dogs based on labeled examples of past pictures. Other applications include detecting spam emails, predicting diseases from medical data, and translating languages.

Reinforcement learning

With reinforcement learning (RL), the agent learns by interacting with an environment, taking actions, and receiving feedback in the form of rewards or penalties. The goal is to learn a strategy that maximizes long-term rewards. RL is most famously used in game-playing AI like AlphaGo, where the system learns effective strategies through trial and error. It also plays a role in robotics (e.g., object manipulation, navigation) and self-driving cars, where the AI adapts behavior based on outcomes of previous decisions.

Self-supervised learning

Self-supervised learning is a form of unsupervised learning where the model generates its own labels from raw data. The process typically involves predicting one part of the input using another part. This method has become essential in modern AI, especially in NLP and computer vision. A common example is using a large body of text to train a language model to predict the next word in a sentence. In vision applications, models may learn by predicting missing sections of an image. These techniques are foundational for today's GenAI systems.

Hybrid learning approaches are sometimes used that combine elements of the methods above. In addition, there are advanced techniques like transfer learning, which allows models to apply knowledge learned in one task to another. However, the four types outlined here form the foundation you'll need to understand before diving deeper in the next section.

ADDITIONAL AI CONCEPTS

Before we move on, you need to understand a few more concepts related to the training and learning process for AI models, as you will encounter these during your AI projects and discussions with team members:

Model features
> Features are variables or individual pieces of information about data that a model uses to learn and make predictions. For example, if you want to predict the price of a car, the features could be brand, model year, color, engine size, etc. For a dataset organized as a table, features can be columns.

Feature engineering
> This is the process of creating, modifying, or selecting the best features from raw data to help models learn better and make more accurate predictions. From a project perspective, feature engineering is usually assigned to data science roles, but it also relies on data engineers to handle pipeline input and ML engineers to handle output (production).

Dimensions
> This concept typically refers to the number of features or variables in the dataset. If you have three features, your data lives in a three-dimensional feature space. So essentially, features are the actual variables, while dimensions describe the count or space those features span. You will hear about high-dimensional datasets, which are very complex, requiring advanced techniques to select the important features and reduce the dimensionality of the data.

Bias
> Bias occurs when a model's predictions consistently differ from the true values, leading to oversimplification or wrong assumptions. The concept of bias is also raised often in discussions of ethical AI, as bias can generate incorrect outcomes that impact specific segments of people. For example, bias is the reason for discrimination in automated hiring or facial recognition systems (*https://oreil.ly/_WmDk*), in which people of specific races and genders can be highly disadvantaged.

Underfitting
> This occurs when a model is too simple to capture the underlying pattern in the data, leading to poor performance. Underfitting can be due to

insufficient training time or inadequate training data, among other causes. To solve this problem, implementation teams can use more complex models, select more relevant features, or decrease regularization (make the model less strict).

Overfitting

This happens when a model learns noise and patterns that are specific to its training data, reducing its ability to generalize to unseen data (i.e., the model becomes too specialized to the training set, so it ends up memorizing too many details and noise instead of learning general rules). Overfitting can be fixed by using more training data, simpler models, or advanced techniques that combine several models.

Variance

This is a measure of how much a model's predictions change when trained on different data, with errors resulting from the model being too sensitive or complex, which causes overfitting.

Cross-validation

This is a technique used to evaluate model performance by splitting data into multiple training and validation sets. You will learn more about the data-splitting process later in this chapter. For now, just know that it is comparable to A/B testing experiments that allow you to get a more reliable estimate of how well your model will perform on unseen data while making the most of the data you have.

Bias-variance trade-off

AI models need to find the right level of complexity to minimize both error due to bias (underfitting) and variance (overfitting). As a project manager, you rely on your data scientists to find the correct balance, but you can learn to evaluate performance metrics to analyze results with your data experts. We will explore what those quantitative metrics look like in Chapter 5, as part of the validation and performance evaluation step.

Epochs

The model can undergo multiple epochs, or go through the entire training dataset, during the training process in order to learn better. Including more epochs in the training process means that the model gets more chances to learn from the data, but too many epochs can lead to overfitting. As a PM, you will be aware that this trade-off impacts not only performance but also training duration and cost. Finding the right balance is key to avoiding project delays and high cloud usage bills.

Explainability, interpretability, and transparency
These concepts relate to how understandable a model is, but they focus on slightly different aspects. *Explainability* is about providing clear, human-understandable reasons for why a model made a specific prediction, based on the features that influenced the outcome. *Interpretability* refers to how easily a person can grasp the overall behavior and logic of the model; good interpretability often implies that the model's structure is simple or intuitive enough. *Transparency* means that the model's inner workings, data, and decision processes are open and accessible, allowing users to see exactly how it functions.

This list is just a selection from the long list of concepts you will learn about in this book. The number of terms can feel overwhelming, but you can become fluent in "AI speak." As we introduce groups of concepts, take your time to understand them, including by taking some notes in your "Chapter 2 Notebook" on page 71 as a way to assimilate and memorize the new lingo.

Now, how do we build new AI capabilities in our projects? What are the key pieces that we need to interconnect to create a system that leverages AI for some intended purpose? Let's explore the main building blocks you need to know as an AI project manager.

Building Blocks for AI Systems

You had a brief sneak peek at AI architecture in Chapter 1, in which you learned about the key elements of a proper architecture, including the complete end-to-end workflow that enables most AI applications. In this section, we will go deep into the key building blocks that you need to know, including a wide variety of AI models. As we don't want to give you just a regular introduction, we will link these concepts to the way you will think through situations in AI project management.

Here we'll explore the types of algorithms that support all the previously mentioned capabilities and the key considerations from an AI project manager perspective. Remember that the type and maturity of the chosen AI models will impact not only the best approach to experimentation and implementation but also the best way to roadmap and unlock any potential blockers, as well as to find the required resources and skills for your project.

MACHINE LEARNING

Due to the mature nature of this area, ML models are a great option for specific unitary tasks that allow, for example, the detection of specific patterns in extensive datasets, the segmentation of specific cohorts of clients, and the classification of binary or other situations based on previously labeled data.

While you will face plenty of situations where internal and external stakeholders may feel more excited about other kind of technologies (e.g., deep learning, generative AI) due to their level of technical advancement or current market attention, ML models are the base for a lot of pragmatic and solid implementations.

From a resources point of view, ML models bring obvious advantages:

- Data science and AI professionals usually learn these techniques during their academic journey.

- There are plenty of code repositories with examples that can be quickly adapted and reused.

- The amount of required data is lower than other techniques.

- The trade-off between performance and compute infrastructure requirements is very friendly.

Machine learning concepts

First, let's review a few statistical and machine learning concepts you need to understand before exploring the different types of ML models in this chapter:

Bayesian probability

A fundamental concept in AI probability, Bayesian probability is a way to measure uncertainty by updating your belief about an event based on new evidence using Bayes' theorem (*https://oreil.ly/jmOgW*). If you've studied statistics in the past, you have encountered this foundational statistics concept. If this topic is new to you, you may want to explore it in detail. But for now, just keep in mind that this is a way to deal with uncertainty when you cannot predict one single value from a complex, real-world situation.

Decision trees

Decision trees are used to predict outcomes by learning simple decision rules from features, forming a tree-like model of decisions. Decision trees split data step-by-step by asking yes/no questions on features to arrive at a prediction. This makes them highly explainable.

Directed acyclic graphs (DAGs)

More complex than a decision tree, a DAG is a type of graph made up of nodes. The nodes are connected by edges that have one direction (from one node to another). They also have no cycles, meaning that you cannot start at one node and follow a path that leads back to the same node. Figure 2-3 shows the difference between a directed tree (on the left) and a DAG (in the center). A graph with cycles would be described as a directed diagram (on the right).

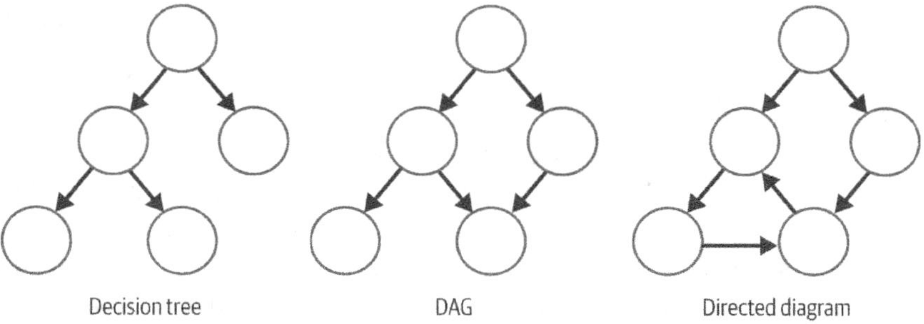

Figure 2-3. Decision tree, directed acyclic graph, and directed diagram

Support vector machines (SVMs)

An SVM is a type of model that finds the optimal *hyperplane*, or boundary, that separates classes. It is based on the idea that *margin* is the distance between the hyperplane and the closest data points (also known as *support vectors*) from each class.

Ensemble methods

These are ML methods in which multiple models are combined to make better predictions than any single model alone. The goal is to reduce potential overfitting and bias that will lead to lower performance in your projects. When several models are combined, the algorithm may gain an understanding of more complex datasets and patterns, resulting in higher-quality final output.

Random forest

A random forest is an ensemble method based on combining several decision trees to reduce overfitting and improve output accuracy. Decision trees are combined by averaging their results (for regression) or using majority voting (for classification models).

Gradient boosting

Another ensemble method, gradient boosting involves building models one after another. Each new model tries to fix the mistakes of the previous ones, often using decision trees. So where a random forest simply combines models, here the goal is to chain multiple models so they improve step-by-step and then combine their multiple outputs. Boosting methods can achieve better performance for certain complex tasks. Keep in mind XGBoost (*https://oreil.ly/ff6bc*), as it is one of the classics and a favorite of data and AI teams. It works well with the kind of structured (tabular) data often found in business contexts and is a clear top performer for multiple use cases.

Bagging

Also known as *bootstrap aggregating*, this ensemble learning technique improves model stability and accuracy by training multiple versions of a model on different random samples of the data and then combining their predictions. The idea is to diversify model input by leveraging multiple parts of the training dataset. For that to work, the dataset needs to be split while maintaining statistical representativeness in each of the resulting datasets.

K-nearest neighbors (k-NN)

This is a technique that predicts the output for a new data point by looking at the k closest points (similar samples) in the training data and choosing the most common label (for classification) or average (for regression). This means that if you wanted to analyze a specific situation, you would check an existing set of samples and find the most similar ones to understand the situation and make a proper prediction.

Dimensionality reduction

Dimensionality reduction is the process of simplifying data by reducing the number of input features while keeping the important information. In practical terms, this means reducing complexity and noise from the original dataset. It also enables higher computational efficiency and potentially better model performance.

Principal component analysis (PCA)
One of the main dimensionality reduction techniques, PCA transforms features into uncorrelated principal components. Basically, it involves translating very complex information into understandable, easier-to-consume pieces. A classic among AI techniques, PCA is likely to be known and loved by your technical team members.

These foundational ML concepts are essential for understanding how various ML models make predictions and manage data complexity.

Machine learning models

Now that you understand some lingo and fundamentals, let's explore the most relevant ML models, organized by each type of task you'll need to be familiar with. Let's start with the unsupervised approaches:

Anomaly detection
In general terms, anomaly detection can help you analyze specific data patterns to find atypical values or outliers. ML models focus on the ability to spot this information from datasets that contain *features* (i.e., characteristics, often represented as columns) related to the client, user, machine, or any other context. From a learning perspective, these techniques are mainly unsupervised, which lowers the barrier to entry created by a need for subject matter expert (SME) knowledge and for data annotation. However, anomaly detection can also be a supervised method if there are already labeled examples of normal and anomalous instances. Here are a couple of anomaly detection techniques you may want to keep in mind when you have a new project that may have a need for them:

One-class SVM
A one-class support vector machine is a type of SVM that is trained on "normal" data to learn the decision boundary of regular observations. It is particularly effective for high-dimensional data with more than one hundred features and is often used in detecting fraud, monitoring system health, and identifying outliers.

PCA-based anomaly detection

Principal component analysis is a dimensionality reduction technique that can also be used to detect anomalies by identifying data points that lie far from the principal components. It is useful when dealing with noise-prone data and works well in cases requiring fast detection with low computational complexity.

Clustering

Clustering is another data-centric and unsupervised approach. You can apply analytical techniques to data to find mathematical values and distances that allow you to cluster, or segment, the data into different groups. As a project manager, note that this is a low-risk approach, as these techniques are pretty mature and rely minimally on human knowledge. For example, you don't need a deep understanding of the business to know how many clusters to look for.

k-means clustering

One popular unsupervised algorithm used to partition data into clusters is k-*means clustering*. This works by minimizing the variance within each cluster. It's efficient, scalable, and useful in customer segmentation, document classification, and image compression, where labels are unknown and pattern discovery is desired.

Both anomaly detection and clustering are useful techniques for concrete scenarios. They are highly accessible thanks to their unsupervised-first approach, which also makes your project implementations simpler. But most of the ML projects out there rely on human knowledge in the form of data labeling and supervised learning. Models that undergo these training methods can replicate a human understanding of reality, and they can reach high levels of performance for numerical and categorical predictions, often referred to as regression and classification tasks. Let's explore the relevant supervised approaches:

Regression

Think of regression as numerical prediction. This ML method estimates the relationships between a dependent variable (the target) and one or more independent variables or features. It is primarily used to predict continuous numerical values such as prices, temperature, sales, etc.

Regressions are based on certain assumptions about the data (e.g., that the relationship between inputs and outcomes is reasonably consistent). If those assumptions don't hold, the results of a regression may be less reliable. Here are a few types of regression you may hear about in your AI projects:

Linear regression

This is a foundational model that predicts continuous variables using linear relationships. It is simple, interpretable, and effective when the relationship between inputs and output is approximately linear. Imagine, for example, predicting a student's final exam score based on hours studied and attendance rate.

Ordinal regression

This type of regression is used when the target variable has a natural order but no fixed interval between values. For example, ordinal regression might be used to predict customer satisfaction ratings (1 = very dissatisfied, ..., 5 = very satisfied) from delivery time and product quality, where the difference between 1 and 2, or 2 and 3, is not defined because they are just categories. (You cannot say that the difference between ratings of 1 and 2 is the same as the difference between ratings of 2 and 3.)

Poisson regression

This regression technique models count data and is appropriate when the target variable represents counts (amounts) or frequency of events. Examples would be a positive number of purchases, clicks, or calls based on specific variables such as active users and day of the week. In this case, the regression models the potential number based on historical information.

Fast forest quantile regression

This is a tree-based ensemble method that uses a group of decision trees designed to predict not just point estimates but also conditional distributions (*quantiles* in statistics) of the target variable. For example, this could help estimate the 90th percentile (the value below which 90% of the data points fall) of house prices in a city based on square footage, location, and year built. It is ideal for uncertainty modeling and risk assessment, because the decision trees handle the complexity and flexibility that this kind of quantile regression needs without assuming a strict mathematical form for the relationship between variables and the target.

Bayesian linear regression

This variant of linear regression incorporates prior distributions over model parameters, enabling it to model uncertainty in predictions. Based on the idea of Bayesian and conditional probabilities, this approach is useful in probabilistic modeling and when interpretability is important.

Boosted decision tree regression

Boosted trees combine multiple weak learners (decision trees) into a strong ensemble model. They are powerful for capturing complex, nonlinear relationships and are robust to overfitting with proper regularization. Remember that boosting models like XGBoost build an ensemble of trees where each new tree focuses on the mistakes of the previous ones, improving accuracy over time. Therefore, we are talking about a sequential and iterative implementation.

Fast forest regression

This is a parallel implementation of a random forest, which, as you learned earlier, is an ensemble of decision trees that output the average prediction of the individual trees. It is nonlinear, relatively fast to train, and robust, making it suitable for a variety of regression tasks.

Classification (binary)

Instead of generating a numerical prediction like regression models do, classification groups and predicts by *classes*, or categories. It could be as simple as classifying emails as "spam" or "not spam" based on features like sender address, keywords, and message length. Or it could be as complex as predicting whether a patient has a particular type of cancer based on high-dimensional data such as gene expression levels, medical imaging data, and clinical history. Some classifcation techniques include:

Naive Bayes

This simple and fast classification algorithm uses probability and assumes that all features are independent. Although in reality this assumption rarely holds, the technique often works well.

Two-class SVM

Like one-class SVM for anomaly detection, two-class support vector machines find the hyperplane that maximally separates two classes in feature space. They are effective in high-dimensional spaces and are robust to overfitting. However, SVMs can become computationally expensive as the number of data points grows, making them less practical for very large datasets.

Two-class averaged perceptron

This simple linear classifier updates weights using the average of all weight vectors obtained during training. Fast and lightweight, it's useful for large-scale or streaming data where interpretability isn't a primary concern.

Two-class logistic regression

Following the same principle as other regression models but adapted to classification scenarios, a logistic regression estimates the probability that a given input belongs to a certain class. It's interpretable, fast, and works well for linearly separable problems and applications like spam detection or churn prediction.

Two-class Bayes point machine

This probabilistic model approximates the average of all hypotheses that correctly classify the data. It's useful when probabilistic output and theoretical soundness (solid and well-established mathematical principles and reasoning) are important, although it's less commonly used than logistic regression.

Two-class decision forest

This model involves an ensemble of decision trees trained via bagging. It offers robustness, handles nonlinear data well, and is suitable for many general classification tasks. The final output is decided by combining the separate model predictions through a "vote." The vote tally can be based on the general number of class votes per model (hard approach) or on the highest class probability voted by the models (soft approach). Voting helps improve accuracy by leveraging the strengths of different models and offsetting individual model errors.

Two-class boosted decision tree

Based on the same pattern as the regression models (XGBoost works well for both regression and classification tasks), this is a powerful classifier that builds trees sequentially, focusing on correcting errors made by previous ones. It excels in accuracy and handles mixed data types well, and it is often used in competitive ML tasks. As a project manager, be aware that this model is a bit more complex and requires more training effort than some others.

Two-class decision jungle

In this variant of a decision forest, the structure is a directed acyclic graph instead of a tree. This design allows for feature sharing between paths and works well for complex decision boundaries.

Classification (multiclass)

Though it is similar to binary classification, relying on similar kinds of algorithms, multiclass classification finds more than two classes or categories. It can be done in various ways, including:

Multiclass logistic regression

This technique extends logistic regression to handle more than two classes, usually via a *softmax function* (a mathematical function that converts raw numerical scores into probabilities for each class). It is interpretable and effective for problems where classes are linearly separable.

Multiclass decision forest

In this ensemble method, each tree votes for a class, and the majority wins. This is an accurate and robust technique for multicategory tasks like image labeling or document classification.

Multiclass decision jungle

Similar to decision forests, the jungle uses a DAG structure that allows node reuse, improving generalization and reducing overfitting on high-dimensional datasets.

One-versus-all multiclass

This is a meta-strategy that breaks down a multiclass problem into multiple binary classification tasks. It allows the reuse of any binary classifier for multiclass settings.

This is a pretty exhaustive list of ML models. For your day-to-day reference as an AI project manager, you can use the summary in Table 2-1 anytime you need to remember the nature of a specific ML model.

Table 2-1. Machine learning models

Task type	Model name	When to use it	AI project manager considerations
Anomaly detection	One-class SVM	When detecting outliers in high-dimensional datasets	Requires only normal class training data; good for fraud and intrusion detection
	PCA-based anomaly detection	When dimensionality reduction is needed; detects anomalies based on variance	Fast and interpretable; assumes linear relationships
Clustering	*k*-means	When grouping unlabeled data into clusters	Simple and scalable; needs the number of clusters defined and assumes spherical clusters
Regression	Linear regression	When predicting continuous values with linear relationships	Very interpretable; weak with nonlinear patterns
	Bayesian linear regression	When uncertainty estimates are needed with linear regression	Adds probabilistic insight; more complex to implement
	Poisson regression	When modeling count-based data (e.g., calls per hour)	Good for prediction of rare events; assumes Poisson-distributed output
	Ordinal regression	When the target has ordered categories (e.g., satisfaction ratings)	Captures order in outputs; less commonly supported in libraries
	Fast forest regression	For robust nonlinear regression tasks	Handles missing values; slower training than linear models

Task type	Model name	When to use it	AI project manager considerations
Regression *cont.*	Fast forest quantile regression	When predicting ranges/quantiles of outcomes	Useful in risk-sensitive domains; more resource-intensive
	Boosted decision tree regression	For complex nonlinear regression problems	High accuracy; sensitive to overfitting and requires tuning
Two-class classification	Logistic regression	For binary classification when interpretability matters	Fast and explainable; poor with nonlinear patterns
	Two-class SVM	For high-dimensional binary classification	Accurate; needs kernel selection and not scalable for huge datasets
	Averaged perceptron	For fast linear classification	Lightweight; not great for nonlinear data
	Bayes point machine	For probabilistic classification	Probabilistic outputs; less commonly used
	Decision forest	When robustness across varied data is required	Ensemble method; less interpretable
	Boosted decision tree	For high-accuracy binary tasks	Often a top performer; sensitive to noise and overfitting
	Decision jungle	For compact models with reused nodes	Efficient; less interpretable than trees

Task type	Model name	When to use it	AI project manager considerations
Multiclass classification	Logistic regression	For simple multiclass classification	Fast and interpretable; less effective for complex data
	Decision forest	For robust multiclass classification	Handles large feature spaces; needs tuning
	Decision jungle	For multiclass tasks with DAG structure	Compact; complexity in understanding internal logic
	One-versus-all	When using binary models for multiclass problems	Flexible; higher training overhead

Remember, these ML models are mature and well-known techniques that fuel plenty of nongenerative AI applications around the world. Your role as an AI project manager will be to bring them to the table anytime a project stakeholder forgets their value as cost-efficient and technically feasible options.

DEEP LEARNING (DL)

We often describe deep learning as a subset of ML or as an expansion of traditional ML capabilities. DL is based on the concept of *neural networks.*

Neural networks are computational models inspired by the structure and function of the human brain. As you can see in Figure 2-4, they consist of layers of interconnected nodes called *neurons,* where each neuron processes input data by applying a weighted sum and neuron activation functions. They are based on the idea of *backpropagation,* a recurrent training process that goes backward from the output layer to the input layer so the model continues to readjust. This is like teaching a neural network by showing it its mistakes and helping it fix them step-by-step.

Neural networks learn to perform tasks by adjusting the mathematical weights through training on data, and they form the foundation of deep learning, with the term *deep* referring to networks of multiple hidden or intermediate layers that can automatically learn complex features and representations from raw data inputs.

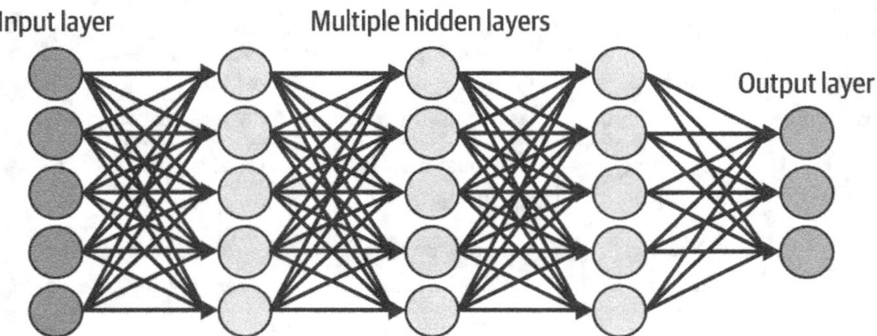

Figure 2-4. Deep learning layers

Compared to other ML models, DL can achieve higher performance depending on the task and conditions, but there are several key considerations:

High data requirements

DL models typically have millions (or even billions) of parameters, making them incredibly powerful but also data hungry. To train these models effectively and avoid overfitting, large volumes of labeled examples must be provided, especially in supervised settings. Without enough data, the model may memorize noise instead of learning meaningful patterns, resulting in poor generalization to new inputs. This is why industries adopting DL often invest heavily in data collection, labeling, and augmentation.

Simplified feature extraction

One of DL's greatest advantages over traditional ML is its ability to automatically learn and extract features from raw data. Instead of manually engineering features (like detecting edges in images or counting keyword frequencies in text), DL models learn hierarchical representations, starting with low-level patterns and combining them into increasingly abstract concepts. This automation significantly reduces the need for domain-specific feature engineering, speeding up development and often improving performance.

Lower explainability

Despite their power, DL models are often considered "black boxes" because their decision-making process is buried in many layers of nonlinear transformations. Unlike with simpler models (e.g., decision trees) that offer clear, rule-based reasoning, it's difficult to pinpoint exactly why a DL model made a specific prediction. This lower explainability can be a drawback in regulated industries like health care or finance, where understanding the reasoning behind decisions is critical, and it has driven research into explainable AI (XAI) methods.

High computational cost

Training DL models often requires powerful hardware like GPUs or tensor processing units (TPUs), which can be expensive to acquire and maintain. Complex architectures and large datasets can lead to long training times, and all of this together will certainly impact your AI project approach and roadmap.

Given their advantages, it will be beneficial for you to keep in mind the various kinds of DL models, which leverage supervised, unsupervised, and reinforcement learning methods, depending on the case:

Neural network regression

Just as with ML, you can perform regression tasks with DL. Neural networks are highly flexible models that can approximate nonlinear relationships between inputs and continuous outputs. They are powerful tools when you have large datasets with complex patterns, and their automated feature extraction is useful for advanced scenarios such as financial forecasting and sensor data analysis.

Feedforward neural network

A *feedforward neural network (FNN)* is the simplest kind of neural network with multiple neurons, lacking any loops or cycles between nodes, and it is optimized for binary classification tasks. It can learn and separate complex patterns in the data, making it well suited for tasks like sentiment analysis and fraud detection.

Two-class locally deep SVM

This combines the SVM (an ML technique) with detailed, learned representations extracted from specific small regions or parts of the input dataset (also known as *local deep features*, obtained via DL models) to improve classification in nonlinear, complex datasets. Accurate output is needed with complex or high-dimensional data.

Multiclass neural network
> This is a multilayer perceptron (MLP) that uses an activation function in the output layer (i.e., softmax) to model probabilities over multiple classes. It excels in problems with high complexity and data variety, such as understanding visual handwriting or performing speech recognition.

Convolutional neural network (CNN)
> These are specialized neural networks designed for processing grid-like data such as images (pixels) or videos (frames). They use convolutional layers (convolutions (*https://oreil.ly/6XVEi*) are a kind of complex mathematical operation) with filters that automatically detect local patterns like edges, textures, and shapes, building hierarchical feature representations. CNNs excel at recognizing spatial structures and are highly efficient, go-to models for computer vision tasks.

Recurrent neural network (RNN)
> RNNs are designed to handle sequential data by maintaining a hidden state or internal memory that captures information from previous inputs, allowing the network to model temporal dependencies. They are widely used for tasks like speech recognition, language modeling, and time series forecasting. However, traditional RNNs struggle with learning long-term dependencies due to issues like vanishing gradients (they become too small) during the backpropagation process, limiting their effectiveness on longer sequences of layers.
>
> Note that techniques like *long short-term memory networks (LSTM networks)* and *gated recurrent units (GRUs)* improve regular RNNs by introducing gating mechanisms that control the flow of information, effectively solving the vanishing gradient problem. This allows RNNs to capture long-range dependencies in sequences of layers and neurons, making them powerful tools for applications involving complex sequential data such as machine translation, speech synthesis, and video analysis.
>
> While newer generative AI techniques are gaining attention, established architectures like CNNs, RNNs, and LSTM remain widely used. For example, CNNs continue to power image classification and quality inspection systems, and RNNs/LSTM are still effective for time series forecasting, speech recognition, and sequential data modeling.

Autoencoder

This type of unsupervised neural network is designed to learn compressed, efficient representations of input data by encoding inputs into a lower-dimensional latent space and then reconstructing them. Autoencoders are widely used for dimensionality reduction, anomaly detection, and data denoising, enabling models to capture essential patterns without requiring labeled data.

Deep reinforcement learning (RL)

Deep RL combines deep neural networks with reinforcement learning principles to enable agents to learn complex policies for sequential decision-making tasks. These agents are not to be confused with the "AI agents" that you hear about everywhere lately, which we'll discuss later in the chapter. These are RL agents that follow some strategy to achieve a specific reward and iterate to optimize a final result. This is not the kind of technology you may see in your day-to-day work as an AI project manager, but it's important to know what it is because deep RL has powered breakthroughs in areas like game playing (e.g., AlphaGo (*https://oreil.ly/2R1-I*)), robotics, and autonomous systems.

Table 2-2 will help you remember all these DL models. Depending on the approach, keep in mind that you will need to balance complexity and time to implementation. As an AI project manager, you will work with your data scientists to understand the potential trade-offs and required training iterations, as these factors will impact the number of days and compute resources allocated for experimentation.

Being intentional at this stage will help you effectively plan your AI project. You'll play a key role in guiding discussions to determine the appropriate level of expertise needed for various tasks. For example, some advanced techniques may require senior data scientists with more specialized training. You'll also help decide when it's necessary to train custom models versus using prebuilt cloud AI services for tasks like image recognition, video analysis, or speech-to-text. Ultimately, the goal is to find the best solution that offers the highest ROI with the lowest possible cost.

For a quick reference, you may want to keep these summary tables along with Microsoft's model cheat sheet from Figure 2-5 close at hand anytime you want to discuss potential ML and DL model choices with your team.

Table 2-2. Deep learning models

Task type	Model name	When to use it	AI project manager considerations
Regression	Neural network regression	For large-scale data with nonlinear dependencies	High capacity; requires careful tuning and more compute
Two-class classification	Neural network (two-class)	For binary tasks with complex patterns	Handles nonlinear features; requires labeled data and compute
	Locally deep SVM (hybrid ML & DL)	For nonlinear binary classification	Combines local and deep features; complex to tune
Multiclass classification	Neural network (multiclass)	For large, nonlinear multiclass tasks	High performance; requires GPU/TPU resources
Image processing	Convolutional neural networks (CNNs)	For images, videos, and spatial data pattern recognition	Efficient at learning local features; needs lots of labeled data and compute
Sequential data	Recurrent neural networks (RNNs)	For sequential data like text, speech, and time series	Captures temporal dependencies; can be slow to train and suffer from vanishing gradients
	LSTM/GRU	For long-range dependencies in sequences	Better than standard RNNs at learning long sequences; more complex
Unsupervised learning	Autoencoders	For dimensionality reduction and anomaly detection	Learns data representations without labels; needs careful design
Reinforcement learning (RL)	Deep RL	For decision making in dynamic environments	Complex training with environment interaction; requires careful reward design

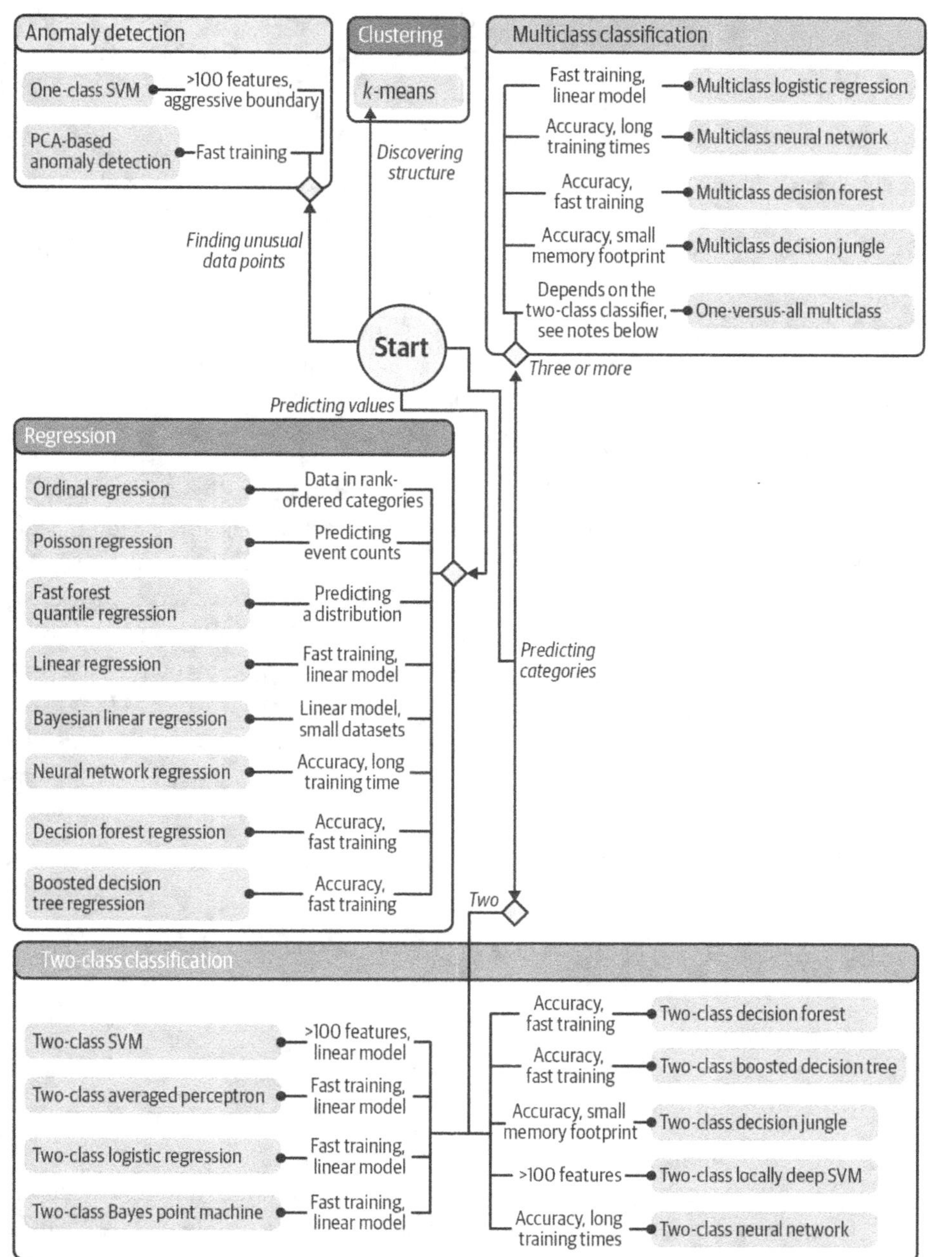

Figure 2-5. Machine learning and deep learning cheat sheet (adapted from Microsoft)

Remember that you, as an AI project manager, are entitled to ask questions and bring potential options to your technical teams. Let's now explore language and generative AI models.

NATURAL LANGUAGE PROCESSING AND GENERATIVE AI

This section covers a series of capabilities and models related to NLP and generative AI (GenAI). While GenAI is not used only for linguistic tasks, there is a clear relationship and even a sort of evolution from traditional NLP technologies to the LLMs fueling models like ChatGPT, Microsoft Copilot, and Google Gemini. You are likely to leverage these technologies for most of your new AI projects, as organizations continue to adopt generative AI. Here are some key concepts you need to know as background for your AI projects:

Tokenization

This is the process of breaking text into smaller units, called *tokens*, such as words or subwords, for easier processing by models. It is similar to the way we learned our mother tongue in school, usually by splitting sentences into several pieces. This is the process of breaking text into smaller units, called tokens, such as words or subwords, for easier processing by models. While we were taught in school to analyze our mother tongue by identifying formal parts of speech like nouns, verbs, and articles, modern AI models often use tokenization as a starting point to focus on entities and intent. By breaking text down into these functional pieces, we can more easily filter out semantically irrelevant information. Some concepts that complement the tokenization process are these:

Named-entity recognition (NER)

A task that identifies and classifies key entities (like names, dates, locations) in text

Intent recognition

The process of identifying the underlying purpose or goal behind a user's input for conversational or search tasks

Stopword removal

The process of filtering out frequently occurring words that usually carry little meaningful information in text analysis (e.g., *the, is, and, but*).

Vectors

Vectors are numerical representations of data (e.g., tokens, entire words, images) in a continuous space with values and coordinates that machines use to perform mathematical operations on this data. From a mathematical point of view, vectors can be 2D or 3D representations used for other, non-AI domains or high-dimensional vector representations (with hundreds or thousands of dimensions) used for AI tasks. A concept closely related to vectors is that of *embeddings*, which represent learned mapping that converts discrete tokens into high-dimensional, dense vectors, capturing semantic relationships between them. For example, a vector for the word *cat* can look like this: `[0.12, -0.34, 0.56, 0.88, -0.45]`, where each number is a coordinate in the embedding space. Similar words like *kitten* or *feline* would have vectors with similar values, reflecting their related meanings. Thus, AI models can spot these relationships to find similarities and related information. This mathematical "closeness" is how AI actually "understands" meaning: it doesn't just match keywords but instead calculates the "distance" between ideas. This is the secret sauce behind modern search engines that can answer what you meant to ask, even if you didn't use the exact right words.

Attention mechanism or self-attention

Self-attention is a method that allows models to weigh the importance of different parts of input data (e.g., specific parts of a text, like key intent and entities) dynamically, improving context understanding in a more efficient manner than traditional language techniques. This is highly technical, but if you want to explore this concept, your main reference is Google's "Attention Is All You Need" paper (*https://arxiv.org/abs/1706.03762*), the real foundation of the modern GenAI era.

Training

While you will learn more about AI model lifecycles in Chapter 5, it is important for you to understand that approaches to model training depend on the type of model. Discriminative (nongenerative AI, e.g., ML or DL) and generative AI models are not trained the same way. For non-GenAI tools, you will rely on one model along with the dataset to train them on a specific type of task. GenAI models, on the other hand, are pretrained by default on a massive amount of information, and the training process follows a different pattern:

Pretraining

In this initial phase, the model learns from vast, diverse datasets to build a broad, general understanding of language, facts, and patterns. This stage equips the model with foundational knowledge and the ability to generate coherent, context-aware text across many topics without task-specific guidance.

Posttraining

After pretraining, the model is adapted and refined for specific tasks or domains. This primarily involves *fine-tuning* on specialized datasets, but other techniques may be used as well, such as reinforcement learning from human feedback (RLHF) (*https://oreil.ly/iHACM*), to improve performance, alignment, and safety in ways tailored to particular applications.

Multimodality

Multimodality in AI refers to a concept similar to multimodal transportation, where for example cargo might be transported first by ship and then by truck. With multimodality, an AI model can process and integrate information from multiple types of data, such as text, images, and audio. It also allows the generation of output in different formats, and it expands the possibilities for your AI projects. Most of the state-of-the-art models from top AI providers are already multimodal.

Retrieval-augmented generation (RAG)

RAG is an approach that enhances generative AI models by allowing them to access external information (e.g., knowledge bases, databases, documentation, websites, etc.) before producing a response. Instead of relying solely on what the model learned during the training, RAG first retrieves relevant content from a trusted source and then uses that information to generate a more accurate and context-aware answer.

In practical terms, this means the AI is not just "guessing" based on past training but grounding its responses in real, up-to-date, or proprietary data. RAG is commonly used in internal knowledge assistants, customer support systems, and document-based Q&A tools, where accuracy and alignment with company-specific information are critical.

Most of your GenAI projects will probably use RAG. Also, you can leverage the same RAG pattern with your external data sources while updating and replacing the models, without losing previous effort that went into the project.

Fine-tuning

Fine-tuning is a different approach to customizing a generative AI model. Instead of retrieving external information at the time of each question, like RAG does, fine-tuning involves further training a pretrained model on a specific dataset so it learns a particular style, domain, or task more deeply. In other words, you update the model itself so it becomes better aligned with your use case.

In practice, fine-tuning is useful when you want the model to consistently follow certain formats, tone, terminology, or domain-specific patterns such as legal drafting, medical documentation, or brand-specific messaging. Compared to RAG, fine-tuning is, at least in theory, better suited for specialized tasks but less flexible when information frequently changes. However, the reality is that most projects rely on RAG patterns. Moreover, fine-tuning doesn't guarantee better results due to its technical complexity. Also, the fine-tuned knowledge is not portable to newer models and versions, a limitation that is a definite drawback from a project investment and ROI perspective.

AI agents

Last but not least, we have AI agents, one of the most trendy topics out there. An AI agent is usually defined as some sort of autonomous system that perceives its environment (e.g., existing tools, potential actions), makes decisions, and performs actions to achieve goals. For example, imagine an agent that retrieves information about customers and autonomously connects to multiple sources until it finds the proper data, without your having to explain every single step required to achieve that goal.

While people and companies use "agents" for pretty much everything, keep in mind that true AI agents are not static workflows that combine a series of steps and tools. Instead, they are automated and autonomous tools that iterate to complete a series of tasks.

The skills your AI teams need may be a little different from those needed for ML and DL technologies, which are more science-focused. We'll go into more detail in Chapter 3, but it's important to know that the industry is now moving toward more engineering-focused roles. There's less need for data science skills, since GenAI models are already trained. In fact, most organizations are now working mainly on connecting existing tools and combining prebuilt models with their own private data. From an AI PM perspective, that means that you will interact more with what we call *AI engineers*, a mix of AI professionals with engineering software development skills, and *cloud professionals* to leverage SaaS infrastructure. Obviously, exactly who you work with depends on the organization and the available team, roles, and individual skills.

Here is a list of models and techniques that will consolidate your NLP and GenAI knowledge. Once again, there's no need to be a technical expert to manage your AI projects, but it doesn't hurt to know about these when you engage in discussions with your team members.

Term frequency–inverse document frequency (TF-IDF)
> TF-IDF transforms text into numerical features by measuring how important a word is to a document in a collection. Additionally, these features can then be used with ML models like SVMs, logistic regression, or naive Bayes for tasks such as spam filtering, sentiment analysis, and topic classification. This approach is lightweight, interpretable, and suitable for small to medium datasets. Certainly, TF-IDF is one of the classic tools for any NLP-enabled project.

Bag-of-words (BoW)
> An alternative to TF-IDF, BoW is a simpler way to represent text data by treating each document as an unordered collection ("bag") of words, ignoring grammar, word order, and context. This means that BoW offers a raw word count (frequency) for a document, which is good for quick baseline models and very simple text classifications.

Latent Dirichlet allocation (LDA)
> LDA is a probabilistic model used for topic modeling, as it can automatically discover hidden themes or topics in a large collection of documents. It's useful for exploring large bodies of text and identifying abstract themes or clusters of documents.

Hidden Markov models (HMMs)

Commonly used in sequence-labeling tasks like part-of-speech tagging and named-entity recognition, HMMs model the probability of a sequence of observed events and underlying hidden states.

Word embeddings via Word2Vec, GloVe, FastText

These models map words to dense vector representations that capture semantic relationships. Pretrained embeddings can be used as input to neural networks or directly in specific tasks.

Sequence-to-sequence (Seq2Seq) models

Seq2Seq architectures are used for translation, summarization, and dialogue generation. They consist of an encoder that processes the input sequence and a decoder that generates the output sequence.

CNNs for text classification

While CNNs are primarily used for images, they can also be applied to NLP by treating text as a 1D signal. CNNs capture patterns in the text and are efficient for tasks like sentiment classification and intent recognition.

Generative adversarial networks (GANs)

A GAN consists of two neural networks (known as the *generator* and the *discriminator*) that compete in a zero-sum game. The generator tries to create realistic synthetic data to fool the discriminator, which attempts to distinguish real from generated data. This adversarial training approach leads to the creation of highly realistic images, videos, and other data types, with applications in image synthesis, style transfer, and data augmentation.

Transformer models

These models have revolutionized data sequence processing via self-attention mechanisms that weigh the importance of all parts of the input sequence simultaneously, enabling efficient parallel processing and better modeling of long-range dependencies. Transformers are the foundation of systems like Bidirectional Encoder Representations from Transformers (BERT) and generative pre-trained transformers (GPTs).

Table 2-3 provides a summary of models likely to be referenced during your NLP and GenAI projects.

Table 2-3. Natural language processing and GenAI models

Task type	Model name	When to use it	AI project manager considerations
NLP preprocessing	TF-IDF	For small/medium-scale NLP classification tasks	Easy to explain; sparse representation; limited contextual info
	Bag-of-words	For basic text models	Fast and simple; ignores order/context
NLP topic modeling	Latent Dirichlet allocation (LDA)	For discovering latent topics in documents	Good for summarization/clustering; needs human validation of topics
NLP sequence labeling	Hidden Markov model (HMM)	For part-of-speech tagging, named entity recognition (NER) in simpler domains	Historically important; largely replaced by deep models
NLP embeddings	Word2Vec	When semantic similarity is needed	Fast, efficient; no context sensitivity
NLP embeddings	GloVe	When general-purpose word vectors are needed	Dense vectors; static (context agnostic)
NLP embeddings	FastText	For subword modeling and rare-word handling	Handles unseen words; larger memory footprint
NLP contextual models	BERT	For tasks needing deep language understanding (e.g., QA, NER)	High accuracy; needs GPU and fine-tuning pipeline
NLP Seq2Seq	Seq2Seq (encoder-decoder)	For translation, summarization, dialogue generation	Flexible for text-to-text; can be complex to train
NLP classification	CNN for text	When local patterns in text are predictive	Efficient; less context aware than transformers

Task type	Model name	When to use it	AI project manager considerations
Generative models	Generative adversarial networks (GANs)	For generating realistic synthetic data	Training can be unstable; requires expertise in balancing generator and discriminator
Natural language processing/ generation	Transformer models (e.g., BERT, GPT)	For NLP and sequence modeling with long-range context	State-of-the-art performance; requires very large datasets and heavy compute

This set of ML, DL, NLP, and GenAI models may represent 95% of the projects you will be managing. However, keep in mind that there are other models that can be interesting for your AI projects:

Recommender systems

Algorithms like collaborative filtering, content-based filtering, matrix factorization (e.g., singular value decomposition or SVD), and deep learning (e.g., neural collaborative filtering) are used to suggest items tailored to user preferences. Real-world applications include Amazon's product recommendations, TikTok's personalized video ranking feeds, and Spotify's playlist creation (e.g., Discover Weekly).

Time series analysis

Techniques such as autoregressive integrated moving average (ARIMA), exponential smoothing, Facebook's Prophet, and LSTM recurrent neural networks model data that evolves over time. They are widely applied in forecasting electricity demand for power grids, predicting stock prices in finance, and monitoring IoT sensor data in manufacturing to detect anomalies.

Optimization (operational research)

Methods including linear programming (using the simplex method), integer programming, dynamic programming, gradient-based optimization, and evolutionary algorithms are used to find the best solution under constraints. Real-world uses include scheduling airline crews and flights to reduce costs, planning efficient delivery routes by companies like UPS and

FedEx, and optimizing hospital staff shifts to balance budgets and patient care.

While there's no need to learn all the details of these models, do remember that they exist. From time to time, you may identify new use cases that require recommendation, time series, or optimization capabilities. Your active collaboration with your data scientists and other technical team members will help the team determine the best approaches.

Conclusion

By now, you should feel a bit more AI savvy, and hopefully you feel more prepared to facilitate group and one-on-one discussions with your technical team members. AI project managers are expected to be familiar with the terms introduced in this chapter and understand the basic nature of the models discussed. As you get practical experience with AI projects, you will gain an additional level of understanding of the complexities and trade-offs of implementation and the impact of different choices on required resources. Only you can decide how technical is "technical enough" for you to contribute to the operational day-to-day of your AI projects.

Your foundational learning is not over! You also need to understand the end-to-end AI project lifecycle, from the preparation of input data sources to other building blocks (such as libraries and frameworks) for your AI architectures. But don't worry: all those will be covered (along with your role during each project phase) in Chapters 5 and 6.

Meanwhile, we'll turn to Chapter 3, where you will learn more about your role as AI project manager and the relationship you'll have with your teams and other stakeholders. The next chapter will be a bit less technical than this one but is equally relevant to your continued upskilling and preparation for AI project management. Keep it up!

Chapter 2 Notebook

The Role of the AI Project Manager

The project manager is arguably one of the most underrated roles in the technology industry. Often seen as an overhead cost to be minimized, people in this role sometimes are made to work on too many projects at the same time and end up getting stretched too thin. Why spend valuable investors' dollars on a role that doesn't directly further the project's progress? After all, PMs aren't the ones training the models, are they?

Unlike traditional software development projects, AI projects are full of uncertainties. Their dependency on high-quality data and the need to constantly retrain the models make the AI project lifecycle look more like a plate of spaghetti than a beautiful linear Waterfall project or iterative Agile sprints. Unfortunately, the engineers and data scientists are often left to make sense of the mess on their own. That's where the need for PMs comes in: to make the plate look less like spaghetti and more like neatly layered lasagna.

So the question is: What if the role of the AI project manager is not just helpful but actually critical to any AI initiative's success? What if the many projects failing around the world could leverage advanced AI PMs with skill sets adapted to the complex nature of these projects to avoid continuous failures, cost overruns, and unfulfilled expectations?

In this chapter, we discuss the role of PMs in an AI project context, going well beyond the tasks of maintaining schedules and creating dashboards. We'll assess the responsibilities and specific skills required to successfully lead and support AI projects.

Project Management and Hybrid Skills

When hiring managers think about the role of an AI PM, they have an expectation that this person will come in and magically make everything make sense. With their special powers, the PM will close up all the gaps that have been hindering development and uncover the answers to every question that leaders have been struggling with. The launch date question we keep getting from stakeholders? The new PM will answer it. What about the solution to the added feature that sales asked for? The new PM will coordinate that. And the resourcing gap we have, will they fill that too? Well, yes, of course they will.

Since the recruitment team cannot post a job description that says "Will fix all our problems," they are forced to come up with a job description with a list of qualifications and skills. In perusing the job postings available on LinkedIn at the time of writing this chapter, we found that most of them are generic and seem to have been repurposed from existing PM job descriptions for traditional software roles. Intrigued, we asked ChatGPT to check out all the active job descriptions of AI PMs available in English on LinkedIn and extract keywords, then rank the keywords in descending order based on occurrence. Figure 3-1 is the result, showcasing the most frequently mentioned responsibilities and skills in current AI PM job descriptions.

Many keywords associated with Agile methodologies, such as Agile, Scrum, and Kanban, top the list, followed by traditional project management tasks like stakeholder management, change management, and risk mitigation. To gain more insight into this phenomenon, wait for Chapter 4, where you will explore the convergence between project management and roles such as scrum master and product owner.

You may also notice that terms more specific to data and AI appear much less frequently in the job descriptions, and when they do show up, they're broad concepts like artificial intelligence/machine learning understanding or data governance. This isn't so much a reflection of the job descriptions themselves but rather of the hiring managers and the organizations as a whole. It suggests that leadership doesn't really know how to articulate what they are looking for in this role. So rather than listing all the problems the AI PM will be solving, they opt to go with the responsibilities and skills they are familiar with. The reality is that managing complex projects is especially challenging when the features sometimes feel like unknown black holes and the definition of success is often a moving target. A lot of the time, teams don't know what they are looking for, but they know what it is when they see it.

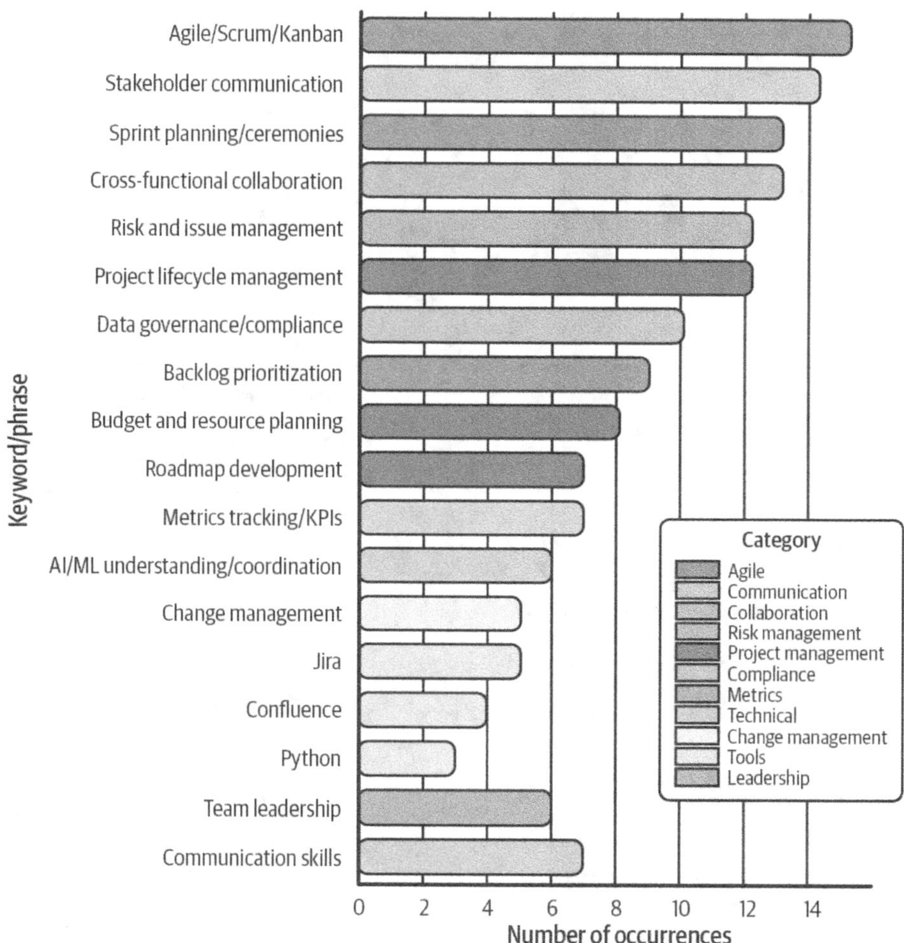

Figure 3-1. Top responsibilities and keywords in functional AI roles (data from LinkedIn)

So before we move on, consider Figure 3-2, which illustrates the mix of skills that we believe an ideal AI project manager should have. Feel free to use the "Chapter 3 Notebook" on page 115 to evaluate your own level of knowledge and experience in each of these areas.

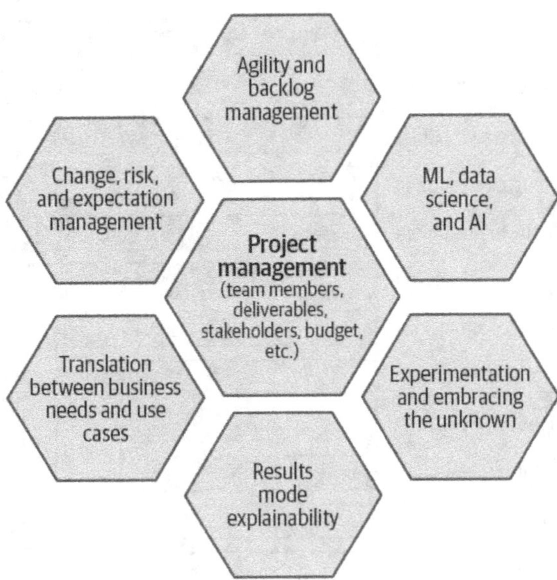

Figure 3-2. AI project management mix of skills

At the end of each of the following sections, you'll have an opportunity to reflect on your current level in each group of skills and document your self-assessment.

AI AND DATA SCIENCE KNOWLEDGE

While it is not necessary for you as an AI project manager to be a data scientist or ML engineer, you must have a solid technical understanding of the fundamental principles of AI, data science, and the underlying technologies. This will enable you to:

Understand the AI project lifecycle
> The AI PM should be familiar with the complete flow of an AI project, which includes data collection and preparation, model development and training, and solution implementation or deployment.

Communicate effectively with the technical team
> Data scientists and engineers work with complex algorithms, massive data-sets, and advanced statistical methodologies. A highly capable AI project manager will be able to interpret their needs, barriers, and progress without relying entirely on simplified explanations.

Make informed decisions

It is essential that the PM understand key concepts such as supervised and unsupervised ML, neural networks, DL, NLP, and the limitations of different types of models. This will enable the PM to make strategic decisions, prioritize tasks, and adjust customer or stakeholder expectations in a realistic manner.

For example, if a team is working on a classification model, you should understand what the terms *accuracy*, *recall*, and *ROC curve* (receiver operating characteristic curve) mean and how these indicators are used to evaluate model performance. With this knowledge, you can help define clear stakeholder expectations about the results and the time required to optimize the model.

Self-evaluation: AI and data science knowledge
☐ Low ☐ Medium ☐ Strong

PROFICIENCY IN AGILE METHODOLOGIES AS ADAPTED TO AI

The AI project manager must not only be an expert in Agile and hybrid methodologies but also be able to adapt them to the specific context of AI projects, which often require greater flexibility and iteration due to the experimental nature of working with data and models. Some competencies in this area include:

Adaptation of sprints and iterative cycles

Since AI experiments may require more time than planned, it is essential to know how to adjust sprints and priorities according to the results obtained, without compromising the delivery of continuous value.

Technical and data backlog management

In AI, tasks often involve a high degree of uncertainty (e.g., data quality issues or a need to adjust models). An Agile AI manager must be able to manage a product backlog that integrates both model development and data management, prioritizing tasks according to their technical and business value.

Flexibility in planning

AI projects often do not have predictable outcomes and may require continuous experimentation. This requires project managers to be comfortable managing ambiguity and adjusting expectations with stakeholders as AI experiments progress.

For example, you could use Scrum with an iterative approach, where each sprint aims to develop and fine-tune an AI model, allowing the results of each cycle to be evaluated and adjusted in real time. In addition, you could implement Kanban to manage task flows related to data preparation or machine learning pipeline refinement. Stay tuned: in Chapter 4 you will learn more about project management methodologies and their suitability for AI project management purposes.

Self-evaluation: Agile methodologies as adapted to AI
☐ Low   ☐ Medium   ☐ Strong

COMMUNICATION AND COLLABORATION SKILLS

An AI project manager must be an excellent communicator. Clear and effective communication is critical to coordinate work across cross-functional teams (e.g., data scientists, software engineers, and business analysts) and to keep stakeholders (e.g., executives, product managers, and customers) aligned. To achieve this, the AI PM must master several key interpersonal and organizational capabilities:

Be fluent in technical and nontechnical communication
> The AI PM must be able to translate technical language into terms understandable to nontechnical stakeholders and, at the same time, grasp the technical needs of the AI team. This skill is crucial to manage expectations and ensure that all stakeholders understand the challenges and progress of the project.

Encourage collaboration among multidisciplinary teams
> AI projects involve diverse specialists, from data scientists to infrastructure engineers. A good PM will be able to facilitate smooth collaboration between the people in these roles and across diverse teams, resolving conflicts and ensuring that everyone is working toward a common goal.

Listen and synthesize needs
> The PM must be able to listen to stakeholders, understand their business needs, and synthesize them into clear technical requirements for the AI

team. They must also be adept at managing expectations, especially in cases where AI experiments do not yield the intended results.

For example, here is a classic situation. During a sprint review, you may need to explain to stakeholders that, although the current model is 85% accurate, the team is working on improving that accuracy by collecting more data and adjusting the model architecture. At the same time, you will need to communicate business priorities to the AI team, ensuring that key metrics reflect strategic objectives.

Self-evaluation: Communication and collaboration skills
☐ Low ☐ Medium ☐ Strong

DATA MANAGEMENT SKILLS

AI projects depend on the quality and quantity of data. Therefore, AI project managers must be familiar with data management and understand the common challenges that arise in this field:

Data preparation

Data cleaning, transformation, and enrichment are crucial in any AI project. The PM must be able to collaborate with the team to identify when data is insufficient or inadequate for the needs of the project and then manage the tasks necessary to improve its quality.

Big data knowledge

Many AI projects require the processing of large volumes of data (big data), so the PM must understand how platforms and tools work to perform distributed processing (e.g., Databricks, Snowflake, Hadoop, Spark) and ensure that the team has the right infrastructure in place.

Data governance and privacy

Given the increasing focus on data privacy and regulations (such as the General Data Protection Regulation, or GDPR, and the California Consumer Privacy Act, or CCPA), the PM must make sure that data is handled in an ethical and legal manner. This involves working closely with compliance teams and ensuring that AI workflows respect regulatory frameworks.

An AI PM can lead the definition of the process to implement an end-to-end data pipeline to guarantee that the data science team has access to clean, well-structured data, while verifying that all applicable privacy regulations are met in the data collection process. In this case, your main interfaces will be your data engineers and data administrators.

Self-evaluation: Data management skills
☐ Low ☐ Medium ☐ Strong

DATA-DRIVEN DECISION-MAKING CAPABILITIES

AI project managers must have a data-driven approach to decision making. This means they must be able to interpret data and metrics, both technical and business, to make informed decisions that optimize project performance. By moving beyond just reading reports and instead using data as a strategic tool, the PM can effectively manage the following responsibilities:

Evaluate model performance
> It is crucial that PMs be able to interpret model performance metrics (e.g., accuracy, F1 score (*https://oreil.ly/wRmao*), recall) and use them to make decisions about whether to further iterate a model, change the approach to development, or prioritize other experiments.

Prioritization based on business metrics
> PMs must be able to tie technical results to business objectives and use data to justify changes in the project roadmap.

Resource optimization
> In AI, resources such as computation time and data can be costly. The PM must be able to analyze the cost-benefit trade-offs of different approaches and prioritize tasks based on expected results.

Say an AI project is consuming a lot of processing time in the cloud without obtaining a significant improvement in model performance. You might do a cost-benefit analysis and decide with your team to discontinue that experiment, redirecting resources toward obtaining new data or testing other types of algorithms.

Self-evaluation: Data-driven decision-making capabilities
☐ Low ☐ Medium ☐ Strong

LEADERSHIP AND CHANGE MANAGEMENT SKILLS

AI projects often involve significant changes in the way organizations use data and make decisions. AI PMs must be effective leaders and change agents, able to manage resistance to change and encourage the adoption of AI technologies. This requires a balanced approach to managing both the internal morale of the technical team and the broader cultural shifts within the company:

Inspire and motivate the team

Since AI projects can be technically challenging and often require many iterations before yielding tangible results, PMs must be able to keep the team motivated, focused, and aligned with long-term goals.

AI adoption management

The PM must also guide the organization through the AI adoption process, ensuring that all stakeholders understand the value that AI can offer and overcoming any internal resistance.

Facilitate cultural change

AI can change the way an organization makes decisions and operates. The PM must be able to lead this cultural change, promoting a data-driven mindset and ensuring that teams adopt AI tools and processes.

These skills are key to your success and that of your team. You will need to inspire and develop meaningful connections with all relevant stakeholders. Developing change management and leadership skills is of course not simple and will take time, which is all the more reason to begin now.

Self-evaluation: Leadership and change management skills
☐ Low ☐ Medium ☐ Strong

Now that you have a better idea of the skill set and footprint of a valued AI project manager, let's analyze your role and responsibilities.

The next section outlines the value proposition, key responsibilities, and related skills of the AI project manager. As you review this material, take time for self-reflection and evaluate how closely your current understanding of what an AI project manager is aligns with these characteristics of the role.

Key Responsibilities of the AI Project Manager

Let's break down the job requirements for AI project managers into key responsibilities and corresponding skill sets. But because of the nascent nature of the role, let's first confirm the value proposition that effective AI project management brings to the organization.

THE CORE VALUE PROPOSITION OF AN AI PM

To be honest, it's not easy to explain the value of a good project manager. Sometimes we PMs feel defensive when we have to explain the role and get people to believe in its value. The business doesn't always think it needs a PM, but when there isn't one, the difference is definitely noticed.

AI PMs work at the intersection of technology, business transformation, and ethics. The job isn't merely to track project progress but to navigate uncertainties, foster cross-disciplinary alignment, and drive strategic and responsible AI implementation. Core responsibilities of this role, therefore, sit snugly at the intersection of the team, the business, and the technical stakeholders. Let's take a moment to understand the ecosystem of stakeholders whose work is directly impacted by the support of the PM.

Managing AI project stakeholders

AI projects are rarely the work of a single superstar. They are more like an orchestra, where each group of stakeholders plays a different instrument. If one section is too loud or another is missing altogether, the music falls apart. For the AI PM, the job isn't just to make sure everyone shows up but to make sure they're all in tune. As we introduce you to various roles, pause to complete the thought experiments posed at the end of each section. These hypothetical but realistic exercises are designed to help you practice your stakeholder management skills in a safe space. There are no right or wrong answers, but jot down some notes about the thought process you follow to reach your conclusion.

Data scientists and AI engineers The data scientists and AI engineers are often the first people we think of when we think about an AI project. They're the ones experimenting with algorithms, playing with datasets, and tuning models until the results start to look promising. Their contribution is obvious: without them, there's no model and no AI. But they are also the group that tends to get lost in the weeds of technical detail, and they need someone to connect their work to the bigger picture.

From the perspective of the AI PM, this is where translation comes in. The PM makes sure that business goals don't get lost in equations and experiments and that the team has what it needs, whether that's access to clean data, enough compute power, or just protection from ever-changing requests. In practice, the PM helps them focus on the right problems and shields them from the chaos outside the lab.

Where AI projects differ from traditional software development is in the constant uncertainty. A data science team may spend weeks chasing down a small accuracy improvement, only to discover that the data isn't representative enough. Or a model that looks promising in training may completely fall apart when exposed to live data. This is frustrating for scientists, but it's also a natural part of AI development. A strong PM creates a safe space where experimentation and failure are expected, while still keeping an eye on deadlines and value delivery.

Another unique AI challenge is explainability. Business stakeholders and regulators often demand to know *why* a model makes its predictions. That's not an easy question for the technical team to answer when they're deep in model architectures. The PM plays a role in bridging this gap by ensuring explainability reviews are built into the process and by helping to translate technical model behavior into narratives that nontechnical stakeholders can understand.

The data science team needs access to customer data before it can begin model training, and the data has not been forthcoming. Weeks are passing, and frustration is growing. How could the PM step in to keep progress moving while the data issue gets resolved?

MLOps and DevOps teams Data scientists may build brilliant models, but without MLOps and DevOps, those models are destined to live in a Jupyter notebook forever. These teams make sure the work is scalable, monitored, and actually usable in production. Think of them as the bridge between "proof of concept" and "real-world impact."

The AI PM's relationship with this group is all about coordination and expectation setting. MLOps teams care about uptime, reproducibility, and integration, while the business often cares mainly about speed of delivery. The PM sits in the middle, balancing ambition with operational reality and making sure there's a common definition of "done" before anyone celebrates.

AI systems bring added complexity for these teams. Unlike traditional software deployments, models degrade over time as data drifts. This means continuous monitoring and retraining pipelines aren't "nice to have"; they're essential for the system to stay relevant. The PM ensures these needs are understood by executives, who may assume a model is a one-time build. Without that support, MLOps often ends up underfunded and under pressure.

When it comes to reproducibility, a model trained on slightly different data or code may produce different results, a phenomenon that can be a nightmare in regulated industries. PMs help create processes where experiments are tracked, versioned, and auditable so MLOps isn't left scrambling when leadership asks why a model decision can't be re-created.

The data science team insists that the model is ready for deployment, but MLOps is flagging concerns about monitoring and reliability. As a PM, how would you handle this tension between pushing forward and slowing down to ensure robustness?

Product owners and business stakeholders If data scientists focus on the "how," business stakeholders focus on the "why." They set priorities, define customer problems, and ultimately decide if the solution is useful. Their success criteria are rarely about accuracy percentages. Instead, they care about whether the AI system saves money, increases sales, or improves the customer experience.

For the AI PM, managing business stakeholders is a constant exercise in translation and expectation management. The PM takes technical progress and reframes it in business language. AI project management includes creating structured feedback loops, bringing in demos and prototypes, and making sure that what's being built lines up with what the business actually needs.

AI adds a twist here: sometimes what the business wants simply isn't technically feasible. A product owner might ask for 100% accuracy in predicting customer churn or a model that makes perfect real-time recommendations based on minimal data. The PM's role is to mediate between ambition and reality, helping stakeholders understand the probabilistic nature of AI without killing their enthusiasm. This means finding creative ways to frame value; even if the system isn't perfect, it may still save millions or unlock entirely new workflows.

There's also the challenge of bias and fairness. Business stakeholders may not anticipate that their requests can have ethical implications. A PM who understands AI can raise these questions in business terms, for example, by asking how an algorithm that disadvantages certain customer groups might affect brand reputation or customer trust. Doing so makes bias a shared business concern, not just a technical footnote.

The product owner insists that the model cover "all customer types," while the data scientists argue that narrowing the model's focus is critical to making progress. How could the PM help bring these stakeholders into alignment and avoid an endless scope-creep battle?

Legal, compliance, and ethics advisors No matter how exciting the technology is, every AI project has to answer the question "Is this allowed?" Legal, compliance, and ethics advisors bring that lens. They worry about things like privacy, bias, and regulatory risk. While they can sometimes feel like the brakes on innovation, their role is to keep the company out of trouble and to ensure the AI system can be trusted.

The PM's role here is to bring these advisors in early and often. Instead of treating compliance like a late-stage hurdle, a good PM weaves it into the project from the beginning. That way, concerns about bias or data use can be addressed before the model is too far along to change.

AI projects introduce issues that compliance teams are still learning to navigate, such as algorithmic transparency or the "right to explanation." Many legal teams don't yet have playbooks for these challenges. The PM adds value by facilitating cross-learning: ensuring that legal advisors understand the technical realities while also pushing technical teams to provide the documentation and evidence that regulators might expect in the future.

There's also the emerging space of AI ethics, which is fuzzier than compliance but just as important. Should an AI system be used to screen job applicants? What about predicting employee attrition? These aren't purely legal questions. They are cultural, reputational, and strategic ones. The PM is often the first to spot when a project crosses into uncomfortable territory and can bring the right advisors together before decisions are locked in.

Midway through development, compliance flags potential bias issues in the dataset. Fixing it now could delay the project by months. How could the PM manage both the risk and the expectations of stakeholders who want to keep pushing forward?

Sponsors, clients/users, and executives Finally, we get to the people holding the purse strings. Sponsors, clients, and executives decide whether the project gets funding, resources, and visibility. They care about strategy, ROI, and timelines—not the nitty-gritty of neural network layers. Their support can make or break a project, but they can also be the hardest group to keep engaged.

The PM supports this group by keeping communication simple, visual, and focused on outcomes. No jargon and no technical deep dives. Just clear connections between what the team is doing and what it means for the business. The PM also needs to surface risks early, ideally with mitigation options, so executives aren't blindsided when something doesn't go as planned.

AI projects challenge executives in a unique way because the results are uncertain and nondeterministic. Unlike traditional IT projects, you can't guarantee that if you invest X, you'll get Y features delivered on Z date. Success is probabilistic. The PM helps executives get comfortable with this uncertainty by reframing discussions around scenarios, trade-offs, and experimentation rather than the binary of success or failure.

Another AI-specific factor is scalability. A pilot project may look impressive, but scaling it across an organization can expose integration challenges, ethical dilemmas, or hidden costs. The PM helps executives understand the difference between a proof of concept and a production deployment, making sure that enthusiasm for the project's potential is matched by realistic expectations.

An executive sponsor demands a project demo for the board in two weeks, but the system is nowhere near ready for a polished showcase. What could the PM do to keep leadership engaged without overpromising or undermining trust?

Building Alignment Across Stakeholders

The challenge for the AI PM is that all these groups often pull in different directions. Data scientists want space to experiment. Compliance officers want to minimize risk. Executives want results yesterday. The AI PM's job is to navigate these tensions without letting the project snap.

That means translating, mediating, and building trust. It's about helping each group see how its work connects to the bigger picture and ensuring no one feels like they're working in a silo. When the alignment works, stakeholders stop being competing voices and start sounding more like a choir.

In conclusion, data scientists innovate, MLOps teams deploy, business stakeholders define value, compliance advisors safeguard trust, and executives provide resources. Each of them matters, but none of them can deliver alone. The AI PM is the conductor who brings them together, sets the tempo, and keeps the music flowing. The better the project manager is at supporting each group, the greater the chance that the AI project will move from a messy proof of concept to something that delivers real, lasting impact.

THE RESPONSIBILITIES OF AN AI PM

The previous section discussing a PM's relationship with project stakeholders has probably given you a glimpse of their priorities and what keeps them up at night. Now let's break down the AI PM's responsibilities and dive into the skill sets that make this role an integral part of the AI team.

The responsibilities of an AI PM can be grouped into three categories corresponding to the three levels of AI management as described in Chapter 1, starting with overall strategic alignment, followed by execution at the team level, and ending with technical and data stewardship. The illustration of these groupings in Figure 3-3 shows how the PM's duties align with organizational strategy, execution, and data stewardship.

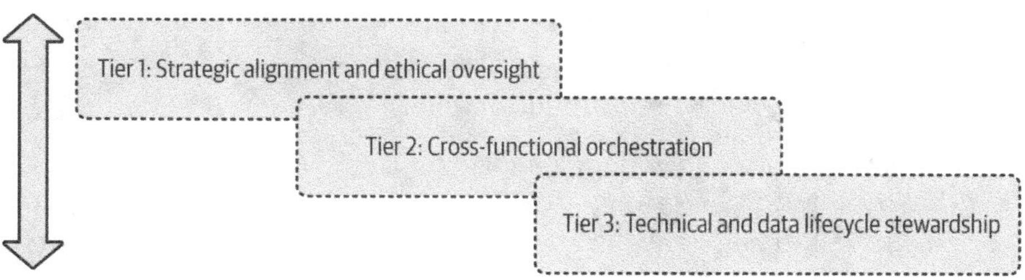

Figure 3-3. The AI PM "responsibility stack"

Organizations that understand the value of PMs ensure that they are in the loop for any updates on the business's strategic direction, and leaders take the PMs' feedback seriously. Not only does including PMs in strategic discussions allow them to connect the dots between strategy and implementation, but it also gives them a channel in which to raise concerns when gaps are identified. Let's break this down into tiers.

Tier 1: Strategic alignment and ethical oversight

The goal of the AI PM's participation here is to drive purpose-driven AI that aligns with organizational priorities and values. Here's what that means:

Aligning the project with the organization's AI vision and KPIs

> PMs have a unique role in which they work not only vertically on a project but also horizontally across the organization. By understanding business goals and the motivations behind them, PMs are integral to identifying AI opportunities with positive ROI and aligning tactical project implementation with the organization's strategic vision and KPIs.

> In the case of product development, this may involve enhancing existing product offerings by adding AI features and capabilities, thus adding value for customers. For the organization's departments, this may mean integrating AI capabilities into existing workflows to optimize day-to-day tasks and free up manual resources for higher-value functions. The more PMs understand the organization's strategic direction, the more capable they are of ensuring that various teams are aligned in their decision making. For the AI PM, this requires the following skills and practices:

> - *Skill group:* Strategic thinking, business acumen
> - *Subskills:* Goal decomposition, business translation
> - *What it looks like in practice:* Instead of starting with AI models, the PM starts projects with problem statements aligned with specific, desired outcomes at the organizational level.

Translating business needs into AI opportunities

> We have heard "We have to use AI" or a similar sentiment many times in executive meetings, although thanks to AI education, this kind of blanket demand is becoming less frequent. PMs have the responsibility to convert such vague direction into measurable objectives and work with business stakeholders to frame the scope and define feasibility. Moreover, not every business goal is appropriate for AI. Depending on organizational stakeholders' level of AI familiarity, PMs may have to navigate uncharted territory, taking stakeholders through an exercise to filter and refine ideas into

implementable AI use cases. This responsibility is composed of the following skills and practices:

- *Skill group:* Outcome ownership

- *Subskills:* Problem decomposition, AI use case framing, objectives and key results (OKRs) mapping, value tracking, prioritization trade-offs

- *What it looks like in practice:* The PM translates ambiguous requests into scoped, business-aligned use cases with measurable KPIs and enterprise OKRs. The PM also identifies when a use case isn't worth pursuing, filtering out hype from viable AI opportunities.

Championing responsible AI practices

PMs have a responsibility to promote best practices in the areas of data governance, ethics, and inclusion at the organizational level. Not everything that *can* be built *should* be built. Part of the job is to ask the question "Should we build it?" PMs make sure that the organization's AI solutions are fair, explainable, privacy respecting, and aligned with evolving legal and ethical standards. The AI PM's responsibilities extend beyond simply flagging issues or asking the right questions. Instead, the PM institutionalizes ethics through processes, checklists, and steering committees. While this starts at the strategic level, PMs have the responsibility to see it through every step of the implementation. This capability breaks down into these core components:

- *Skill group:* Responsible AI stewardship

- *Subskills:* Bias/risk literacy, ethical escalation, regulatory awareness

- *What it looks like in practice:* The AI PM flags issues related to consent, fairness, and discriminatory risks in data and leads bias audits of the model.

Manage stakeholder expectations and cross-functional priorities

As an AI PM, you will need to align executives, business units, technology teams, and users on what AI can deliver and what it *can't* deliver, all while navigating competing interests and power dynamics within the organization. This responsibility may be one of the trickiest to master. It often extends beyond simply explaining the situation to include providing ongoing training on AI literacy and expectation setting for various levels of stakeholders. Given additional external factors such as pressure from investors, clients, or an intense competitive market, PMs must hone their hard and soft skills to steer the organization toward success. Achieving this relies on the following set of skills and practices:

- *Skill group:* Stakeholder expectation management, influencing without authority

- *Subskills:* Value framing, risk storytelling, communication tailoring, soft power, narrative persuasion, emotional intelligence

- *What it looks like in practice:* The AI PM reframes a low-accuracy model not as a failure but as a prototype that can be used to identify new product opportunities. They also facilitate alignment meetings between legal (concerned with bias) and product (focused on time to market) to reach agreement on acceptable deployment criteria.

Some of these responsibilities may reside with program managers or other roles with similar names, some of whose responsibilities overlap with those of project managers. While exactly which responsibilities fall into which job may vary from one organization to another, it is simply a fact that AI PMs need to be involved at the strategic level in order to be able to perform effectively at the implementation level.

Tier 2: Cross-functional orchestration

The goal of the AI PM's participation at this level is to facilitate implementation across business, technical, legal, and research domains to ensure that execution is feasible, cohesive, and resilient. This orchestration requires the PM to act as the "connective tissue" of the project, proactively aligning specialized workflows with the broader organizational mission.

Coordinating diverse roles within and among teams

AI projects involve cross-functional teams with diverse skills; team members may include data scientists, data engineers, MLOps professionals, backend developers, UX researchers, business analysts, legal experts, product managers, and more. Each specialty comes with its own vernacular and perspective on the project. Misalignment across these groups can lead to redundancy, delays, technical debt, and ethical oversights. It is the PM's job to translate and mediate across these diverse perspectives, ensuring that the gaps are bridged. Communicating clearly is simply not enough. PMs must enable mutual understanding among experts despite all the changes and uncertainties that are a given in AI projects. The key ability is to be able to create shared meaning in highly abstract environments. Great AI PMs design for friction rather than react to it. In practice, this responsibility requires:

- *Skill group:* Cross-functional coordination, domain translation, mutual understanding enablement, conflict anticipation and resolution

- *Subskills:* Perspective awareness, workflow facilitation, handoff design, conceptual alignment, terminology unification, shared vocabulary building

- *What it looks like in practice:* The AI PM identifies that when data scientists say "model performance," they mean F_1 score, but when business leaders hear it, they expect revenue impact. The PM bridges these different interpretations by working with both groups to codefine a "business-ready" model. The PM uses dual-language updates (i.e., technical and plain language) to engage multiple stakeholders. In addition, they anticipate cultural or professional misalignments and preempt them with proactive design. They also explain legal/compliance constraints to engineers and explain experimentation constraints to nontechnical executives.

The tactical implementation of this activity is outlined in detail in "Managing AI Teams" on page 97 later in this chapter.

Protecting researchers' bandwidth while ensuring the delivery timeline

One of the unique aspects of AI projects is the seemingly never-ending research. Data scientists are usually the ones in charge of researching and iterating on the algorithms that are the heart and soul of AI solutions. This activity is complex and vulnerable to distractions from within (e.g., their own research leading them down a rabbit hole) and without (e.g., stakeholders asking them to investigate issues seen in previous versions or other products). Because training and tuning algorithms is a dependency to downstream validation and production, getting sidetracked delays the project as a whole. PMs must take an active role in creating and maintaining an environment in which team members can perform at their best. This includes rigorously assessing bandwidth and identifying anything that uses it unproductively. The AI PM uses the following key skills and activities:

- *Skill group:* Navigating external pressure, minimizing context switching

- *Subskills:* Prioritization despite distractions, executive shielding, message control, preserving focus time, coordination batching, async-first culture

- *What it looks like in practice:* The AI PM pushes back diplomatically on a sales VP's demand to "launch GenAI in Q3" by presenting phased delivery options with clear risks. They may also set up an operating rhythm that accommodates deep work for ML researchers, sprint reporting for the product team, and asynchronous compliance reviews.

Creating feedback loops across model development, product usage, and performance monitoring

Just as orchestra members come together with their different instruments to perform a beautiful symphony, AI project team members do the same with their skills. Everyone depends on every other specialty's input and skills to achieve positive results. AI PMs play an active role in making sure the collaboration is tight and productive. This means creating strong and proactive feedback and reiteration loops across teams, facilitating light but effective processes, and encouraging an extreme ownership mentality. PMs must ensure that feedback from data, product, user behavior, and system performance flows fluidly and continuously between stakeholders. They do this by orchestrating short-cycle and high-frequency communication that triggers rapid adjustments in design, modeling, and deployment strategies. This translates into the following skills and actions:

- *Skill group:* Tight iteration enablement

- *Subskills:* Feedback loop architecture, signal pathway optimization, removal of barriers, actionability, learning-oriented delivery culture

- *What it looks like in practice:* The AI PM builds feedback-to-response pipelines, not just feedback inboxes. They also create an environment of psychological safety where team members feel comfortable admitting to gaps, normalizing test—fail—learn cycles, and celebrating loop closures in sprint demos. PMs may also map feedback touchpoints across roles and stakeholders and identify who owns each type of loop.

Owning the project backlog, Agile events, and delivery processes—all tailored to the AI development cycle

PMs are in charge of building the infrastructure, processes, and rules of engagement among the team members involved in the project, including those involved in day-to-day operations as the project heads toward the finish line. Some of these activities include setting up a hybrid Agile framework and associated events, owning the project backlog, roadmapping milestones and sprints, facilitating technical deep dives, and driving delivery. Some may say that all these activities are part of the basic responsibilities of any PM, but the reality is that this skill domain is one of the most difficult to master in an AI context. Many of the frameworks popular in technical development come from software development, and they are simply not applicable without being adapted to the pace and complexity of an AI project. Key skills and examples for this include:

- *Skill group:* AI delivery infrastructure design and execution

- *Subskills:* AI-adapted Agile design and facilitation, structuring the AI backlog, AI-focused and nonbinary definition of done, delivery health tracking

- *What it looks like in practice:* The AI PM defines "done" in layered terms, ensuring that deliverables include not just working code but performance thresholds, explainability requirements, and retraining triggers. They may also split a backlog item when model training fails due to mislabeled data, so the team launches a patch now and schedules relabeling for the next sprint.

The final bucket of core responsibilities for AI PMs centers on the very core of AI projects: the data. While software projects focus on workflows and integrations, AI projects live and breathe data. Whether you are building an ML predictive model, NLP model, or a chatbot, your algorithm depends on data. PMs lead data-driven efforts on both the strategic and tactical level.

Tier 3: Technical and data lifecycle stewardship

The goal of the AI PM's involvement in Tier 3 is to understand, support, and de-risk the model or data pipeline lifecycle. This level of stewardship requires the PM to act as the primary guardian of data integrity, ensuring that the technical foundations of the project remain stable as the model evolves.

Understanding and tracking data dependencies and quality

Garbage in, worse garbage out. As you saw in Chapter 2, the results of an AI project are only as good as the data it's built on. PMs must understand where the data comes from, who owns it, and whether it meets the standards needed for modeling. PMs are responsible for collaborating with data providers/owners to map the data's lineage and promote a culture of understanding source systems, transformation steps, and update frequency. Awareness of how the data is obtained and processed is a responsibility of everyone involved in the project, as it informs both the solution and its societal impact.

Additionally, each of the AI system function's dependencies on the data is integral to the success of the project, be it in the training, tuning, or validation steps. It is the PM's job to collaborate with the team to flag any issues with volume, format, bias, or completeness. The PM must rigorously map the data, ensure its availability and usability, and guide the team in ensuring its governance throughout the AI project lifecycle. Here's what that looks like in terms of skills and application:

- *Skill group:* Data governance and quality management

- *Subskills:* Data lineage mapping, data quality metrics monitoring, data privacy and ethical framework implementation

- *What it looks like in practice:* The AI PM maintains an up-to-date data lineage map and tracks data quality metrics on a shared dashboard. In addition, the PM facilitates the resolution of data issues as part of the modeling lifecycle.

Working with teams to scope feasibility, minimum viable products (MVPs), and performance metrics

While at the strategic level, PMs are responsible for asking whether a product should be built, at the project level, they are responsible for working with teams to set a realistic definition of what "done" looks like for the model (i.e., the agreed-upon success metrics for accuracy, F1 score, latency, confidence thresholds, etc.). Together, the stakeholders must reach consensus on a minimum viable model (MVM) that delivers enough value to launch a pilot. For more discussion of this process, see Google's article "Framing an ML Problem" (*https://oreil.ly/Uxr7i*). This breaks down into the following skills and practices, which allow the PM to translate high-level consensus into technical execution:

- *Skill group:* Model scoping, identification of success metrics

- *Subskills:* Defining performance targets, minimum viable model scoping, domain-specific benchmarking

- *What it looks like in practice:* The AI PM cohosts working sessions with data scientists and product leads to establish clear success thresholds. In addition, they guide the various teams through establishing an agreed-upon MVP scope, ensuring that it's linked to business goals, and maintain a definition of done for the model.

Supporting reproducibility, documentation, and versioning efforts

AI PMs are responsible for establishing and enforcing processes and a culture that prioritizes reproducibility and auditability. In AI projects, *reproducibility* refers to the ability to consistently replicate model behavior and performance under the same conditions. Keeping track of changes made to the code, data, models, and metrics configurations throughout the lifecycle helps to ensure reproducibility. With the fast-moving nature of AI projects, model failures may emerge well after a change was made, so using best practices for traceability, such as version control, allows teams to diagnose and fix such problems more efficiently. Accountability is especially important in highly regulated domains such as finance, health care, and the public sector. This PM responsibility is composed of the following skills and practices:

- *Skill group:* AI reproducibility and auditability practices

- *Subskills:* Model and data versioning discipline, experiment tracking and metadata logging, enforcing end-to-end traceability

- *What it looks like in practice:* The AI PM's responsibilities include implementing a standard such that every model release has a model card that summarizes the release's purpose, metrics, limitations, and provenance. Moreover, in postmortems, AI engineers can trace any output back through the exact data and code that produced it, satisfying both internal QA and external regulatory audits.

Managing experimentation cycles and model readiness gating

A common pitfall in AI projects is the endless experimentation loop. Because modeling is explorative and iterative, avoiding this rabbit hole involves setting clear decision points, locking evaluation datasets and metrics to ensure fair comparisons, and enforcing risk-aware iteration limits so teams avoid the "infinite tuning" trap. The PM ensures that experiments are consistently logged with tools like MLflow or Weights & Biases, collaborates with data scientists to preregister evaluation protocols, and applies readiness checklists that cover performance, fairness, interpretability, and reproducibility. Before the project advances to the next stage, the PM convenes stakeholders for a go/no-go review (i.e., the launch decision), turning what could be an open-ended research exercise into a disciplined, accountable decision-making process. This capability breaks down into these core components:

- *Skill group:* AI experimentation and validation governance

- *Subskills:* Structured experimentation design, comparable evaluation protocols, readiness criteria definition, risk-aware iteration limits

- *What it looks like in practice:* The AI PM ensures that the team uses tools like MLflow, Data Version Control (DVC), or Weights & Biases to track experiments and artifacts. They also work with the data scientists to preregister evaluation metrics (e.g., precision, accuracy, F1) and lock in datasets to ensure fair comparisons. In addition, the PM may set explicit readiness gates and review the project's status with relevant stakeholders before advancing to the next stage.

Overseeing launch plans, CI/CD, and post-launch model health monitoring

The launch of a product or feature is a highly anticipated event. PMs play a key role in shaping model deployment strategies, managing expectations with stakeholders, and coordinating the launch plan. This may include final validations, a shadow deployment, a canary release, and other advanced deployment techniques. PMs must coordinate with MLOps to ensure that the model is containerized, tested, and integrated with the CI/CD pipeline for operationalization. For the AI PM, getting the team to think about release and postrelease risk is a way to form a robust strategy and tactical deployment approach.

This means shaping not just the launch event but the entire operational reliability plan around it. The PM coordinates with MLOps to ensure that models are containerized, integrated into CI/CD pipelines, and validated through staging, shadow, or canary releases before full rollout. A structured production-readiness checkpoint verifies packaging, benchmarking, and integration tests, while monitoring dashboards are put in place to track both infrastructure metrics (latency, uptime) and model health indicators (data drift, prediction confidence, fairness). Post-launch, the PM drives incident response planning, ensuring that the team can detect anomalies quickly and roll back if needed. In this way, the PM turns deployment into a managed, low-risk business event rather than a leap of faith. In practice, this responsibility requires:

- *Skill group:* AI deployment and operational reliability

- *Subskills:* Deployment strategy orchestration, verification of production readiness, post-launch performance monitoring, incident detection and response planning, AI lifecycle performance governance

- *What it looks like in practice:* The AI PM leads a production-readiness checkpoint that confirms the project passes model-packaging, performance-benchmarking, and integration tests. The PM also leads coordinated deployment sequencing and ensures that monitoring dashboards are set up to track both technical metrics (latency, uptime) and model-specific metrics post-launch.

MANAGING AI TEAMS

AI PMs wield different skill sets and focus on different responsibilities depending on the challenge the team is facing. This section will address the tactical toolbox available to the AI PM when it comes to managing AI teams.

Managing an AI team is where the theory of project management meets the real-world complexity of data, models, and humans. No two AI teams look the same. One week you're managing researchers who are fine-tuning a transformer model, and the next you're mediating between compliance and engineering about data retention policies. The job of the AI PM isn't to master every technical detail but to design how information flows, how people collaborate, and how progress becomes visible even amid uncertainty.

When you walk into your first AI project, it won't be long before you notice where the points of friction are. The data scientist explains that "recall on the minority class dropped to 0.61." An engineer responds with a concern about idempotent endpoints. Compliance asks if the dataset even has a lawful basis for use. The business lead, meanwhile, just wants to know: "So, can we launch or not?"

With each role speaking its own dialect and communicating its own priorities, the AI PM acts as a systems designer for human collaboration. You will shape how each role works together toward a meaningful outcome. Early on in your career, your goal will likely be to establish rhythm, visibility, and shared understanding among your team members. As your experience grows, you will begin to take on the challenge of scaling those systems, embedding autonomy, accountability, and responsible AI practices into the team's and organization's DNA.

Coordination with technical roles

Given the multidisciplinary ecosystems in technology, AI PMs are responsible for creating shared meaning and avoiding misalignments. Let's explore how PMs can achieve this.

Establishing common understandings In practice, this starts with:

Stabilizing communication loops
> Set a predictable weekly cadence for planning, experiment review, and demos. Determine dependencies and risks, and fill in the gaps where connections between roles don't come naturally.

Translating between domains
> Use dual-language summaries, harnessing the language of both the technical and business teams to align understanding.

Defining readiness
> Standardize the definition of "done" and design handoffs so that done means the same thing to data scientists, engineers, MLOps, and compliance.

Building lightweight artifacts
> Capture experiments, versioning, dependencies, decisions, and readiness checks in shared visual trackers/boards.

Automating visibility
> Use dashboards or knowledge graphs to highlight stale experiments or missing steps, not just reporting. Configure the dashboards to highlight stalled work or recurring risks.

Protecting focus
> Shield data scientists' time and focus from constant context switching by centralizing inbound requests.

If you get these foundations right, you can prevent a huge amount of staff churn. Instead of long meetings where people talk past each other, you'll have short touchpoints that generate decisions, artifacts that maintain memory across sprints, and a shared language that survives role changes.

Establishing cadence and flow A successful AI team is able to convert exploration into progress. That's easier said than done since the concept of scheduling doesn't match up with the rhythm of an AI team. The AI PM, therefore, must focus on the predictability and closure of work in progress. The goal is to provide the team with a light structure that supports rigorous review and continuous improvement. Here is a simple framework for establishing this cadence:

Define your iteration timebox

Whether it's a 1-week, 10-day, or 2-week sprint, each iteration should open with alignment, include a focused review at the midpoint, and end with reflection and demo. You need to break down time into a measurable unit that is large enough that progress is visible but not so large that the team loses its way.

- *Iteration start (Day 1):* Clarify the sprint's objectives, the decisions required, and any visible blockers.

- *Midpoint:* Review experiments in progress using concise one-pagers with sections such as hypothesis, dataset version, metrics, and decision (continue, pivot, pause).

- *Iteration end (Day N):* Showcase tangible outputs, perhaps by demoing a prototype, performance benchmark, or insight. Don't forget to document a decision in writing for the next iteration.

Measure learning velocity

Track how quickly hypotheses convert into validated insights.

Automate signals

Set up your dashboards so they highlight stalled work or recurring risks.

Shift toward a growth mindset

Treat the team's cadence as a feedback mechanism for organizational learning, not as a reporting schedule.

Integrate reflection

Run short "learning reviews" across technical, ethical, and user dimensions. Think of these as progress-focused retrospectives.

Designing handoffs between roles One thing that differentiates a great PM from an average one is the effort they spend in trying to understand the pain points each role experiences in relation to its counterparts. PMs can help grease the wheels by adapting processes intelligently. A practical way to start is to:

- Define explicit readiness criteria before each transition:
    - *Data science → Engineering:* Inputs, latency expectations, sample data
    - *Engineering → MLOps:* Container image, rollout plan, monitoring specs
    - *MLOps → Compliance:* Lineage, model card, retention policy
- *Embed readiness gates in the process:* Automate quality, bias, or reproducibility checks before approval.
- *Visualize dependencies:* Use mapping tools to expose friction points.
- *Run micro-retros:* After each major handoff, log any issues that slowed delivery and note how the process might be streamlined next time.
- *Integrate ethics by design:* Include compliance checkpoints in every transition gate/review.

Scaling practice and culture Once you've got your basic setup in place, go ahead and launch your first iteration. As you get to know your team, including their work and their preferences, your focus will shift from enforcing a certain process toward facilitating collaboration. In this way, you will merge structure with context, producing a foundation that is tailored to your team's needs. Here are some of the activities you can leverage to enhance the team's operating framework:

Spread the culture
> Mentor peers, publish internal guides, and standardize ethical reviews.

Evolve governance
> Introduce lightweight reproducibility audits and bias reviews.

Close the feedback loop
> Treat every project not as a deliverable but as an evolving capability within the organization's AI ecosystem.

Evolution of roles due to GenAI

The rise of GenAI has quietly rewritten how AI teams work. The old model of sequential, specialized roles no longer fits. What was once a straightforward relay between research, engineering, and deployment has become something much more fluid. Teams that used to build algorithms now find themselves shaping behavior. The systems they manage don't just execute logic anymore; they generate language, images, and ideas. Managing this new kind of capability is less about building models and more about steering intent.

GenAI has fundamentally changed how teams approach their work. The focus is no longer on constructing intelligence from scratch but on aligning pre-trained models with human goals. Data scientists, who once spent their time experimenting with architectures and features, now focus on curating prompts, evaluating responses, and fine-tuning models using human feedback. Engineers face new challenges around latency, context management, and safety in complex API-based systems. For PMs, success is no longer measured by how closely outputs match a predefined requirement but by whether the system behaves in a way that aligns with human expectations, business value, and ethical responsibility.

These shifts have blurred the boundaries between disciplines. Teams now work in overlapping cycles rather than passing work along in a straight line. A model's behavior, user feedback, and compliance review often evolve together. Everyone from data scientists to product leads to legal advisors interacts with the same system in motion. That makes coordination a daily act of translation, not just across technical domains but also across different understandings of what "good" looks like. The AI PM's role is to keep those conversations connected, ensuring that science, engineering, and ethics stay in step rather than competing for attention.

Emerging disciplines and the new shape of collaboration

As this new way of working takes hold, entirely new disciplines are emerging. Prompt engineers and model interaction designers focus on how generative models interpret instructions and express tone. AI operations teams extend traditional MLOps practices to include ongoing monitoring of model behavior, retraining cycles, and feedback loops. Responsible AI leads have become the ethical counterparts to technical leads, defining fairness thresholds, reviewing model outputs, and helping teams make decisions that balance innovation with accountability. As these new responsibilities crystallize, familiar roles are being reshaped and entirely new ones are emerging. Table 3-1 summarizes how core roles are evolving to meet the demands of the GenAI era.

Table 3-1. Evolving roles in the GenAI era

Role	Traditional focus pre-GenAI	Evolving focus in the GenAI era	Emerging competencies
Data scientist	Building and optimizing models through custom architectures and features	Steering foundation models through prompt design and behavioral fine-tuning	Prompt engineering, reinforcement learning from human feedback, qualitative evaluation, data curation
MLOps engineer	Automating pipelines, ensuring scalability, and maintaining reproducibility	Managing model deployment, latency, context windows, and continuous retraining	Behavioral monitoring, safety guardrails, lifecycle governance
Product manager	Translating business needs into features and KPIs	Defining and measuring desired model behavior's alignment with user intent	Behavioral KPIs, prompt evaluation, human feedback integration
Engineer (software/ backend)	Integrating APIs, building infrastructure, and maintaining performance	Embedding and scaling generative models within applications	Inference optimization, traceability, safety and compliance integration
Responsible AI/compliance lead	Reviewing fairness, privacy, and legal compliance post-development	Embedding ethical oversight throughout the AI lifecycle	Bias and alignment auditing, transparency frameworks, responsible experimentation
Prompt engineer/ model interaction designer	This role didn't exist before the generative AI era	Designing prompts and interaction flows that shape model responses	Linguistic precision, conversational design, model behavior tuning

As you can see, the PM's role has evolved alongside these new functions. While the AI PM may not write prompts or build evaluation frameworks, they create an environment in which these roles can connect effectively. The PM ensures that creativity doesn't outpace governance and that compliance doesn't smother experimentation. Their job is to maintain balance, to hold space for exploration while keeping delivery purposeful and responsible.

Across all these roles, the skill set is shifting toward higher-level abstraction. Teams are moving from building to steering, from optimizing for accuracy to designing for trust. Technical performance still matters, but it now shares the stage with interpretability, transparency, and social impact. Managing data has expanded into managing context by understanding how examples, prompts, and feedback shape the model's behavior and the user's experience.

In mature teams, collaboration in the GenAI context feels less like a series of handoffs and more like an ongoing dialogue. Researchers monitor model drift and behavioral changes, engineers strengthen guardrails, product managers interpret user sentiment, and compliance teams ensure traceability and fairness. The PM connects these threads into a single learning rhythm where every release teaches the team something new about how the system behaves and why.

Leadership in this environment has become an act of sensemaking. The PM's work isn't just to keep things on track but to help the team interpret what the system's behavior is revealing. A poor response from a model isn't just a defect; it's a signal that there is something to learn about the data, design, or framing. This role demands both curiosity and calm, especially when the outcomes are uncertain.

GenAI hasn't erased traditional roles; it's just made them more porous. The strongest teams operate like adaptive systems, learning from their models as much as they teach them. The PM's role is to make that learning intentional, ethical, and tied to purpose. Managing AI teams today isn't about getting projects out the door faster. It's about guiding intelligence that grows, behaves, and evolves alongside the humans who build it.

AI team gaps analysis

Imagine this common scenario: a GenAI pilot project was coming along smoothly but then started to fall apart when it met real-life users. The model performed well in testing but inconsistently when deployed in production. The data scientists say there are issues in fine-tuning drift, the MLOps engineer blames unclear retraining criteria, and compliance has just realized that no one documented which model checkpoint was deployed. You as the AI PM are setting up meetings to get to the bottom of it, and timelines are slipping. The business is asking questions the team can't seem to answer.

What's happening here isn't that the team members aren't good at their jobs. It's an invisible structural issue. The team has all the necessary skills, motivation, and good intentions, but somewhere between all the tactical implementation tasks, accountability got lost. This is what an AI team gap looks like in practice: it's not a missing person or role but a missing bridge.

Visualizing the gaps AI teams rarely follow a clean blueprint. They tend to grow around immediate delivery needs. Then, over time, this ad hoc structure starts to show cracks, with recurrent errors and fuzzy ownership.

The AI PM's role is to step back and make those gaps visible. One of the simplest ways to do that is to use a visualization tool, such as a *capability heatmap*, that plots skills against responsibilities. It doesn't evaluate people; it evaluates functions. By taking this approach, you guide the conversation away from judging individual team members and instead show how complete or incomplete the system itself is. A heatmap may reveal patterns such as that the team has strong research and modeling but weak data governance, or mature deployment pipelines but no clear process for behavioral evaluation. Table 3-2 shows a sample capability heatmap.

Table 3-2. Example of an AI team capability heatmap

Capability area	Data science	MLOps/ engineering	Product/ design	Responsible AI/ compliance	Overall maturity
Data quality & stewardship	Mature – robust preprocessing & data validation	Partial – lacks lineage documentation	▲ Minimal involvement	Partial – reviews late in process	Developing
Model experimentation & traceability	Mature – uses MLflow for tracking	Mature – version control and CI/CD in place	Some visibility into metrics	▲ Limited oversight of documentation	Developing

Capability area	Data science	MLOps/ engineering	Product/ design	Responsible AI/ compliance	Overall maturity
Prompt engineering & model behavior tuning	Strong fine-tuning and evaluation expertise	Supports infrastructure but limited behavioral metrics	Designs prompts and user testing	Reviews after incidents	Developing
Deployment & monitoring	Supports evaluation but not deployment	Mature pipelines and monitoring	Involved during launch only	Limited to compliance audits	Strong
Responsible AI & governance	Considers bias testing ad hoc	Ensures technical safeguards only	Limited literacy in RAI	No formal framework	Weak
User feedback & post-launch learning	Collects feedback data but rarely loops it back	Monitors metrics in production	Integrates user feedback into roadmap	Reviews compliance signals only	Developing

A visualization like the one in this table can help facilitate your conversation with your team, and perhaps the wider organization, on how to upskill team members or fill in the gaps.

Recognizing risk clusters Capabilities gaps rarely exist in isolation. They cluster and create compound risks. Some of the more common patterns tend to fall into a few familiar categories: reproducibility gaps that create compliance and traceability risk, data stewardship gaps that surface later as bias or inconsistent performance, responsible AI gaps that expose ethical or reputational vulnerabilities, and human-centered design gaps that make technically sound models feel misaligned or untrustworthy.

These patterns often show up together. For instance, a team may skip versioning while fine-tuning a generative model, only to discover later that different prompt templates were deployed across regions, causing inconsistent user experiences and a compliance issue with explainability. What looks like a small process oversight quickly becomes a chain of risks that affect delivery, governance, and trust.

The AI PM's task is to notice these early and trace how they connect. A missing documentation step in MLOps can slow retraining cycles. An untracked prompt change can invalidate user feedback. A late-stage compliance review can block release. These aren't random failures; they're systemic signals of capability misalignment.

The AI PM responsibility stack outlined earlier provides a useful way to diagnose where those signals originate:

Tier 2 (cross-functional orchestration)
> Miscommunication or friction between roles that means decisions get lost or delayed

Tier 3 (technical and data stewardship)
> Weaknesses in documentation, versioning, or data governance that erode reproducibility and accountability

When delivery slows or quality drifts, it usually traces back to one of these two layers. Recognizing that pattern early allows the PM to shift the team's focus from fixing symptoms to strengthening the system itself.

Turning gaps into growth Finding a gap tells you where the system is weak. Turning the gap into growth is about learning how the system can adapt. The most effective AI PMs don't just close gaps; they build teams that learn faster than the gaps can reappear. You can think of the process as four interlocking forces that keep the teams learning, as shown in Figure 3-4.

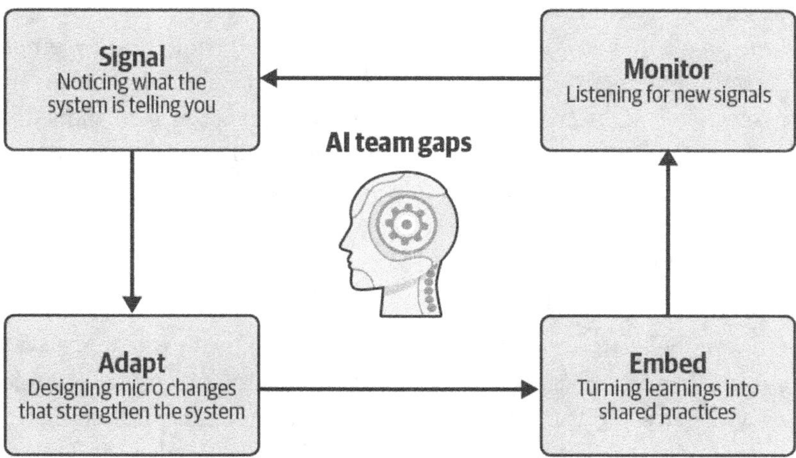

Figure 3-4. Continuous learning loop that enables closure of AI team gaps

This framework illustrates how teams convert detected weaknesses into adaptive growth by continuously signaling, adapting, embedding, and monitoring:

Signal—Noticing what the system is telling you

Every gap is a signal of something larger. So instead of asking "What went wrong?" ask instead "What is this revealing about how our system works?" A reproducibility problem might be a sign of missing traceability in MLOps. Or a late legal review might be a signal that compliance isn't embedded in the process early enough. The PM's job is to read those signals with curiosity, not urgency.

Adapt—Designing micro changes that strengthen the system

Once the signal is clear, the team makes a small, deliberate adjustment or micro adaptation. It might be as simple as versioning prompt templates, linking user feedback to experiment tracking, or adding a one-page ethical check before deployment. Each tweak builds muscle memory and subtly shifts how the team operates. But what about major changes? Should the team restructure? In the spirit of continuous adaptation, you will focus on incremental and implementable changes. Leave major overhauls to the organization.

Embed—Turning learning into shared practices

Learning only becomes growth when it's made visible. PMs memorialize each improvement with a living artifact, such as a checklist update or a retrospective insight. These small acts of documentation turn individual lessons into collective knowledge. But beyond documentation, the PM makes these improvements part of the day-to-day practice, which eventually turns into a process, and that process, when followed often enough, turns into second-nature instinct.

Monitor—Listening for new signals

Once embedded, the team starts detecting new patterns. Gaps evolve. Old weaknesses resurface in new forms. It can feel a bit like Whac-a-Mole. The AI PM helps the team sense these shifts so they can respond faster each time. Over time, the loop tightens, signals surface earlier, and adaptation becomes more intuitive, not just for the PM but also for the team members.

When this loop is active, maturity stops being about how perfect the process is and starts being about how quickly the team learns and how effectively insight travels across disciplines. Remember that this isn't simply a sequence of actions. It's a rhythm of awareness, adaptation, and reinforcement. The speed of adaptation and learning is a true KPI of organizational intelligence. It's how high-performing AI teams stay resilient despite the constantly increasing pressure to keep up with a fast-paced industry.

Bonus Track: ADRIAN Framework for AI PM Hiring

If you are reading this book, that means that you are either managing (or planning to manage) AI projects or making sense of the complexity of AI project management to build and scale your organization. If the latter, then you will need to evaluate internal and/or external talent. You may recall the ADRIAN framework from Chapter 1. It is reproduced here in Figure 3-5 because you can use it to evaluate how close your candidates are to the ideal profile of a modern AI project manager from both a soft skills and a methodology perspective.

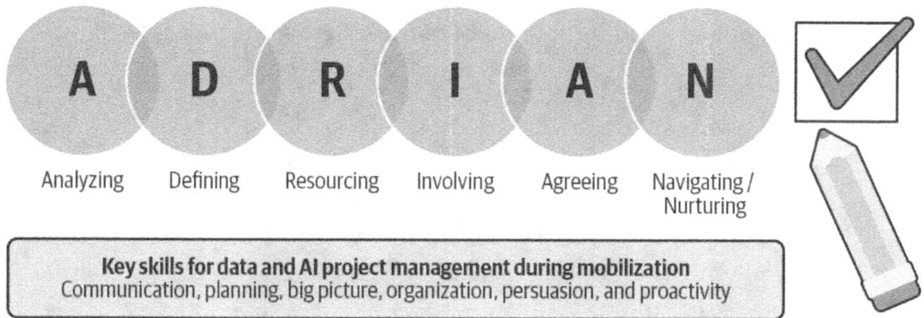

Figure 3-5. The ADRIAN framework as hiring checklist

Add this framework to your toolkit and use it as a checklist during your hiring and reskilling activities. In addition, you can use the following skill descriptions and interview questions as a guide when evaluating the skill sets of current employees and job candidates, as well as when assessing your own readiness as a professional AI PM:

Analyzing

The ability to deeply understand business problems and translate them into AI-relevant opportunities. This includes assessing data availability and quality; identifying technical and organizational constraints; evaluating feasibility; and anticipating risks related to ethics, bias, scalability, and performance.

Potential interview questions:

- Can you describe how you evaluate whether a problem is suitable for an AI solution?

- How do you assess data quality and availability at the start of an AI project?

- Tell me about a time you identified a major risk early in an AI or data project. How did you handle it?

- How do you account for ethical, bias, or regulatory risks in AI projects?

Candidate evaluation: Business problem and analysis skills
☐ Low ☐ Medium ☐ Strong

Defining

The ability to clearly define project scope, objectives, success criteria, and KPIs. An AI project manager must frame well-structured use cases; align them with business value; and ensure expectations are realistic in terms of timelines, costs, and AI maturity.

Potential interview questions:

- How do you define success for an AI project? What metrics do you use?

- Describe how you turn a vague business request into a well-defined AI use case.

- How do you manage stakeholders who have unrealistic expectations about AI capabilities?

- Can you give an example of how you refined project scope to increase impact?

Candidate evaluation: Project definition skills
☐ Low ☐ Medium ☐ Strong

Resourcing

Expertise in identifying and securing the right mix of skills, tools, data, and infrastructure. This includes coordinating data scientists, ML engineers, domain experts, IT, and external vendors while ensuring access to datasets, cloud platforms, and MLOps capabilities.

Potential interview questions:

- What roles do you consider essential in an AI project team, and why?

- How do you handle resource constraints such as missing skills or limited data access?

- Describe a time when you had to work with external vendors or cloud platforms for an AI project.

- How do you balance speed, cost, and quality when allocating resources?

Candidate evaluation: Project resourcing skills
□ Low   □ Medium   □ Strong

Involving

Stakeholder engagement and collaboration skills. The AI project manager must actively involve business owners and end users as well as legal, compliance, and technical teams to ensure shared understanding, adoption, and trust in AI solutions.

Potential interview questions:

- How do you ensure that business stakeholders remain engaged throughout an AI project?

- Can you describe a situation where stakeholder misalignment threatened a project?

- How do you involve end users in AI solution design and validation?

- How do you communicate complex AI concepts to nontechnical audiences?

Candidate evaluation: Stakeholder involvement skills
□ Low   □ Medium   □ Strong

Agreeing

Ability to facilitate alignment and decision making across diverse stakeholders. This includes managing priorities, trade-offs, and dependencies; negotiating scope and timelines; and ensuring clear commitments to deliverables and responsibilities.

Potential interview questions:

- How do you drive decisions when stakeholders disagree on priorities?

- Describe a time when you had to say no or deprioritize a feature.

- How do you ensure commitments are respected in a fast-changing AI environment?

- What techniques do you use to align teams around a common road-map?

Candidate evaluation: Agreement facilitation skills

☐ Low   ☐ Medium   ☐ Strong

Navigating

The ability to operate in conditions of uncertainty and complexity. This involves proactively removing blockers, adapting plans to changing data or model performance, managing organizational resistance, and guiding teams through change and ambiguity.

Potential interview questions:

- Tell me about an AI project where assumptions changed midway. How did you adapt?

- How do you handle organizational resistance to AI adoption?

- Describe a situation where you had to remove major blockers for your team.

- How do you stay effective when outcomes are uncertain or models underperform?

Candidate evaluation: Skills for navigating ambiguity

☐ Low   ☐ Medium   ☐ Strong

Core transversal skills

Depending on the context of your organization and team, you may want to adapt this list to the specific soft and hard skills you are looking for. Some of these critical skills include:

- Clear, structured, and persuasive communication with both technical and nontechnical audiences

- Ability to plan, organize, and coordinate work across multiple teams

- Strategic and big-picture thinking combined with execution focus
- Influence, negotiation, and facilitation skills
- Proactivity, adaptability, and continuous learning in fast-evolving AI environments

Potential interview questions:

- How do you balance long-term AI strategy with short-term delivery?
- Can you give an example of how your communication skills helped unblock a complex situation?
- How do you keep yourself up-to-date with AI trends without losing focus on delivery?
- What does proactivity mean to you in the context of AI project management?

Candidate evaluation: Core transversal skills
☐ Low ☐ Medium ☐ Strong

One final takeaway: the mix of skills you can get from candidates for AI project management roles can differ enormously depending on their academic background, professional experience, and level of knowledge and proficiency in the different areas of knowledge you have explored in this chapter. Don't let any preconceived ideas you have interfere with your consideration of candidates whose backgrounds may not be what you expect. Also, use the hiring process as input for the 30-, 60-, and 90-day upskilling plan you will develop with your new AI PMs. A structured upskilling process will help them close any skill gaps and become well-rounded contributors to your team.

Conclusion

AI projects challenge many of the assumptions that traditional project management was built on. Progress is rarely linear, success is often probabilistic, and the work continues to evolve long after launch. In this environment, the value of the AI project manager is not found in rigid plans or perfect forecasts but in an ability to navigate ambiguity, connect disciplines, and guide intelligent systems toward meaningful outcomes.

Throughout this chapter, we have seen that the AI PM is far more than a scheduler or a coordinator. This role operates at the intersection of strategy, execution, and stewardship. At the strategic level, the PM helps organizations move beyond vague ambitions of "doing AI" toward purpose-driven initiatives aligned with business goals, ethical principles, and long-term value. At the execution level, they orchestrate collaboration across diverse roles, translating between technical depth and business intent while protecting focus and momentum. At the technical and data level, they act as stewards of the AI lifecycle, ensuring that data quality, reproducibility, experimentation discipline, and post-launch monitoring are treated as first-class concerns.

What makes this role uniquely challenging is that none of these responsibilities can be performed in isolation. Strategic alignment breaks down without executional rigor. Technical excellence loses value without business relevance. Speed becomes dangerous without governance and ethical oversight. The AI PM reconciles the tension between these levels, not by eliminating it but by designing systems, processes, and conversations that allow teams to learn and adapt responsibly.

As generative AI reshapes how teams build, deploy, and interact with intelligent systems, the PM's role becomes even more central. With blurred boundaries between research, product, engineering, and compliance, leadership increasingly takes the form of sensemaking. The AI PM helps teams interpret signals, learn from failures, and turn uncertainty into insight. In doing so, the PM transforms gaps into growth and projects into capabilities.

Ultimately, successful AI delivery is not just about building smarter systems. It is about building organizations that can learn, govern, and evolve alongside those systems. The AI project manager is a key enabler of that organizational maturity. When the PM is empowered to operate across strategy, people, and technology, AI initiatives are far more likely to move beyond fragile proofs of concept and become trusted, impactful solutions that endure.

In the next chapter, you will learn about the EMED methodology and how it can help you manage the end-to-end needs of your AI projects in an efficient and standardized manner.

Chapter 3 Notebook

Applied Approach to AI Project Management

In this chapter, we shift our discussion from the high-level management of AI teams to the specific methodologies required to succeed in AI delivery.

Building on the human and organizational foundations you learned about in the previous chapter, we'll explore applied methodologies that help AI project managers bring structure to uncertainty. The primary focus is on learning how to apply frameworks like EMED (exploration, mobilization, execution, and delivery). We'll examine how to use this model to guide a project from initial definition to final completion, finding the right balance between Agile, Lean, and traditional Waterfall approaches (Figure 4-1).

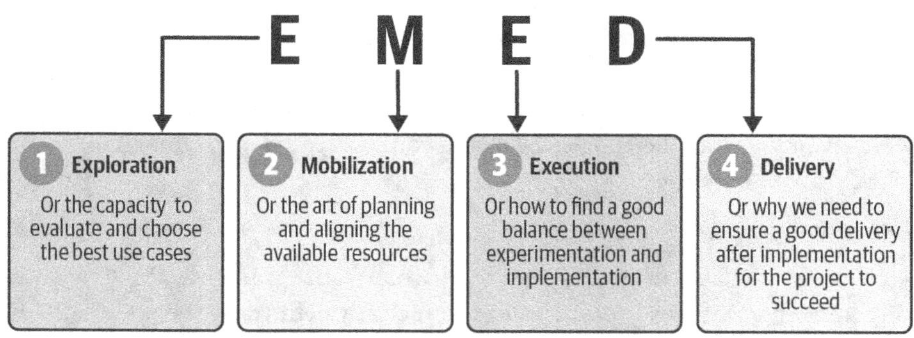

Figure 4-1. EMED methodology for AI project management

Additionally, we'll discuss how to design workflows that integrate responsible AI best practices into every stage of execution. By the end of this chapter, you'll understand how to choose, adapt, and combine methodologies that make AI projects not only deliverable but repeatable and aligned with business and ethical objectives.

Remember, the importance of having a methodology mindset when managing uncertainty, iteration, and accountability in AI delivery is due to the intrinsic nature of these projects. While they are similar to regular technology and software initiatives, they also bring complexities and unknowns that are intimidating for most business and technical professionals out there. Your role is to provide the leadership and structure necessary to navigate these challenges and achieve your project goals.

The EMED methodology detailed in the next section serves as the foundation for the lifecycle and tooling considerations we'll discuss in Chapters 5 and 6.

The EMED Methodology for End-to-End AI Project Management

Successful and efficient AI project management requires structuring work into clearly defined phases. The EMED methodology bridges the gap between corporate strategy and project execution, facilitating the identification and prioritization of potential use cases. In addition, a phased structure helps to plan and mobilize the necessary resources, manage stakeholder expectations, and ensure an orderly and effective implementation.

Each phase, from initial exploration to final delivery, provides a framework to assess progress, mitigate risks, and ensure that the project is generating tangible value for the organization. And best of all, this multi-phase approach converges with existing PM methodologies, allowing you to adapt them to the unique complexities of AI initiatives.

PHASE 1: EXPLORATION

To successfully launch the exploration phase of your AI project, it is crucial to align the organization's overall strategy with clearly defined AI project objectives, thereby ensuring that the solution addresses concrete business priorities.

To navigate this phase effectively, follow these core steps:

1. *Conduct technical ideation*

    Identify potential use cases and document them based on their expected business impact, technical feasibility, and scalability.

2. *Map data sources*

    Identify and consolidate relevant data sources, mapping them to proposed use cases to ensure data availability and suitability for modeling.

3. *Prioritize and select*

    Rank use cases based on your assessments and choose the most viable candidate for implementation.

4. *Select a pilot scope*

    Start with a focused pilot project of limited scope and medium technological complexity to validate the value proposition while minimizing initial risk.

5. *Establish value objectives*

    Explicitly state the primary driver for the project, whether it is cost reduction through automation, revenue growth via personalization, or new business opportunities through advanced analytics.

6. *Perform exploratory data analysis*

    Analyze data patterns and detect anomalies to validate assumptions and guide model selection for the subsequent phases.

7. *Evaluate data quality*

    Assess data for accuracy, completeness, and consistency, as these factors directly dictate model performance.

Let's explore the details of all these phases, including useful templates and assets, so you can use them as a multistep checklist for your new AI projects.

Strategic alignment of AI

At the organizational level, economist Michael Porter's generic strategies (Figure 4-2) comprise a strategic analysis framework that shows the various ways in which organizations can gain a sustainable competitive advantage. Porter identifies three primary strategic positions: cost leadership, differentiation, and focus. These represent the distinct paths a company can take to position itself against competitors within the market.

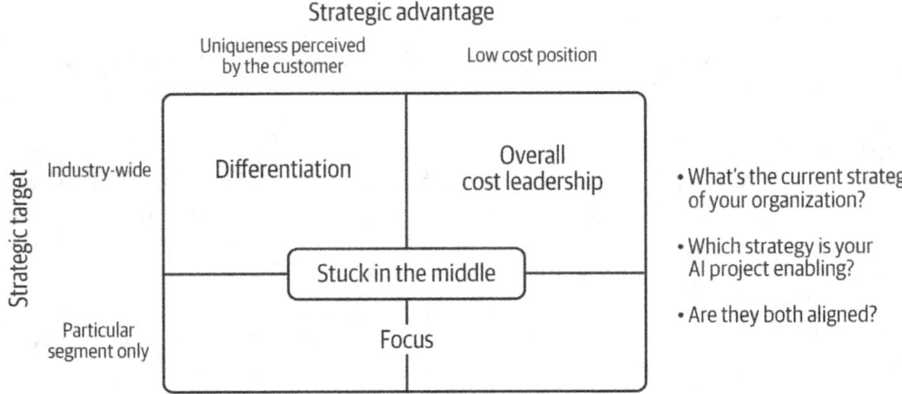

Figure 4-2. Porter's generic competitive strategies

AI serves as a powerful lever for executing these strategies, whether through aggressive cost reduction or the creation of highly differentiated products. As a project manager, you must first understand your organization's strategy to make sure that new AI use cases directly support it. This is important because a significant number of projects fail not due to technical limitations but due to a lack of alignment with corporate goals.

Let's now dive into several AI-related examples that will illustrate how your work as an AI PM can support alignment with your company's strategic direction.

Cost leadership An organization pursuing the cost leadership strategy focuses on being the most cost-efficient supplier within an industry. So that the company can offer lower prices than the competition, its priority becomes reducing production or service delivery costs without compromising quality.

Companies with this strategy seek to optimize processes, increase operational efficiency, and reduce costs on a large scale, and AI can leverage automation and data to achieve all these goals. Common examples include:

Process automation

Technologies such as robotic process automation (RPA) and NLP automate repetitive manual tasks. For example, customer service can be automated via intelligent chatbots or document processing, significantly reducing labor costs and minimizing human error.

Supply chain optimization

With AI, companies can analyze large volumes of real-time and historical data to forecast demand, manage inventories, and optimize distribution routes. This reduces costs associated with excess inventory or product shortages.

Predictive maintenance

In sectors such as manufacturing, ML algorithms can analyze patterns in sensor data to predict equipment failures before they occur. This minimizes downtime and reduces unplanned maintenance costs.

Energy optimization

In energy-intensive operations, such as factories or data centers, AI can optimize energy consumption, resulting in significant savings.

Ultimately, justifying your AI initiatives within a cost leadership framework will rely on these three pillars:

Reduced operating costs

AI reduces the need for human intervention in repetitive, low-value tasks.

Improved efficiency

Automation and real-time analytics allow for faster, more proactive changes, avoiding unnecessary expenses.

Scalability
> AI-based solutions can scale without operational costs growing at the same pace, allowing companies to offer products or services at lower prices.

Whatever the AI use case and project are, as the AI PM, you must facilitate rigorous discussion with all relevant executive, business, and technical stakeholders. It will be critical to identify potential cost levers that will justify the initiative, especially for organizations with a strong cost advantage in the market (e.g., Ryanair, Costco).

Differentiation The differentiation strategy involves offering a product or a service that is perceived as unique in the market, thus justifying higher prices. Differentiation can be based on quality, innovative features, design, or customer service. Some of the most famous examples of companies that pursue this strategy are Apple or Dyson.

AI enables organizations to personalize and enhance the customer experience, as well as innovate products and services that other competitors cannot offer, creating a unique value proposition. Here are some ways in which AI can support differentiation:

Personalizing the customer experience
> Using AI, companies can analyze data on customer behaviors and preferences to deliver highly personalized experiences. For example, Netflix uses AI to recommend content based on each user's viewing habits, thereby improving customer satisfaction and engagement.

Product innovation
> AI enables companies to develop smarter and more efficient products. One example is autonomous vehicles that use AI algorithms to improve safety and driving efficiency, creating a significant differentiator in the automotive industry.

Advanced virtual assistants
> Companies such as Amazon and Google have integrated virtual assistants such as Alexa or Google Assistant, which use advanced AI to allow users to interact with their devices in a natural way. These solutions offer a more efficient and intuitive user experience than traditional portals, resulting in significant product differentiation.

Improved customer service

AI can optimize customer service by creating intelligent chatbots or proactive support systems that anticipate customer needs and provide solutions before problems arise. This improved service can be a key differentiator.

In this case, the direct benefits of leveraging AI are:

Barriers to imitation

AI can enable innovative solutions that are technically complex and data dependent, making them difficult for rivals to replicate quickly.

Improved customer loyalty

By offering highly customized or innovative products or services, companies can improve customer loyalty and justify higher prices.

Superior user experience

Using AI to anticipate customer needs or to deliver more seamless and natural interactions enhances the user experience, which reinforces brand perception.

When planning a new project for your company or a client, you can anticipate the potential differentiation advantage that AI will bring to them. While you can combine these benefits with cost-saving levers, a differentiation-led value proposition will resonate most strongly with executives in highly innovative organizations.

Focus approach The focus strategy involves concentrating on a specific market segment, either geographically, demographically, or based on a product niche, and serving it more effectively than competitors. A focus approach can be either cost-based or differentiation-based. AI can help you identify and thoroughly understand specific market segments through detailed data analysis. This makes it possible to offer solutions that are more tailored to the needs of those segments, either through extreme customization or by optimizing costs within that niche. Here are some examples of how AI is used to support the focus approach:

Hyperpersonalized targeting

AI can enable highly specific market segmentation by analyzing demographic, behavioral, and geographic data. For example, an online fashion retailer could use AI to personalize marketing campaigns to target customers in precise age groups or those with specific shopping behaviors.

Specialized products or services

AI can help companies create specialized products for unique market segments. For instance, some health care startups are using AI to develop personalized treatments based on the genetic data of a small group of patients with a condition.

Prediction and microtargeting in marketing

Using predictive ML techniques, companies can focus their marketing efforts on audiences that are more likely to convert, improving the ROI in advertising and marketing. Platforms such as Facebook and Google Ads use AI to enable advertisers to target audiences.

The benefits that AI can bring to the organization using a focus approach can be a source of inspiration for new projects and even internal initiatives within your organization:

In-depth customer knowledge

AI enables detailed insights into the needs and preferences of a niche market, enabling better tailoring of products or services.

High satisfaction in niches

By using AI to improve products or services targeted to a market niche or segment, companies can achieve higher customer satisfaction and loyalty.

Limited competition

Specializing in a niche creates higher barriers to entry, and AI can help maintain this edge by continuously refining the service based on proprietary data.

AI, when aligned with a clear business strategy, becomes a powerful enabler that allows organizations to optimize operations, offer innovative and customized products, and achieve a sustainable competitive advantage. Thus, Porter's generic strategies can be effectively applied to motivate AI projects, whether the goal is to reduce costs, differentiate products, or target market niches. These strategies provide a framework to propose relevant AI projects to clients and executives. By aligning technical initiatives with these business pillars, you can present arguments in the language of your stakeholders, for instance, by demonstrating how a project's benefits will directly support the performance goals and incentives of your executive sponsors.

Your success in integrating these strategies depends on how well you align technology with strategic objectives. In your hybrid role as an AI PM, you facilitate the business-technical dialogue necessary to generate high-probability AI projects tailored to your organization's context. Let's now see how you can help your teams prioritize the most relevant projects.

Use Case Prioritization

The value-versus-complexity prioritization exercise is a useful tool that helps teams and organizations prioritize initiatives and projects according to their expected impact (value) and difficulty of implementation (complexity). Prioritizing in this way helps optimize decision making by identifying the projects that are most feasible and generate the greatest benefits, allowing resources to be managed efficiently.

There are a variety of techniques that can be used for prioritization (e.g., voting, stakeholder consensus), but AI teams usually leverage 2 × 2 matrices like the one shown in Figure 5-8 in the next chapter.

Regardless of how it is done, the value versus complexity analysis is organized around two main axes or criteria:

Value

> Represents the expected benefit or impact that the project can generate for the business. It can be measured in financial terms (ROI, cost reduction, and revenue growth), metrics (such as efficiency improvements or customer satisfaction), competitive advantage, or strategic impact. *Low value* means an initiative will have relatively little impact on the business or users, and *high value* means the project can generate a significant change or create a high return.
>
> To measure the value of an AI project, analyze its expected impact in terms of efficiency, cost reduction, process improvement, or customer experience. In addition, consider how the project aligns with the company's strategic objectives. For example, an AI model that automates the analysis of large volumes of financial data can save time and avoid human error, outcomes that are of high value in a financial services company.

Feasibility

> This dimension refers to the project's technical difficulty, the resources required (human, technological, and financial), and the possible risks or uncertainties involved. *Low complexity* means the AI project is relatively

easy to implement, requires fewer resources, or relies on well-understood and available technologies. On the other hand, *high complexity* means the initiative requires a high investment of time, resources, or advanced technical knowledge and/or carries a higher level of uncertainty.

The level of feasibility and complexity in AI projects depends on several factors, such as access to quality data, the need for advanced infrastructure (cloud computing, GPUs, etc.), the availability of data science experts, and the need for frequent testing and tuning. The key factors to consider are:

Data availability and quality
> Most AI projects (with the exception of GenAI ones) depend on the availability of large amounts of clean, labeled data. If the data is not available or requires a lot of processing, the complexity of the project increases.

Technical capabilities of the team
> The team's technical knowledge and experience with AI tools and techniques are key factors. An experienced team can reduce the complexity of technically challenging projects.

Risks and uncertainty
> In AI, uncertainty about results (since some models may not work as expected) and risks associated with the deployment of the technology (ethical issues, data privacy, regulatory compliance) also influence the assessment of complexity.

If you combine both value and feasibility factors, you get four clusters of projects that will help you categorize and prioritize your AI initiatives:

Quick wins—high value and low complexity
> These are the most attractive projects, as they generate high value with relatively little investment of resources and effort. Examples of potential quick wins include the implementation of already-trained AI models or the use of prebuilt solutions that optimize processes or make automatic decisions quickly. What falls into this category depends not only on the nature of the project but also on the technology available and the AI maturity of your organization (e.g., a visual recognition system can be easily implemented if

you already have a cloud platform for visual AI). As an AI PM, you will welcome these opportunities.

Strategic projects—high value and high complexity

These projects can generate significant impact but only with considerable investment of time, technology, and talent. Examples of strategic projects might be the development of a personalized recommender system based on advanced deep learning techniques or the design of a complex, large-scale prediction model. Although difficult to implement, these initiatives can transform the business if they're successful. These projects can be very valuable for your portfolio and individual growth as an AI PM, so keep an eye open for them and advocate for them when your company and team context allow it.

Routine tasks—low value and low complexity

These projects are easy to execute but have limited impact. Although you should not devote too many resources to them, they can be useful to optimize minor operations or as initial steps toward more ambitious objectives. Depending on how you manage resources in your company, you may want to allocate some capacity to implement these projects as a way to gain experience and generate internal traction.

Wrong project choices—low value and high complexity

These are resource- and time-intensive projects that do not promise great value to the organization. Ideally, they should be avoided or postponed until resources are available or value can be increased. An example might be the development of an experimental model that has no clear application or may not be cost-effective. From a career perspective, you should avoid these to maintain stakeholder trust.

You can structure prioritization as a multistep process, using each step as an opportunity to align ideas and stakeholders. Make sure you handle those steps carefully to achieve a good output in terms of expected value and realistic expectations. As the AI project manager, you will be facilitating discussions with executive sponsors, technical folks, and business experts. Use this checklist to guide these discussions.

Steps in the Project Prioritization Process

- [ ] *Project identification:* List all possible AI initiatives that the organization could develop.

- [ ] *Value assessment:* Measure the potential impact of each project in terms of key business metrics.

- [ ] *Complexity assessment:* Consider factors such as resources required, data availability, development time, and risks.

- [ ] *Placement in a matrix or ordered list:* Classify the projects in the appropriate quadrants of a 2 × 2 matrix or categories in a list.

- [ ] *Strategic decision:* Focus efforts on projects that fall into the "quick wins" and "strategic projects" quadrants while avoiding or postponing those of low value and high complexity.

You will revisit this prioritization in richer detail in Chapter 5 as a way to integrate this decision process into your end-to-end project lifecycle. Let's now explore one of the factors that impacts the level of feasibility of your AI projects: the data.

Impact of data on AI

The performance of an AI system is inextricably linked to the quality of its underlying data. Depending on the type of AI architecture used, the volume and nature of the required data will vary, but its role as a critical building block remains constant. Data quality factors serve as the criteria for determining if a dataset is adequate for meeting project objectives.

The following are the main data quality factors:

Accuracy

This reflects how correctly the data represents the real-world values it is intended to model. Inaccurate data, such as mismatched sales figures, leads to erroneous forecasts and biased results.

Completeness

Are all necessary data points present? Missing values, such as customer contact information, forces algorithms to make incorrect assumptions, reducing overall reliability.

Consistency

Data must not present contradictions across different datasets or sources. Inconsistent records, such as multiple identification numbers for a single customer, cause models to produce contradictory or inaccurate outputs.

Timeliness

This relates to whether data is current and relevant to the appropriate temporal context. Outdated information, like five-year-old sales data used for current trend predictions, often renders a model ineffective.

Relevance

Data must be appropriate and useful for the specific problem being solved. Irrelevant variables add noise to a model, degrading its effectiveness and accuracy.

Accessibility

This measures the ease with which systems and users can obtain and use data, including real-time availability and interoperability. Inaccessible or unreadable databases can delay or block AI development.

Validity

Data must comply with predefined rules, formats, and standards. Invalid data, such as an age field containing a value of 150, triggers errors and prevents correct algorithmic processing.

Uniformity

Also known as *format consistency*, this reflects whether the data follows a single structure (e.g., a uniform DD-MM-YYYY date format). Heterogeneous formats lead to processing failures and statistical grouping errors.

Traceability

This is the ability to track the origin, transformations, and modifications of data throughout its lifecycle. Data lineage ensures transparency and auditability, which are essential for building trust in AI results.

Integrity
This refers to the correct structure and relationship between different datasets. Compromised integrity causes algorithms to generate incorrect inferences by relating erroneous data points.

Reliability
This concerns the credibility and verification of the data source. Models trained on unreliable or unverified sources are prone to bias and inaccurate decision making.

It's essential to ensure that data meets these quality criteria, as data quality directly impacts the effectiveness, accuracy, and reliability of AI models. A high-quality dataset provides a solid foundation for informed decision making and for the development of robust predictive models and algorithms. We will revisit some of these factors in Chapter 5 as part of our recommendations for analyzing the quality of your AI projects' input data sources.

Data analysis and profiling

Exploratory data analysis is a foundational approach that combines statistical techniques and data visualization to investigate and understand the fundamental properties of a dataset before applying predictive models or making business decisions. Depending on whether you're looking at it from a technical or a business point of view, EDA has slightly different objectives, but they complement each other to ensure that the full value of the data is realized.

The technical perspective As a technical approach, EDA focuses on understanding the statistical and structural properties of data. This initial analysis allows data scientists and analysts to identify patterns, anomalies, and relationships between variables and to assess data quality. EDA is usually performed by technical professionals, but as an AI project manager, you can guide the analysis with business-related questions and hypotheses. The main objectives of the technical approach are:

Understanding of data structure
Identify data types (categorical, numeric, ordinal, etc.), find the distribution of values, detect missing values, and estimate possible out-of-range or erroneous values.

Detection of patterns and relationships

EDA allows the discovery of correlations, dependencies, or other relationships between variables (features) within the dataset. This includes looking for linear and nonlinear relationships that could be useful for further modeling.

Identification of outliers

Outliers can affect the interpretation of data and the performance of ML models. Detecting them and deciding how to deal with them is critical.

Evaluation of the distribution of variables

How variables are distributed (e.g., normal distribution, skewed, etc.) determines whether it is necessary to transform the data before applying it to models.

Assessment of data quality

Aspects such as completeness, accuracy, and consistency of the data are reviewed to identify problems that may require additional preprocessing, such as imputation of missing values or cleaning of dirty data.

Some of the tools and techniques used in technical EDA include:

Data visualization

Graphs such as histograms, box plots, scatter plots, bar charts, density plots, and correlation plots help to visualize relationships and key features of the data.

Descriptive statistics

Measures such as mean, median, mode, standard deviation, interquartile range, and percentiles, among others, allow summarizing and describing the characteristics of the variables.

Correlation matrix

This is used to measure the linear relationship between different numerical variables by highlighting correlated features, allowing teams to understand how variables influence each other and detect potential redundancy that could affect model performance.

Missing value analysis
Use this technique to identify variables or records that have incomplete data and determine whether it is necessary to impute or delete those rows or columns.

For example, imagine you have a dataset containing information about a retail store's sales. The technical side of EDA would involve examining the distribution of sales by plotting a histogram, exploring the relationship between product price and sales using a scatter plot to identify possible correlations, detecting anomalies in daily sales through cash flow diagrams to uncover outliers, and analyzing monthly sales patterns to determine whether they exhibit seasonality.

The business perspective From a business perspective, EDA is used to translate raw data into actionable insights or findings that can improve strategic and operational decisions. The main objective is to understand how data can influence business performance and how it can help make evidence-based choices. In this case, the main objectives are:

Identification of opportunities and risks
EDA enables business leaders to identify patterns of behavior that may signal new market opportunities or risks to which the business may be exposed.

Customer segmentation
Analysis can reveal segments or groups of customers with similar behaviors, allowing for more targeted and personalized marketing and sales strategies.

Operations optimization
By detecting patterns in operational data, such as logistics, inventory levels, or sales trends, the business can make adjustments that improve efficiency and reduce costs.

Trend detection
Identifying behavioral patterns or changes over time, such as seasonality in sales or the evolution of customer behavior, allows proactive planning and decision making.

Evidence-based decision making

EDA enables business decisions to be based on concrete evidence and not just intuition or assumptions. This ensures that actions are aligned with actual data.

The tools and techniques used include:

Key performance indicators

KPIs allow the exploration of data to extract key business performance indicators, such as conversion rates, revenue per customer, and sales growth.

Dashboarding and executive visualization

Presenting key findings visually (through dashboards or reports) is crucial for business decision makers to interpret results and take corrective or strategic action.

Market segmentation

Customers can be segmented according to their buying patterns, behavior, or demographics, allowing for customized offers or products.

Anomaly detection

Business managers can detect unexpected events, such as drops in sales or unusual customer behavior, and make quick corrective decisions.

For example, imagine an online retailer uses sales, web traffic, and customer behavior data to perform EDA from a business standpoint. The analysis might reveal that customers in certain geographic segments spend more on specific product categories, that sales numbers experience seasonal drops during particular months (prompting adjustments to marketing campaigns during those periods), and that some products sell more quickly when paired with discounts, enabling the retailer to refine and optimize its pricing strategies.

Similar to technical EDA, a business analysis is very important for your AI projects. You should take a lead role in organizing the strategy to obtain data insights, then cross-reference those findings with qualitative knowledge gained from interviewing business experts and clients.

EDA connects the technical and business sides of the organization. Analysts and data scientists perform technical EDA to ensure that data is ready and well understood before proceeding to modeling or data-driven decisions. Technical analysis provides insights that are then translated into information of value to the business. You are responsible for connecting both sides to get a 360-degree analysis of your data sources before starting AI projects.

PHASE 2: MOBILIZATION

In this phase, you secure the foundation for execution by aligning all necessary resources before the project begins. This includes provisioning the required infrastructure, technical tools, and environments, as well as identifying additional data sources. You must assemble the right team, ensuring that each member has the appropriate competencies and a confirmed level of effort. At the same time, effective stakeholder and change management are critical to prepare the organization for the project's outcomes. Key decisions regarding the technology stack and productivity and development tools are finalized in this phase, supported by a concise and effective communication plan to keep all parties aligned and informed.

A successful AI project depends on integrating its technical and human elements, beginning with a robust foundation of infrastructure.

Required infrastructure

Infrastructure, which provides the technical basis on which AI projects are executed, includes the hardware, software, and cloud services necessary to store, process, and analyze large volumes of data. Establishing this foundation requires a strategic selection of components designed to handle the unique computational intensity and security demands of machine learning workflows:

Processing power
> AI projects often require high computational power, especially for training complex models such as deep neural networks or GenAI. In general terms, we talk about GPUs or TPUs.

Specialized AI services
> Many organizations use cloud services such as Amazon Web Services, Google Cloud AI, or Microsoft Azure. These platforms offer preconfigured infrastructure, AI APIs, and managed services that enable model development, training, and deployment at scale.

Data architecture and networking

AI often requires storing large volumes of data (how much depends on the type of AI), so scalable and efficient systems are essential for both on-premises solutions and cloud platforms. Furthermore, fast and stable networks are critical for seamless data transmission between systems.

Security and governance

Protecting sensitive data and securing transmission channels are nonnegotiable components of the infrastructure stack.

Tools and technologies

As you'll learn in Chapter 6, a cohesive set of technological tools is required to manage each phase of the project lifecycle. This productivity environment, which is typically selected by the technical team, generally includes:

Programming languages

Python remains the most widely used language in AI due to its large community, libraries, and ease of prototyping. R is also frequently used in statistical analysis and machine learning.

Libraries and frameworks

Commonly used libraries and frameworks in ML and DL include Keras, PyTorch, and TensorFlow, which are widely adopted for building and training neural networks. For traditional ML and simpler models, Scikit-learn is the preferred Python library, while Keras serves as a high-level API for rapid, user-friendly prototyping on top of TensorFlow.

Visualization tools

Tools such as Plotly, Matplotlib, and Seaborn are used for data exploration, while Tableau and Power BI help communicate model results to business stakeholders.

MLOps/LLMOps platforms

Operationalizing machine learning is crucial for bringing AI models into production. Tools such as MLflow, Kubeflow, and DVC help manage the deployment, monitoring, and continuous updating of models in a production environment.

People and competencies

A diverse and highly qualified team is essential to the success of an AI project. The roles required span both technical and business areas. For example, data scientists are responsible for designing and training AI models, conducting statistical analyses, and running experiments, drawing on skills in advanced statistics, machine learning, and data visualization. Data engineers focus on preparing data and building reliable data pipelines to ensure that datasets are clean, well structured, and readily available, while also managing storage and distributed processing. Machine learning engineers, performing what is often referred to as MLOps, concentrate on deploying, scaling, and maintaining models in production by implementing automated retraining and monitoring processes as new data arrives. Infrastructure and DevOps specialists configure and maintain the technical environments needed for AI development, applying expertise in cloud computing, containerization technologies such as Docker and Kubernetes, and networking. Also, ethics and compliance officers play a critical role in ensuring that AI systems adhere to data privacy regulations, such as GDPR, and are designed to avoid harmful bias.

That said, the arrival of GenAI technologies has changed the panorama of AI roles and skills. As shown in Figure 4-3, familiar roles have evolved into new ones that are more adapted to the new era of pretrained models (e.g., AI engineers and prompt engineers).

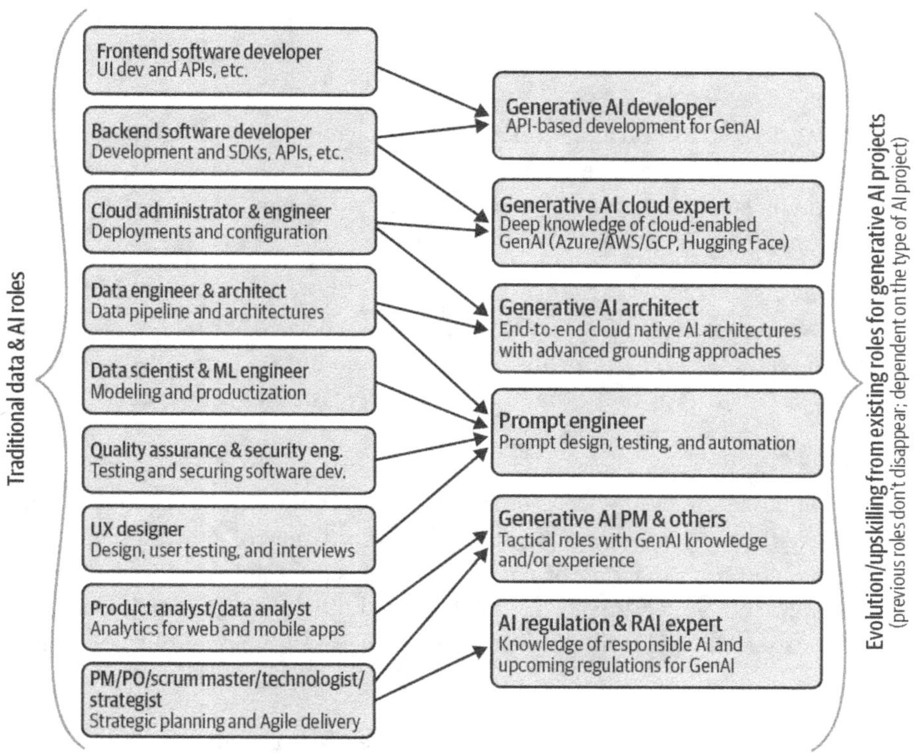

Figure 4-3. Evolution of AI roles

Data sources

Data is the foundation of any AI project. If data is incorrect or insufficient, AI models will not be able to generate good results. Cultivating a strong "data culture" involves the following steps:

1. *Data acquisition*

    Data can come from a variety of sources, such as internal databases, APIs, IoT sensors, social networks, and business transactions. Data collection must be efficient and appropriate for a business problem to be solved.

2. *Data cleaning and preparation*

    A large portion of time in AI projects is spent on data cleaning. Data must be cleaned to remove null values and duplicates and to correct inconsistencies. This step also includes the imputation of missing values and removal of outliers.

3. Data annotation

For supervised learning models, the labeling or annotation of data is required. In some cases, this process can involve a significant amount of human labor, although platforms such as Amazon Mechanical Turk or automated tools can be used to speed it up.

4. Ensuring a balanced dataset

It is essential to ensure that the dataset is balanced, as biases in the data can lead to inaccurate or discriminatory results. To avoid this, conduct a thorough analysis of the quality and representativeness of the data.

Scientific approach

The development of AI projects requires a scientific approach based on the experimental method. This process involves the formulation of hypotheses, experimentation, and the validation of results. To navigate the inherent uncertainty of AI development, project managers must treat the lifecycle as a series of structured inquiries, moving through the following phases of the scientific method:

Hypothesis formulation

Before building a model, it is crucial to clearly define the problem you are trying to solve by formulating hypotheses and determining which variables can be predictive.

Experimentation

The AI model–training process involves performing multiple experiments with different algorithms, hyperparameters, and features. An iterative cycle is used to tune the model and improve its performance.

Model validation

For ML or DL projects, cross-validation should be performed to verify model accuracy and avoid overfitting. Tools such as TensorBoard or Weights & Biases can help to visualize the experiments and track the results.

Evaluation metrics

The metrics used vary according to the type of problem (e.g., classification or regression). Common evaluation metrics include precision, recall, and area under the receiver operating characteristic curve (AUC-ROC) for classification tasks and mean absolute error (MAE) and mean squared error (MSE) for regression models. You'll explore these metrics further in Chapter 5, but here are some baseline concepts you may want to keep in mind:

Confusion matrix

This is a fundamental tool used to visualize the performance of a classification model by summarizing the number of true positives, false positives, true negatives, and false negatives, which in turn enables the calculation of key evaluation metrics (Figure 4-4).

	Actually positive (1)	Actually negative (0)
Predicted positive (1)	True positives	False positives
Predicted negative (0)	False negatives	True negatives

Figure 4-4. Confusion matrix for classification tasks

For example, imagine a situation in which you have a model that classifies pictures of cats and dogs. If the pictures are difficult to interpret, you may have situations in which the prediction is wrong. The confusion matrix summarizes the model's performance by categorizing results into four different types:

- *True positives and true negatives* are the "correct" classifications: what is predicted matches reality. For example, the model predicts that a picture is of a dog, and it is, or the model predicts the picture is not of a dog, and it isn't.

- *False positives and false negatives* are the "incorrect" classifications. For example, the model says a picture shows a dog, but it is actually an image of a cat, or the model says a picture is of something other than a dog, but it actually shows a dog.

By tracking these outcomes over N trials, you can calculate metrics like precision, recall, F1 score, and AUC-ROC. In general terms, you get a percentage metric that helps you quantify and explain the level of performance.

Human evaluation

In many AI applications, automatic evaluation alone is often insufficient, making human evaluation an important metric. Users manually assess the quality, consistency, or creativity of the model's outputs. This is the case for all types of AI models, including LLMs.

System performance

In addition to specific AI metrics, general system performance as measured by time and efficiency metrics is essential in scenarios where real-time performance matters. This includes *inference time*, which measures how long the model takes to generate a prediction, and *resource usage*, which tracks the consumption of memory, CPU, and GPU during training or inference.

Ethical and legal aspects

AI raises several ethical and legal challenges that must be integrated into your requirement validation process. Besides AI-first regulations such as the EU AI Act, you must address the following core pillars:

Biases in models

AI models can amplify existing biases in the data. Therefore, it is critical to ensure that models are fair and do not discriminate against certain groups.

Data privacy

It is important to comply with regulations such as GDPR and CCPA, which protect users' privacy. Personal data must be handled with care and, in some cases, anonymized.

Transparency and explainability

Decisions made by AI models must be understandable, especially in areas such as health care, finance, and the public sector, where transparency is essential. While the degree of explainability depends on the model's complexity (e.g., opaque versus interpretable), transparency regarding the process is essential.

These key elements intertwine to form the technical, human, and organizational foundation necessary to successfully execute an AI project. Proper planning, along with the right choice of tools and infrastructure and a multidisciplinary team, will be essential to maximize the value generated by AI in your organization.

In our experience, the exploration and mobilization phases are the most critical. By nailing these two stages, you effectively filter out poor project choices and eliminate unrealistic resource expectations. While there is still a significant journey ahead, successfully completing these phases accounts for roughly 60%–70% of a project's potential success. With the foundation secured, let's move to the third phase.

PHASE 3: EXECUTION

The execution phase focuses on finding the balance between experimentation and implementation. It begins with *sprint zero*, the critical period where you transition your team from part-time involvement to full-time dedication and establish the project's operational foundations.

Preparing your sprint zero

As an AI PM, use sprint zero to solidify these seven key pillars:

Kickoff session

Begin with a structured kickoff session to align all stakeholders on the project's vision, objectives, scope, and success criteria. This session should establish clear work agreements, including roles and responsibilities, decision-making authority, communication channels, meeting cadence, and escalation paths. If resource gaps or feasibility concerns persist after the mobilization phase, use this session to finalize backup plans.

Initial work agreements

The beginning of your project's execution phase is an opportunity to align on team norms, expectations around collaboration, and how uncertainty and experimentation will be handled throughout the project. Keep in mind that AI projects are complex, so establish working agreements early to align the differing workflows of scientists and engineers.

Structured project schedule

This is not specific to AI, but it is very important to avoid additional complexity in AI projects. Define and share a realistic and transparent project schedule that outlines key milestones, iteration cycles, dependencies, and review checkpoints. The schedule should balance the need for predictability with the experimental nature of AI development, allowing room for learning, iteration, and rework. Clear timelines help manage stakeholder expectations while providing the team with a shared roadmap for execution.

Defined management methodology

Clearly explain and align the team on the chosen PM approach, whether it is Agile, hybrid, or specifically adapted for AI workflows. This includes clarifying how work will be planned, prioritized, executed, reviewed, and adjusted over time, as well as how experimentation, research spikes, and model iterations fit into the overall delivery process. We will share our recommended methodology later in this chapter.

Agile tracking tools

Implement PM assets such as backlogs, task boards, sprint plans, and lightweight dashboards to provide visibility into work in progress, dependencies, and blockers. These tools should simplify coordination across roles, support frequent inspection and adaptation, and reduce the need for excessive status meetings by making progress and risks visible to the entire team. Depending on your company and team context, you may have the possibility to choose the toolset. However, our honest recommendation is to adapt to whatever project-tracking tools your technical team feels comfortable with. The key outcome is that they provide project updates and document their knowledge, so see which applications are appealing to them and go with those.

Baseline evaluation metrics

Establish early agreement on clear, easy-to-understand model evaluation metrics to create a shared baseline for assessing model performance. Using simple metrics at the start helps align technical and nontechnical stakeholders on what constitutes acceptable progress and prevents misinterpretation of early experimental results.

The premortem exercise

Conduct a premortem exercise in which the team (including technical folks, clients, and executive stakeholders) assumes the project has failed and works backward to identify potential causes, including data quality issues, integration challenges, unrealistic expectations, ethical risks, and organizational constraints. This proactive risk assessment encourages open discussion, surfaces hidden assumptions, and allows the team to define mitigation strategies before problems materialize during execution.

A recurrent takeaway from our clients and students is that AI projects, despite their uncertainty, are relatively similar to any complex software implementation. Your primary goal is to create a project environment that facilitates your technical team's work by choosing the correct project dynamics and day-to-day tooling. Much like team sports, your success depends on how you adapt your methodology to the specific backgrounds and skills of your contributors. By reusing established PM frameworks while tailoring them to the AI context, you can maintain focus on your goals during the execution phase.

Analyzing and adapting to the project context

You don't need to reinvent the wheel, but you must use your PM skills to analyze the overall environment in which your project will unfold, including your organization, your team's maturity, and the technology stack, to determine how the project will be executed and tracked.

Here is our advice for adapting and optimizing your PM methodology:

Define iteration periods

> Every company has a different innovation pace. Some work in one- to four-week sprints, while others plan long-term roadmaps, especially in product-led environments where multiple teams must align. Regardless of the choice, define and confirm the iteration length and expectations (e.g., demos, client reviews, and decision gates) and share them up front with all stakeholders.

Assess project maturity

> Don't assume your team's experience level. Take time to discuss and review their understanding of the proposed methodology. You may find that data scientists or AI engineers can act as "project ambassadors," facilitating meetings or managing backlogs. On the other hand, if the team lacks experience with these methodologies, use this as a coaching opportunity. Remember that habits like task documentation are intuitive but require time and daily practice to materialize.

Decide on the rollout strategy

> Depending on the organizational context and level of maturity, you can implement your methodology all at once or progressively. For example, if a company is new to both AI and Agile, trying to master everything simultaneously may be overwhelming. So try starting with small changes, like implementing sprints without using specific methodologies such as

Scrum, and use simpler documentation tools before moving to advanced platforms.

Stay pragmatic

When you configure your project setup, remember that you don't need to go 100% into specific methodologies or frameworks. Instead, use what works and remove whatever you consider unnecessary or too complex. For instance, we have removed meetings like sprint retrospectives when their outcome wasn't critical for a specific project phase. Maintain a balance between structure and the flexibility required for AI experimentation.

Supporting experimentation

One of the key challenges of the execution phase is to enable experimentation without losing focus on delivery. In AI projects, experimentation is often related to science-heavy tasks such as model training and testing, advanced prompt engineering, and safety adjustments.

If the value of these activities is justified, your main goal here is to find a way to define the scope of those experimentation periods. You can achieve this by answering the following questions and allocating a budget of time and resources within your project roadmap:

Who is responsible?

Clearly identify the individuals or roles responsible for the experimentation (e.g., specific data scientists or ML engineers). This ensures accountability by avoiding ambiguity around ownership.

What is the goal?

Define the precise objective of the experimentation, such as validating a modeling approach, testing data feasibility, improving a specific metric, or de-risking a technical assumption.

What is the resource ceiling?

Set explicit limits on time, budget, and computational resources to prevent experimentation from becoming open-ended and to protect overall project timelines.

What are the performance thresholds?

Establish clear success criteria by defining both the target (optimal) performance and the minimum acceptable threshold required to proceed to the next phase.

What is the impact of a delay?

Assess the impact of delays on the project timeline, including stakeholder expectations, costs, and downstream milestones, and define escalation or decision points

What is being blocked?

Identify dependent tasks or teams that cannot progress until the experimentation is completed, and plan contingencies to minimize bottlenecks or idle time.

Keep in mind that owners of some of these experimentation tasks will often perceive them as interesting technical challenges. Help these team members understand how critical it is to achieve the best possible results in the allocated time to avoid general project delays. During your roadmap and sprint plannings, try to help the lead technical team member define the key periods, including potential iterations, experimentation alternatives, and decisions if an experiment doesn't go well.

Preparing users for adoption

A fundamental truth of AI projects is that they are complex, often intimidating, and frequently misunderstood by clients and end users. You and your team may know all the details, including features and specific advantages, but the people who will use the outcome of your AI project will need to understand things before adopting new tools.

Many PMs delay change management until the end of the project, but this is often too late. To reduce resistance and build confidence, integrate the following assets into your roadmap from the earliest experimentation phases:

UX interviews

Conduct interviews early on to gather insights into user needs, pain points, and expectations. You can use mockup tools like Figma or Balsamiq, or prototyping platforms like Lovable or Bolt, to visualize the solution. This allows you to customize the interface and incorporate "human-in-the-loop" controls, giving users the power to override AI decisions when necessary.

Continuous testing and feedback

Incorporate regular testing cycles and gather feedback to refine the AI solution, ensuring that it meets user needs and performs effectively. There is no single formula for this, but depending on your project's duration, try to schedule at least two testing and feedback periods. This will help you close the gap between the AI project outcome and the user expectations.

Solution demos and user training

During and especially at the end of the execution phase, offer hands-on demos and training sessions to familiarize users with the AI solution, boosting confidence and encouraging adoption. This is key for them to fully embrace the outcome of your AI project and to guarantee a positive perception.

Once again, don't wait for the end of the project. By engaging users early and often, you progressively alleviate concerns and ensure the organization is ready to embrace the final outcome.

Expanding the communication channels

In AI projects, there is no such thing as "too much" communication. Involved stakeholders are often a mix of excited, concerned, and curious. Regardless of the context, all of them will enjoy timely and proactive communication channels to get all the information they need to understand how the project is going. We recommend the following channels to maintain transparency and alignment:

Sprint-specific meetings

Later in this chapter, we will go into some detail about dedicated sessions, such as sprint reviews, that are designed to review progress, discuss AI-specific hurdles, and validate assumptions with key stakeholders.

Centralized documentation

Maintain a shared, living space with project goals, decisions, model changes, limitations, risks, and FAQs to ensure transparency and self-service access to information. Keep in mind that this can include not only project-level decks but also technical documentation in an internal knowledge management platform (e.g., Confluence, wiki).

Weekly summaries

Send concise updates highlighting achievements, upcoming work, risks, decisions needed, and key learnings to keep everyone aligned without overwhelming them.

Targeted one-on-ones and office hours

Enable private conversations with critical stakeholders to address sensitive concerns or gather feedback that may not surface in a group setting. Protect your technical team by handling these discussions yourself, involving them only when their specific expertise is required to resolve deep technical doubts.

Remember, being reactive will only create issues during project execution, including continuous questions and escalations that will impact your team's ability to deliver the project on time.

PHASE 4: DELIVERY

The way you present your AI project results is as important as the outcome itself. We have seen projects that were technically average but perceived as extraordinary due to excellent communication, but we've also seen exceptional work that went undervalued because of poor delivery.

This last phase ensures a professional and seamless transition once execution concludes. Focus on these three pillars to solidify the perceived value of your work:

Formalized deliverables

Every single asset created by your team is valuable. Make sure you define the list of items and the way to transfer or share them. Some examples include code repositories, experimentation notebooks, and technical documentation (especially for model experimentation and testing and data pipeline creation).

Knowledge transfer

Documentation is often neglected in the final rush to launch. Make sure you allocate time and resources during the final weeks of your project so your team members can work on this. If the project is being handed over to another organization, facilitate formal training sessions to ensure a smooth transition.

The final readout

Much like the project kickoff meeting, prepare a final readout session with all relevant stakeholders. This may include a live demo, evaluation of project success, and lessons learned for future projects. In commercial contexts, a successful readout is the perfect moment to propose follow-up initiatives or new collaborations.

These simple steps will ensure an elegant conclusion of the project and an increased perceived value from key stakeholders, especially in commercial contexts in which your team will deliver a solution to another team or company.

With the four phases of the AI project lifecycle established, we will now explore how to adapt PM methodologies to fit this framework. If you are already a certified professional (e.g., PMP, CSM), you may find the fundamentals familiar, but applying them within AI-specific constraints is where the real nuance lies. If you are new to project management, this section will provide a vital foundation for any future AI or software initiative you undertake.

Useful Project Management Methodologies

Let's now analyze the existing PM methodologies and their potential role in and contribution to your AI projects. We will highlight their pros and cons and conclude both this section and the chapter with our recommended hybrid approach, tailored for the unique demands of AI development.

WATERFALL: A FOUNDATIONAL APPROACH FROM TRADITIONAL PROJECT MANAGEMENT

Waterfall, one of the earliest formalized PM methodologies, follows a linear and sequential approach. The philosophy behind Waterfall is that each phase of the project should be completed before the next phase begins, making it a structured, predictable, and step-by-step process. This methodology is ideal for projects where the requirements are clearly defined from the outset and are unlikely to change.

Waterfall was first introduced in 1970 by Winston W. Royce, who described it as a process with clearly defined phases. Initially, it was conceived for engineering projects, particularly software development, and it has since been widely adopted across many industries. This methodology assumes that requirements are well understood up front and that changes to the project scope are unlikely once the process begins.

Although Agile has gained popularity, Waterfall remains widely used in certain industries and project types, particularly those that involve predictable workflows, like construction, manufacturing, and some aspects of software development. It offers a relatively rigid framework and is suited for projects where change management is minimal.

As you can see in Figure 4-5, the key phases in the Waterfall approach are requirements, design, implementation, testing, deployment, and maintenance.

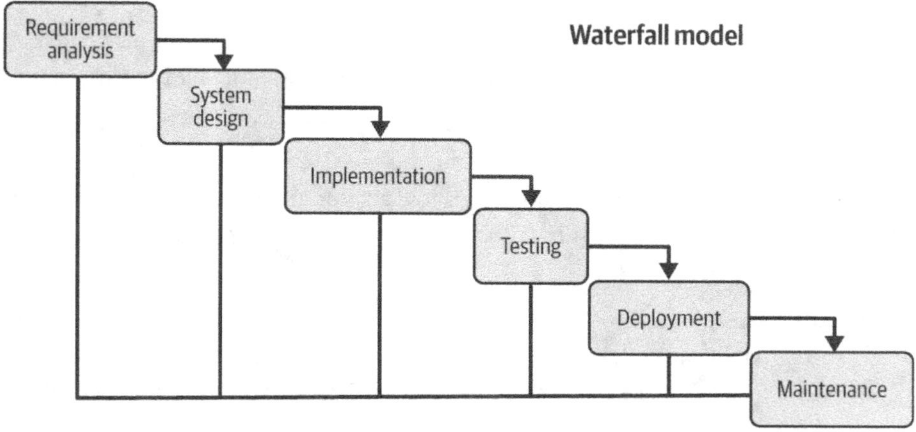

Figure 4-5. Waterfall phases

1. *Requirement analysis*

    Collecting and documenting all stakeholder needs

2. *System design*

    Defining the technical architecture and design plans based on those requirements

3. *Implementation*

    The actual coding and development of the system

4. *Testing*

    Verifying the product against the original specifications

5. *Deployment*

    Delivering the final product to the client

6. *Maintenance*

    Handling updates and fixing issues post-launch

While AI projects are characterized by uncertainty and experimentation, Waterfall offers several assets that are useful to retain in a hybrid approach:

Predictability

Having predefined phases makes it easier to estimate timelines, budgets, and resource needs. Accurate estimates are essential during the exploration and mobilization phases.

Clear milestones

The sequential nature of Waterfall allows you to track progress against firm completion dates, which is critical in commercial contexts with strict delivery deadlines.

Disciplined documentation

In regulated industries like finance or health care, Waterfall's emphasis on recordkeeping ensures compliance and provides a vital reference point for future maintenance.

Well-defined roles

Each phase has defined roles and responsibilities, reducing ambiguity about what each team is accountable for.

Stakeholder clarity

Nontechnical stakeholders often find linear timelines easier to follow, though you must proactively manage their expectations when AI experimentation causes deviations.

That said, there are several reasons to avoid full reliance on Waterfall during your AI activities:

Lack of flexibility

In AI, requirements are often refined based on experimental findings. Waterfall makes it costly and difficult to revisit a previous phase once it is finalized.

Delayed feedback

Testing occurs only at the end of the effort. In AI development, discovering a data quality or model performance issue this late can lead to project failure.

High risk of failure

If an issue is discovered late in the process, it can result in substantial delays and increased costs. The fact that the rigid structure doesn't allow for easy course correction is one of the key reasons you will need to introduce other methodologies.

Customer involvement

Stakeholders are often disconnected from the process between the requirements and deployment phases, increasing the risk that the final model won't meet their actual needs.

Overemphasis on up-front planning

The heavy emphasis on up-front planning can stall progress if the team spends too much time trying to predict every outcome in an inherently unpredictable field.

If you want to formally master these foundational principles and show that you have done so, several certifications are highly regarded:

Project Management Professional (PMP)

Offered by PMI (Project Management Institute), PMP is one of the most widely recognized certifications for project managers. It covers traditional Waterfall methods extensively and is useful for anyone working with structured, plan-driven projects. At the same time, it also offers robust coverage of Agile approaches.

PRINCE2 (PRojects IN Controlled Environments)

This is a widely used process-based methodology for PM that is heavily based on Waterfall principles. It is particularly popular in Europe and is often perceived as an alternative to the PMP. It is useful for individuals working in more structured, predictable project environments.

Certified Associate in Project Management (CAPM)

Also offered by PMI, this certification is ideal for beginners and focuses on core Waterfall principles, providing foundational knowledge for managing traditional projects. If you have zero PM experience, the CAPM could be a great option for you.

Keep this in mind as we discuss combining methodologies in your hybrid AI PM approach: while many discard Waterfall due to its lack of flexibility, its focus on planning and documentation offers advantages for your AI projects. Let's now explore the modern methodologies currently driving most AI projects.

AGILE: AN ADAPTIVE PM APPROACH

Agile is an iterative and incremental approach to PM that focuses on flexibility, adaptability, and continuous collaboration between teams. It emerged in software development, but its popularity and success have led it to be adopted in a wide variety of industries, such as product management, professional services, marketing, and, more recently, AI.

Agile is based on a set of principles detailed in the Agile Manifesto (Figure 4-6), which prioritizes people and interactions over processes, functional software over extensive documentation, and responsiveness to change over rigid planning.

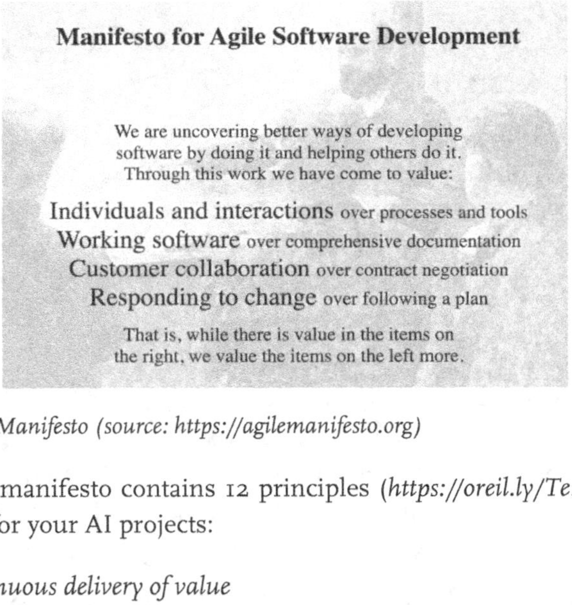

Manifesto for Agile Software Development

We are uncovering better ways of developing
software by doing it and helping others do it.
Through this work we have come to value:

Individuals and interactions over processes and tools
Working software over comprehensive documentation
Customer collaboration over contract negotiation
Responding to change over following a plan

That is, while there is value in the items on
the right, we value the items on the left more.

Figure 4-6. Agile Manifesto (source: https://agilemanifesto.org)

While the manifesto contains 12 principles (*https://oreil.ly/Te1QS*), these are the most vital for your AI projects:

Early and continuous delivery of value
> Agile focuses on the rapid, ongoing release of features that provide immediate value. Rather than waiting for the entire project to be ready for launch, the team delivers small, functional increments. This creates a steady flow of early feedback from users, allowing you to pivot as needs emerge and to redirect the project to deliver even more value.

Adapting to change

One of the most important principles of Agile is accepting change as a natural part of development. Requirements may evolve as your understanding of the customer deepens or as new technologies emerge. Rather than strictly following a predetermined plan, Agile encourages rapid adaptation so that teams can react to these changes without affecting the quality of the final product.

Iteration and incrementing

Instead of working on the entire product at once, Agile teams work in short cycles called iterations or sprints, which generally last two to four weeks. At the end of each iteration, a functional increment of the product is produced that can be presented to stakeholders. This allows you to evaluate progress frequently and adjust the project's direction as necessary.

Continuous collaboration with the customer

Unlike traditional approaches where customers are only involved at the beginning (to define requirements) and at the end (for deployment), Agile promotes constant collaboration with the customer throughout the project lifecycle. The customer or product owner works closely with the team to prioritize and define which features will be developed in each iteration. This ensures that the team is aligned with the customer's expectations at all times.

Self-organizing, cross-functional teams

Agile promotes the idea of self-organizing, cross-functional teams. Instead of relying on a project leader to assign tasks, the team has the independence to decide how best to accomplish the work. In addition, teams are often made up of people with different skill sets who can collaborate to solve problems holistically and quickly.

Constant feedback

At the end of each iteration, Agile teams conduct reviews (demos) and retrospectives. Reviews allow stakeholders to see the progress of the product and give feedback on what has been built. Retrospectives, on the other hand, are meetings in which the team reflects on its work process, identifying what worked well and what needs improvement. This constant feedback loop fosters a culture of continuous improvement.

By embracing these principles, teams can move away from rigid planning toward a more adaptive execution model. As a direct consequence of this, when the Agile approach is properly understood and implemented, it brings key advantages to your project environment, all of them highly relevant for AI implementations:

Flexibility and responsiveness

Agile allows teams to adapt to changes quickly. This is especially useful in projects where requirements may not be completely defined from the outset or where the environment is constantly changing.

Continuous improvement

Regular iterations and constant review of work processes and the product under development foster continuous improvement, in terms of both product quality and team efficiency.

Increased customer satisfaction

Continuous collaboration with the customer and the delivery of frequent functional increments ensure that the final product meets customer expectations, leading to higher satisfaction and lower risk of errors or misunderstandings. Once again, this is a great way to evangelize and facilitate adoption of your AI project outcomes before the final delivery phase.

Risk reduction

By working in short increments and delivering partially complete functionality, teams can identify and address potential problems much earlier than they would in a traditional Waterfall project. This significantly reduces the risk of catastrophic failures at the end of the project, which—if we're being honest—are very likely to happen in AI projects without proper risk analysis and mitigation processes.

Transparency and visibility

The Agile methodology promotes transparency, as all stakeholders have access to the progress of the project and can see the results of the work done at the end of each iteration. This ensures that the team, project leaders, and customers are aligned at all times. In AI projects, this openness is invaluable for helping nontechnical stakeholders understand complex technical work, model results, and potential roadblocks. Don't underestimate the value of being transparent and explaining complex AI details for the stakeholders to understand and accept the solutions you and your team will bring to the table.

Agile is not without its challenges, particularly in corporate environments:

Lack of predictability

Because Agile is based on constant adaptation and change, it can be difficult to predict exactly how long a project will take or how much it will cost until you're fairly well down the path toward launch. That is where combining Agile with some Waterfall touches for a pragmatic, hybrid approach may strike a good balance.

Need for customer commitment

Ongoing collaboration with the customer is key to Agile success, but this also requires a level of customer commitment that is not always easy to obtain. If customers are not available to provide constant feedback, the project can get sidetracked. And if they don't learn to accept some degree of uncertainty, neither Agile nor AI is a good fit for them.

Keep in mind that Agile itself is more of a mindset or philosophy than a single methodology or rigid set of rules. Under the Agile umbrella are several methodologies and frameworks, including Kanban, Scrum, Lean, and Extreme Programming (XP).

Kanban: A visual flow approach to Agile work management

Kanban is an Agile method designed to optimize the flow of work by visualizing tasks, limiting work in progress (WIP), and enabling continuous delivery of value. Originating from the Toyota Production System (TPS), Kanban was initially created to improve manufacturing efficiency and later was adapted to knowledge work such as software development, operations, and AI projects.

At the core of Kanban is the Kanban board (Figure 4-7), a visual representation of the workflow where tasks move through defined stages, making progress, bottlenecks, and priorities visible to the entire team.

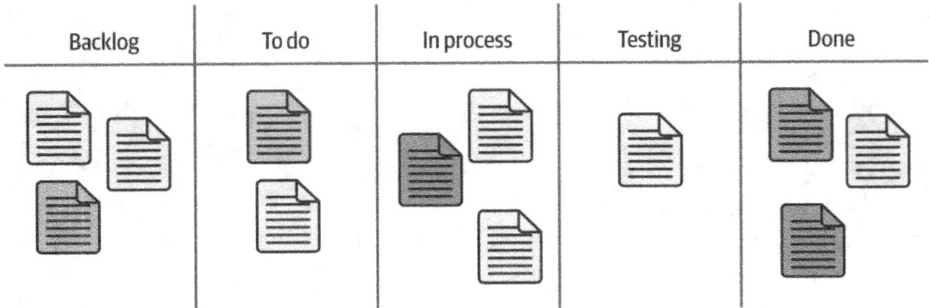

Figure 4-7. Example of a Kanban board

Kanban does not rely on fixed iterations (sprints) or predefined roles. Instead, it uses a pull-based system in which new work is started only when there is available capacity, reducing overload and improving predictability.

Kanban is guided by key principles such as visualizing the workflow, limiting work in progress to reduce multitasking and delays, managing and improving flow, making process policies explicit, and fostering continuous improvement through small, incremental changes. You can customize the different workflow stages to include various review, testing, and validation gates, or keep it simple with a three-part structure of pending, in progress, and completed.

This approach makes Kanban particularly effective in dynamic environments with changing priorities, ongoing support tasks, or AI- and data-driven projects where flexibility, transparency, and steady delivery are essential. As you will see by the end of the chapter, you can leverage Kanban before and after the execution phase of your project to keep things simple while still tracking progress and pending tasks.

Scrum: An Agile framework for project management

Scrum (*https://scrum.org*) is one of the most popular frameworks within the Agile approach to project management, especially in software development, although its use has spread to other areas such as product management, marketing, and, more recently, AI. Scrum enables teams to tackle complex problems while focusing on delivering high-quality products in an efficient and collaborative manner.

Scrum was developed in the 1990s by Jeff Sutherland and Ken Schwaber, who introduced it as a framework for adaptive and Agile software development. Inspired by the Agile mindset, Scrum takes its name from the term used in rugby to describe the formation in which players group together to retrieve the ball, symbolizing the collaboration and teamwork needed in development projects. The Scrum framework was made official in 1995 and has since evolved through the publication of The Scrum Guide (*https://oreil.ly/LFy6M*), a highly recommended reading available in a vast variety of languages that describes the essential roles, events, and artifacts of this approach.

Scrum is characterized by its focus on incremental and rapid delivery of work, transparency, inspection, and continuous adaptation. It is ideal for projects where requirements change frequently or are not fully understood from the outset, which is common in dynamic environments like AI projects. Unlike Kanban, Scrum introduces the idea of specific iteration periods (sprints) and requires a bit more operational effort and understanding of the methodology.

Like other Agile methodologies, Scrum is based on several key principles that guide its implementation:

Transparency

All important aspects of the process should be visible to both team members and stakeholders. This includes visibility into project progress, risks, and team expectations. Transparency builds trust and facilitates informed decision making.

Inspection

Scrum teams regularly review progress toward project objectives and the status of the work. This continuous inspection makes it possible to detect problems or deviations as early as possible in order to make immediate adjustments. Meetings such as sprint reviews are fundamental to this principle.

Adaptability

Based on the feedback obtained from the inspection, the team must be prepared to adjust the plan, processes, or work in progress. Adaptability ensures that the team responds to changes in the environment or customer needs without losing focus on product quality.

For it to work, Scrum uses three key components: roles, events, and artifacts. Together, these elements provide the structure for effective Scrum implementation (Figure 4-8).

Scrum process

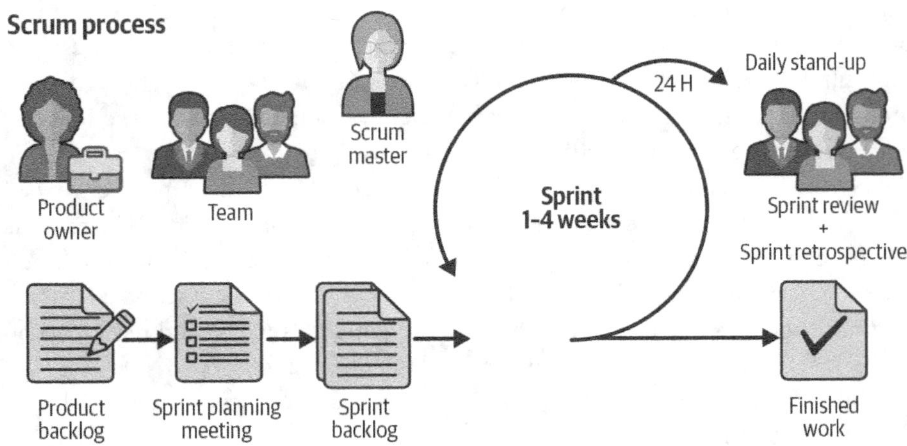

Figure 4-8. Scrum framework and components

Roles: The people Scrum introduces a small, cross-functional team with well-defined roles. The Scrum team is autonomous and is organized to manage work collaboratively. It usually has a few types of members:

- The *product owner (PO)* maximizes product value and manages the product backlog. They act as the bridge between the team and stakeholders, prioritizing tasks that deliver the most value.

- The *scrum master* is a facilitator who ensures that Scrum practices are followed and removes obstacles that block the team's progress.

- The *development team* is a self-organizing group (typically three to nine people) with the technical skills to design, build, and test the increment. In AI projects, this includes data scientists and ML engineers.

Keep in mind that there is theory and there is practice. For example, the number of folks in the development team will really depend on your AI project scope and resources. And your official role as AI project manager can include some PO or scrum master responsibilities, depending on the team setup. Ideally, you can take on both the PM and PO roles, as your main goal will be to control the high-level roadmap and the sprint-level backlog. In that case, one of the technical leads in your team could potentially be the scrum master, but it again depends on how your team is organized and their actual understanding of the Scrum methodology.

Scrum events Events in Scrum create a structure for inspecting and adapting the work, ensuring that the team stays aligned and focused on the objectives. The main events are:

Sprint
> The heart of Scrum, this is a fixed-time cycle (one to four weeks) in which a portion of the project is completed.

Sprint planning
> This is a meeting at the start of a sprint to decide which backlog items will be tackled based on priority and team capacity.

Daily scrum
> A 15-minute daily stand-up, its purpose is to align on progress and identify blockers. Each team member answers three basic questions: What did I do yesterday? What will I do today? Are there any impediments in my way?

Sprint review
> Scrum members demonstrate the completed work to stakeholders at the end of the sprint to gather feedback.

Sprint retrospective
> This is a private team meeting to reflect on the process and identify improvements for the next cycle. (In AI projects, we sometimes limit these to maximize the time that technical members have to build product.)

Artifacts: The tools Scrum uses certain tools that provide visibility into work in progress and help align teams and stakeholders around project goals:

- The *product backlog* is a prioritized list of all the features, enhancements, bug fixes, and tasks needed to develop the product. It is constantly evolving as new requirements arise or priorities are adjusted. The PO is responsible for managing and prioritizing the product backlog. From a PM perspective, this end-to-end product backlog represents the entire set of tasks required for your AI project roadmap.

- The *sprint backlog* is a subset of the product backlog that the team commits to complete during a sprint. It includes the tasks selected for the sprint and a plan for how to accomplish them. It is managed by the development team and changes as work is performed within the sprint. You will work with your team to decide the scope of the sprint backlog, usually during the sprint-planning meetings.

- The *increment* is the functional version of the product at the end of each sprint. It must meet the definition of "done" agreed upon by the team, meaning that the product is ready to be released or presented to stakeholders. Each increment builds on the previous one, leading to the creation of a complete final product at the end of the project.

Keep in mind that the look and feel of the backlog depends on the PM tool you use, but you can see an illustrative example in Figure 4-9.

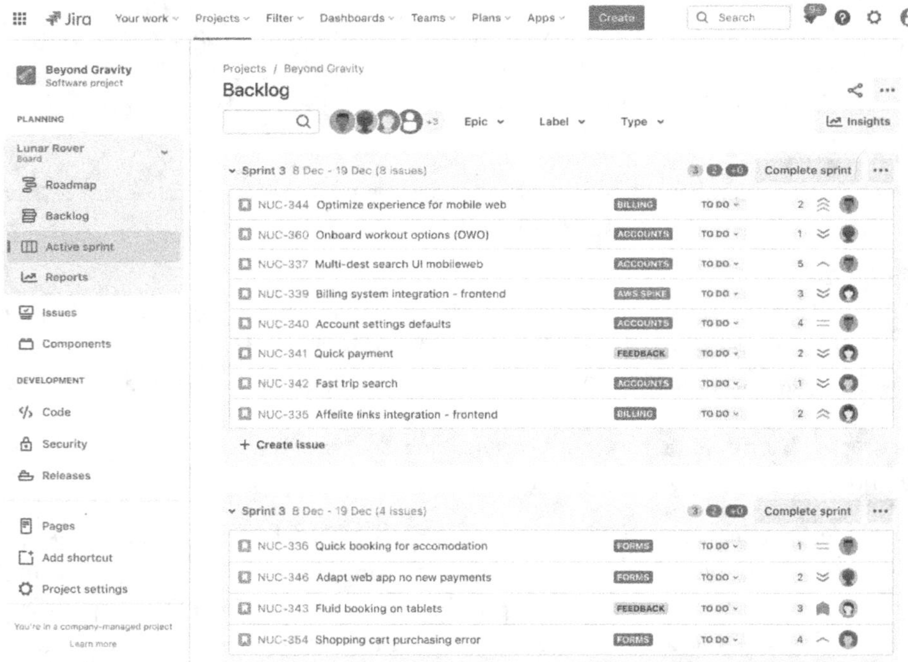

Figure 4-9. Illustrative example of a Scrum backlog (source: Atlassian)

If your organization and team are new to Agile methodologies and don't understand why Scrum would be a good collaboration framework, try to educate them and explain all the relevant components. To motivate adoption, focus on the core value of this methodology in the context of a complex AI project:

Rapid adaptation to change

Scrum enables teams to adapt to changing requirements and customer feedback quickly and efficiently. By working in short cycles and receiving frequent feedback, the team can make continuous adjustments.

Continuous improvement

Periodic retrospectives help the team identify areas for improvement in their work process, which fosters a culture of continuous improvement.

Frequent value delivery

At the end of each sprint, the team delivers a functional increment of the product, which ensures that stakeholders see tangible value throughout the project.

Close collaboration

Well-defined roles and frequent meetings ensure effective collaboration among the development team, the PO, and stakeholders.

Visibility and transparency

Scrum provides a high degree of visibility into project progress, as all team members and stakeholders can see what is being done and what remains to be done.

Just as with the general Agile methodology, the main potential complication involves managing commitment, key dates, accurate estimations, and organizational impediments.

Also, keep in mind that this methodology relies heavily on the dedicated role and commitment of the product owner. If you want to make sure the backlog-level work is properly done, it is a good idea for you to learn the fundamentals and adopt that functional role as part of your AI PM journey. The PO must be engaged and available to make quick decisions and prioritize work because without a strong PO, the team can lose focus.

If you're interested in mastering this side of the role, certifications like the CSPO (*https://oreil.ly/RoG1m*) (from the Scrum Alliance) or the PSPO (*https://oreil.ly/ORRyE*) (from Scrum.org) are excellent ways to upskill.

Lean: An approach to maximize value and reduce waste

Lean is a management methodology that focuses on maximizing customer value while minimizing waste. Its roots are in the post-WWII automobile industry; engineers at Toyota, most notably Taiichi Ohno and Shigeo Shingo, developed the Toyota Production System (*https://oreil.ly/NImW_*) to optimize workflows in an era of extreme resource scarcity. They eliminated any activity that did not add direct value, a practice later formalized as *Lean* in the 1990 book *The Machine That Changed the World* (*https://oreil.ly/MQ63U*).

Lean is based on the idea that everything that does not add value to the final product or service is waste (or *muda* in Japanese) and should be eliminated. The goal of Lean is to continuously improve the workflow by identifying and eliminating this waste, enabling organizations to deliver high-quality products or services more quickly and efficiently.

Lean is based on five fundamental principles that guide its implementation:

1. *Define value from the customer's perspective*

   Value is defined solely by the customer, and only activities that directly contribute to the delivery of that value should be considered part of the production process. Everything else is waste that should be minimized or eliminated. This is highly relevant in AI project management, as you need to define the key technology pieces that will bring the most value to the end users.

2. *Value chain mapping*

   The *value chain* is the complete set of activities required to take a product or service from conception to delivery to the customer. In this step, all stages of the process are mapped to identify those that do not add value (waste). The objective is to optimize each stage of the value chain to maximize efficiency, and you can combine this with the EMED methodology to spot unnecessary or low-value activities that will distract your AI project team from achieving the project's key value and goals.

3. *Create continuous flow*

   Once waste has been identified and eliminated, the next step is to ensure that work flows seamlessly through each phase of the process. This means eliminating bottlenecks, dependencies, and wait times that slow down the process. A seamless flow ensures that the product or service can move from one stage to another efficiently and without interruption. Keep this in mind, especially when you deal with dependencies between stages or even between individual tasks (e.g., your data scientists are blocked because they are waiting for the output of a data engineering task). As an AI project manager, you need to use the mobilization phase to analyze and optimize this flow in advance.

4. Establish a "pull" rather than a "push" system

Instead of pushing work through the process based on predictions or a rigid schedule, Lean promotes a *system pull,* in which products or services are created only when they are needed, based on actual customer demand. This minimizes excess inventory and ensures that only what will be used or consumed is produced. This principle is perhaps less relevant for an AI project but may be applicable to future iterations and improvements.

5. Continuous improvement (kaizen)

The final principle of Lean is the relentless pursuit of improvement. This process, known as *kaizen,* involves all members of the organization in constantly identifying areas for improvement and implementing small incremental changes. Through *kaizen,* organizations can continuously improve their processes, products, and services, leading to greater efficiency, reduced costs, and increased customer satisfaction. Like the previous principle, this is potentially relevant to your AI projects in terms of iterations and improvements.

Lean traditionally identifies seven types of waste. While one (inventory) applies primarily to physical factories, the other six are highly relevant to the "digital factory" of an AI project:

1. Overproduction

Building more features than the user needs (e.g., unused data or code that hasn't been deployed)

2. Transportation

Moving data between systems unnecessarily

3. Extra processing

Overcleaning data or overoptimizing a model beyond what is required for the business case

4. Waiting

Delays due to slow approvals or resource shortages

5. Motion

Inefficient workflows or switching among too many tools

6. Defects

Low-quality data or model errors that require costly rework

Ultimately, adopting a Lean spirit means keeping your AI project focused on actual value propositions. There are countless technical rabbit holes that can lead a project astray; your role is to use tools like user interviews and feedback loops to ensure that every hour of development directly serves the customer.

Extreme Programming: An approach for software development

Extreme Programming is an Agile software development methodology that emphasizes flexibility, quality, and responsiveness to change. It was created in the mid-1990s by Kent Beck, along with Ward Cunningham and Ron Jeffries, as a response to common problems in software projects such as delays, changing requirements, and poor code quality. XP seeks to improve software productivity and quality through a series of practices focused on constant collaboration between developers and customers, continuous delivery of functional versions of the software, and continuous improvement of the code through refactoring.

Unlike other methodologies that may focus more on long-term planning or rigorous processes, XP focuses on maximizing adaptability to change and on rapid delivery of functional software that meets customer expectations. The key to XP is to take certain software development principles and practices "to the extreme," by adopting practices that have proven to be effective and applying them in a more disciplined and intensive manner.

XP is based on a set of fundamental principles that guide teams in creating high-quality, adaptable software that is aligned with customer needs. Key XP principles include:

Communication
> Team members and stakeholders engage in constant face-to-face interaction to solve problems effectively.

Simplicity
> The team builds only what is necessary for today and avoids "overengineering" for hypothetical future scenarios.

Feedback
> The team relies on continuous delivery to gather early and frequent insights from the customer.

Courage
> Teams are empowered to make bold decisions, such as scrapping a flawed design or pivoting when a solution isn't working.

Respect

    The organization fosters an environment in which every contributor's unique skills are valued and stakeholder concerns are genuinely addressed.

The reality is that XP is very aligned with what you will experience in any software development and AI project, so it feels more like a consequence of a modern development environment and less of a methodology you need to implement.

XP practices are grouped into three areas that are highly applicable to the technical complexity of AI.

Engineering practices (technical excellence) The following are technical aspects of XP that are relevant to your AI initiatives:

Test-driven development

    Tests are written before the code. This practice ensures that every feature is validated immediately and improves overall code reliability.

Pair programming

    Two developers work at one workstation; one writes code while the other reviews in real time. This increases collaboration and catches errors early.

Continuous integration

    Code is merged into a shared repository several times a day. This ensures that everyone works on the most current version and minimizes integration headaches.

Constant refactoring

    The team continuously cleans and optimizes code without changing its external behavior, ensuring that the system remains flexible and easy to read.

Management practices (delivery and review) General approaches to delivery and review that will help you manage your AI projects are these:

Small releases

    Delivering functional increments frequently allows for rapid customer feedback and keeps the team focused on high-value tasks.

Planning game

> In this collaborative exercise, the team and customer prioritize features for the next iteration, ensuring that the most important work is tackled first.

Short feedback cycle

> Iterations are typically one to two weeks, allowing for near-instant alignment with stakeholder expectations.

Design practices (managing complexity) These practices are relevant to creating interfaces and systems that are as simple as possible. Thus, they are invaluable to AI projects that are inherently highly complex. They include:

Simple design

> The team creates the most straightforward solution that satisfies the current requirement.

Shared metaphor

> A simple, common language or analogy is used to describe how the system works so that developers and nontechnical stakeholders are on the same page.

Collective code ownership

> Any team member can modify any part of the code. This reduces bottlenecks and ensures that the whole team is responsible for the project's health.

XP is less a rigid set of rules and more a byproduct of high-performing development environments. While it yields high-quality software, it requires a disciplined team and a committed customer.

To make this discussion as pragmatic as possible, let's now combine all these methodologies and explore our applied, hybrid approach to AI project management.

Recommended Hybrid Approach

By leveraging the stages of the EMED methodology, you can build a workflow that is both disciplined and flexible. Because there is no universal way to manage every AI project, your goal is to be pragmatic: combine the strengths of various methodologies while discarding any component that doesn't support your specific goals.

As illustrated in Figure 4-10, you can combine the key planning principles of Waterfall methodologies and the flexibility of Agile approaches.

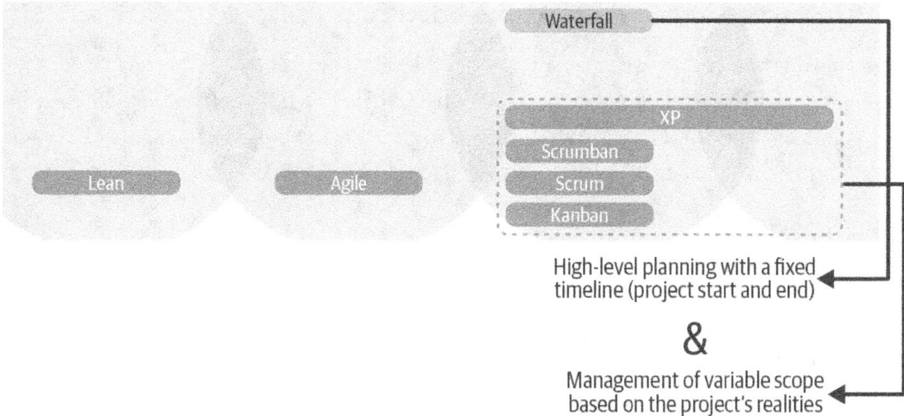

Figure 4-10. Combination of PM methodologies

While every project is unique, Figure 4-11 outlines the mix we use for the vast majority of our AI initiatives.

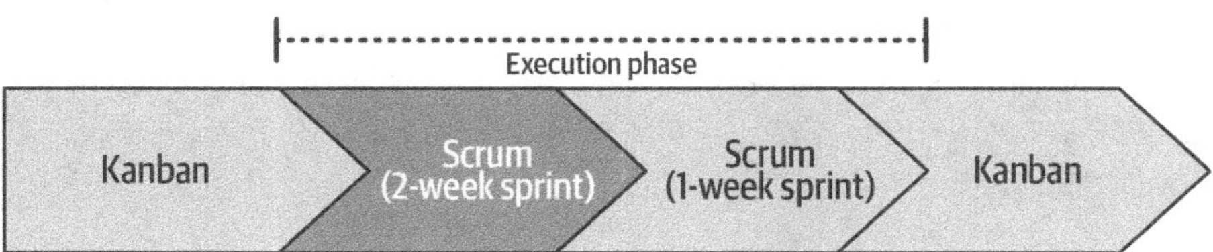

Figure 4-11. Recommended approach

This isn't a magic formula, but it provides a reliable balance for most scenarios:

Exploration and mobilization (Kanban)
> Before the main execution begins, use a simple Kanban board to track preliminary tasks like exploratory data analysis, resource acquisition, and functional checklists. This keeps the "startup" phase organized without the overhead of formal sprints.

Execution (Scrum lite)

During the core development phase, we recommend two-week sprints. This provides enough time for technical members to dive into model training while allowing you to course-correct every 14 days.

Execution wrap-up (one-week sprints)

Toward the end of execution, we often shift to one-week cycles. This helps tighten the focus on final testing and pending experiments when the backlog is thinning out.

Delivery (Kanban)

Once development is complete, return to a simple Kanban board to track knowledge transfer, migrations, and final documentation.

Conclusion

Reflect on all the possibilities and try to create your own approach based on your management style and your team's maturity level. It usually takes a few AI projects to truly develop your own gut feeling for what works. Once you start to see what does and doesn't work, you will be able to take these foundations to the next level.

Take a moment to add your notes to the "Chapter 4 Notebook" on page 169. In the next chapter, we shift back to a more technical focus: the end-to-end AI lifecycle. This discussion will complement the EMED methodology you learned about here by providing a deeper look at the technical stages your project will navigate.

Chapter 4 Notebook

PM Considerations During the Technical AI Lifecycle

The previous chapter detailed an applied methodology and concrete stages from an AI project management perspective: the project before it becomes a project, the key turning points, and the proper way to finalize and deliver the implementation.

Now, we will revisit some technical concepts to complement what you learned in Chapter 2, where you were introduced to specific AI models and technologies. Here, you will learn more about AI tasks and project management responsibilities along the entire technical lifecycle.

The Notion of an AI Lifecycle

An *AI lifecycle* is a framework for mapping the stages of an AI project, from an idea's conception to the application's end of service. There are many versions of AI lifecycles out there. Some focus on the input/output between stages, and others deep-dive into the workstreams that are relevant to each project stage. Some are created for technical purposes, and others see the entire implementation from a compliance perspective. Ultimately, if you compare different versions, you will start to see some key patterns emerge. As a project management professional, you have likely encountered project lifecycles already, so this concept is not completely new. The key goal here is for you to understand all the stages and typical tasks and to connect them to the tactical AI management, strategy, and technical levels from Chapter 1.

The notion of an AI lifecycle is not fully standardized at the industry level. Depending on your company's context and level of maturity, you may already have an internal conception or even a documented standard for the lifecycle. In many cases, this can be a bottom-up, official, or semi-official specification defined by your technical teams that establishes the sequence and scope of tasks for their AI projects.

However, as an AI PM, you may find yourself in organizations and on teams where no such standard exists. Perhaps the steps are there but no one has thought about listing and connecting them. If that's the case, you may get some inspiration from the AI lifecycles you will see in the following pages. Specifically, you will learn about different variations from technical, compliance, role-based, and industry vertical perspectives.

We won't go into granular detail about each lifecycle, as we will cover a specific AI lifecycle in depth later in this chapter, but you can use this chapter as a reference to check anytime you need to ideate new AI project processes in your organization.

TECHNICAL AI LIFECYCLES

This set of lifecycles provides classic resources for structuring technical project stages and tasks. Some of them come from traditional data-driven projects, and others are adapted to the reality of ML and GenAI initiatives. The common pattern among these lifecycles is a sequential series of activities from beginning to end while leaving room for iteration. Iteration can occur at the end of the project for future upgrades or within a specific step of the lifecycle, such as intermediate model experimentation.

Cross-Industry Standard Process for Data Mining (CRISP-DM)

The CRISP-DM (*https://oreil.ly/C8T7K*) in Figure 5-1 is a classic methodology for data mining (extracting insights and patterns from data) and data science projects in general. It follows a sequence from business understanding to data and modeling tasks, followed by an evaluation based on the initial hypotheses and requirements, and wraps up with deployment or productization.

The general aspects of this methodology are still relevant to most data and AI projects. Variants like CRISP-ML(Q) (*https://oreil.ly/5edGj*), for quality assurance and risk control in ML projects, are also very useful for an AI PM to make sure technical implementations align with performance and compliance requirements.

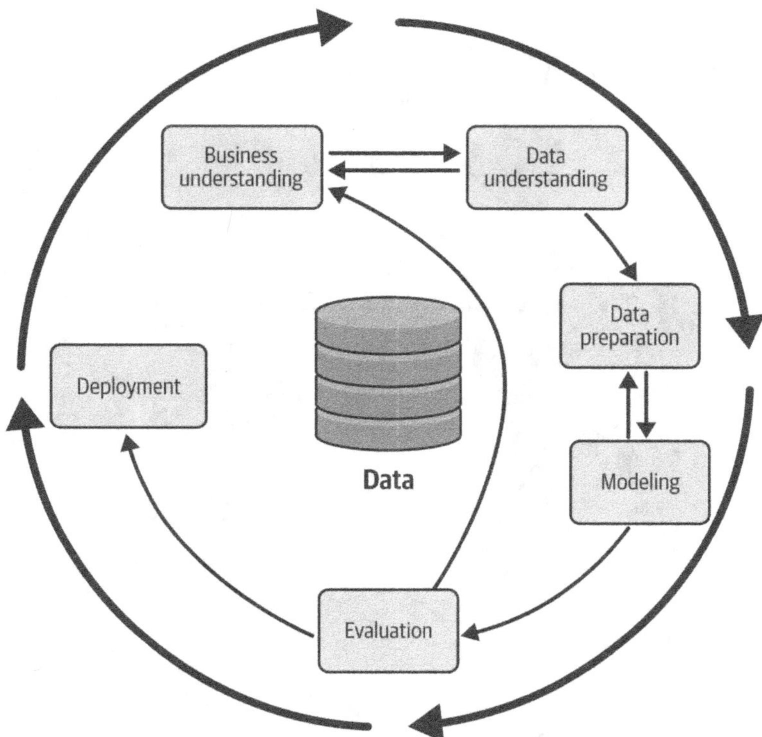

Figure 5-1. Cross-Industry Standard Process for Data Mining

Microsoft's Team Data Science Process

The Team Data Science Process (TDSP), shown in Figure 5-2, is a methodology by Microsoft. It is not only a data science lifecycle but also a specification for a standardized project structure with directories and documents, as well as recommendations for managing analytics and storage infrastructure.

The goal is to streamline processes, making it easier for the team members to find information about their projects. TDSP also includes some tools for initial data exploration and baseline modeling. This is a great resource for your team members and for internal alignment on specific steps, roles, and responsibilities.

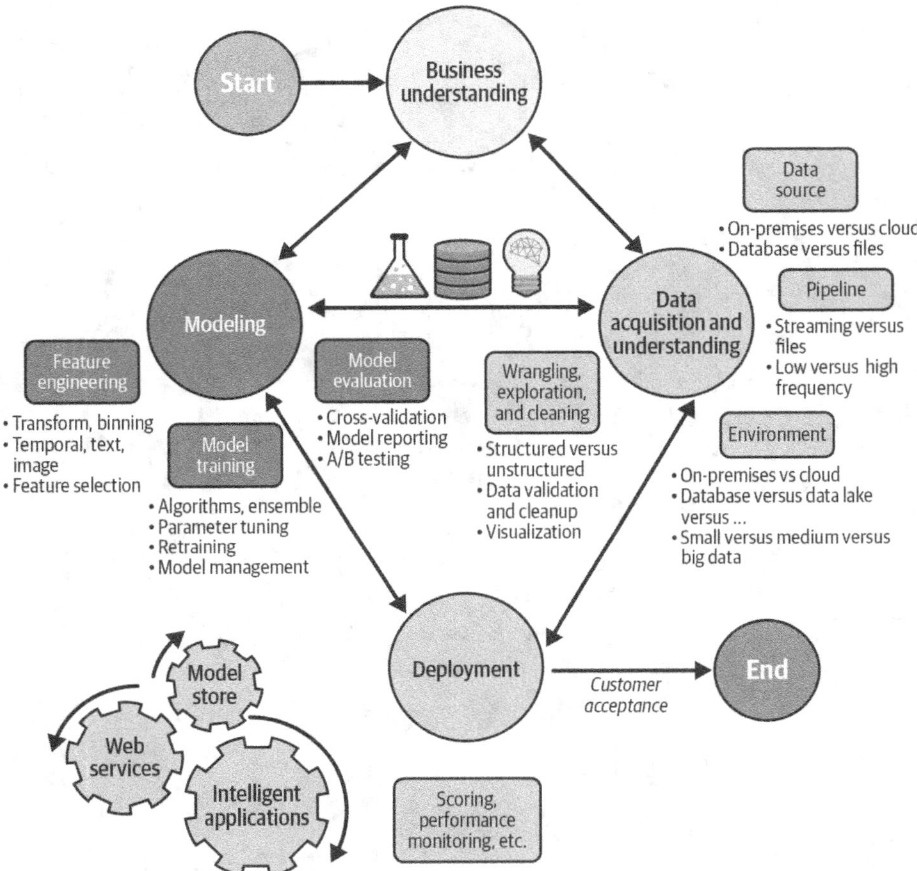

Figure 5-2. Microsoft's Team Data Science Process

MLOps lifecycle

A bit more technical and granular than the previous two examples, the MLOps (*https://ml-ops.org*), or machine learning operations, lifecycle, shown in Figure 5-3, is more oriented to post-implementation, end-to-end operations that help track datasets, models, and versioning as well as technical performance and reliability. You may have a dedicated ML engineering team that supports this level of implementation, or it may be a new area of work for your organization.

Regardless of how advanced your team is, the key areas you need to remember (especially when compared to other lifecycles) are the notions of store as a specific repository of experiments, features (input for datasets), and metadata.

Equally important is the idea of model registry, which allows you and your team to tag and manage versioning at scale.

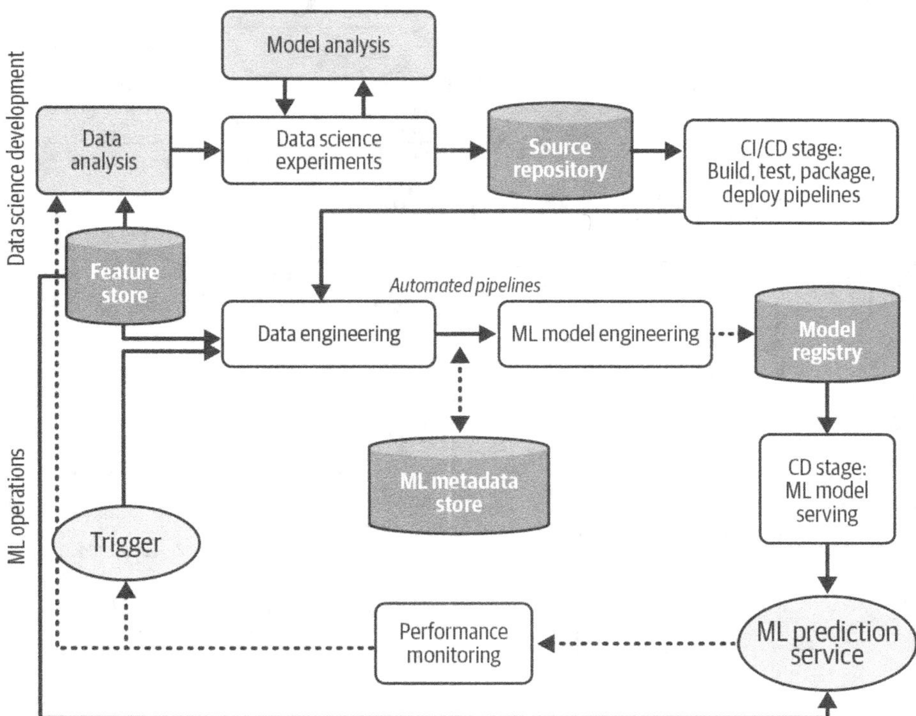

Figure 5-3. MLOps lifecycle (ml-ops.org)

Evolution to GenAIOps/LLMOps

The notion of MLOps has progressively evolved to the idea of GenAI operations, which is an adapted series of steps for systems that rely on LLM operations and other GenAI models. As Figure 5-4 shows, ML and GenAI operations share common steps, such as preparing data sources, deployment, and monitoring. The main difference lies in the role of the model provider in comparison with the adopter. If your organization is adopting LLMs from hyperscalers (e.g., Microsoft, AWS, Google), the dataset will mostly be used to retrieve information and to fine-tune the model for very specific tasks. This is because the model has already been trained by its provider, using datasets that cover an extensive data scope. However, if you work with a traditional ML model, your company's data is a fundamental asset used to train it from an earlier stage.

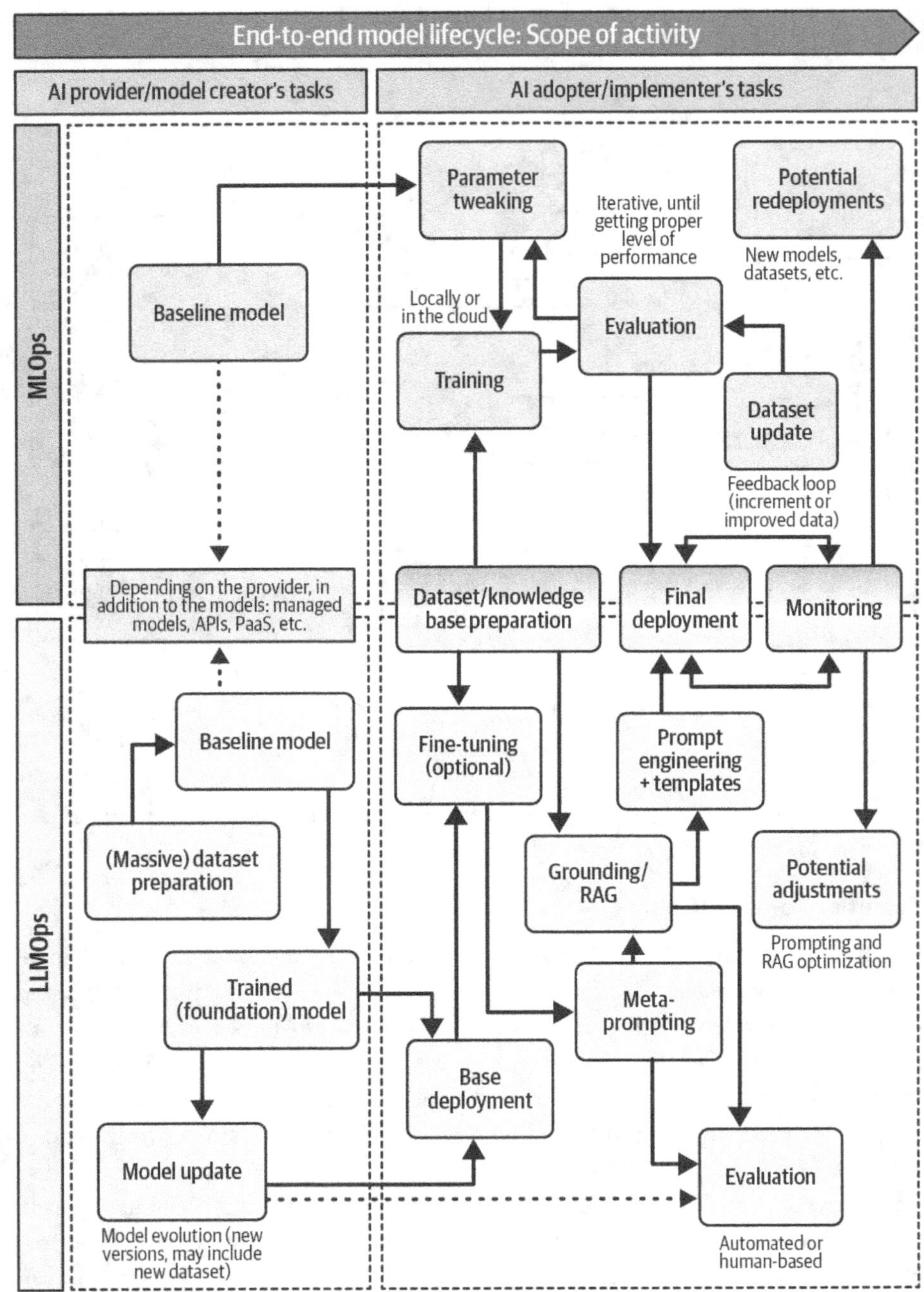

Figure 5-4. Comparison of MLOps and LLMOps

Your role as an AI PM is to make sure you understand the end-to-end operations of your project and ensure that they are properly mapped to your project backlog, especially for projects moving from proof of concept to production.

Let's now explore some other lifecycles that rely on these technical principles, looking through a compliance lens.

OTHER AI LIFECYCLES

As you saw in Chapter 3, your role as AI PM includes supporting governance and responsible AI (RAI) activities, and you may even take a leading role as an RAI champion. A key goal of any AI governance program is alignment with compliance requirements, including regulatory frameworks and international standards.

Here is a selection of compliance-oriented lifecycles and role-based lifecycles that will help you identify which team member does what for each project stage.

NIST AI framework's lifecycle

The National Institute of Standards and Technology (NIST) is a nonregulatory agency based in the United States that creates and promotes standards for a variety of topics, including artificial intelligence (*https://www.nist.gov/artificial-intelligence*). Its AI Risk Management Framework (AI RMF) (*https://oreil.ly/2KoLH*) is a recommended methodology for managing both traditional and GenAI implementations.

The AI RMF includes an AI lifecycle (Figure 5-5) with project stages with different areas of focus and stakeholders. One of the main differentiators of this version is the notion of AI test, evaluation, validation, and verification (*https://oreil.ly/JuuiL*) (TEVV), which focuses on specific actions and assets that help reduce the potential risks at each project stage.

From a project management perspective, this lifecycle can clarify the AI governance and risk management topics that you will need to include in your project roadmap, such as model testing, impact assessments, and audits.

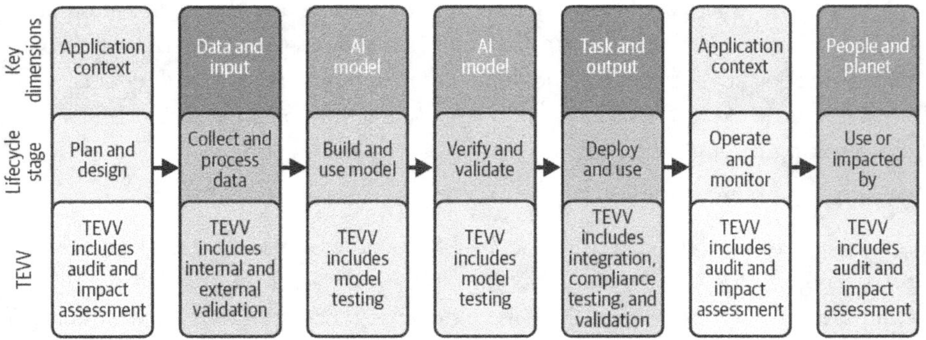

Figure 5-5. NIST AI lifecycle stages

Lifecycles from ISO standards

International Organization for Standardization (ISO) standards are internationally recognized best practices that allow companies to align with requirements for internal and external audits. In AI, being ISO certified means you adhere to certain standards of technical and company-level documentation and other processes related to AI lifecycles.

Specifically, ISO/IEC 5338: AI System Life Cycle Processes (*https://www.iso.org/standard/81118.html*) contains the standard for the AI lifecycle from conception to decommissioning, in addition to other project, technical management, and third-party agreement processes. Similarly, ISO/IEC 8183: Data Life Cycle Framework (*https://www.iso.org/standard/83002.html*) presents another version of the lifecycle with a deeper focus on data activities (planning, acquisition, preparation, and decommissioning).

Note that due to the copyrighted nature of these standards, we cannot include the visualizations of them here. If you and your organization are considering them, you will need to first purchase the specifications and then explore the lifecycle visuals and descriptions.

Other relevant resources

The AI project management live course (*https://oreil.ly/FF41q*) from this book's authors is highly recommended because its content complements this book with live roadmapping and planning exercises. Also from O'Reilly are other books by a wide array of experts. If you want to connect the AI lifecycle not only with activities but also with specific team roles, there are two resources you may want to bookmark and explore later:

- *Operationalizing AI* by John J. Thomas, William Roberts, and Paco Nathan (O'Reilly) maps the AI lifecycle along with the roles involved at each project stage. As you can see in Figure 5-6, this can serve as a template for an initial mapping of stages and roles.

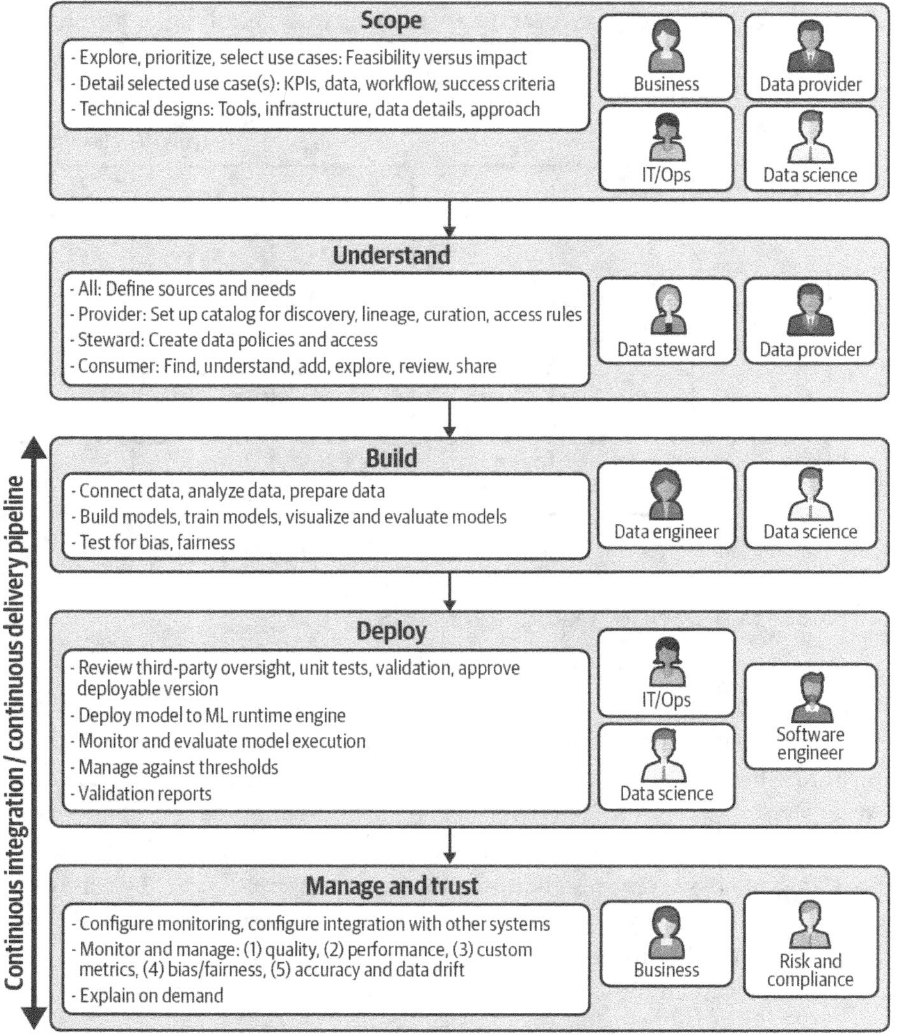

Figure 5-6. Stages and roles in the AI lifecycle (Operationalizing AI, 2021)

- The "skills versus needs" matrix in Figure 5-7 is from *Agile AI* by Carlo Appugliese, Paco Nathan, and William Roberts (O'Reilly). Like the AI team gaps analysis from Chapter 3, this matrix is a helpful tool to use before starting a project in order to evaluate the activities and skills that will be required and map them to specific people on your team. This is very useful if you are planning project resources and you want to detect any knowledge gaps on your team that may require further upskilling or hiring.

	Data prep	Visualization	Feature engineering	Modeling	Production systems	Troubleshooting
Riley						
Parker						
Ali						
Jordan						
Taylor						

Figure 5-7. Skills matrix for AI projects with example team members (Agile AI)

AI Project Management Considerations by Stage

So far in this chapter, you have explored some established project lifecycles. If you are new to managing AI implementations, these best practices and references can be very useful. If you are already experienced, this review will support your future backlog creation activities by helping you understand the main stages and activities that you can then evaluate and split into multiple stories and tasks.

The second part of this chapter focuses on the stages of an AI project based on a standard six-step process that we will use as a simple guide. For each step, we will explain the main activities and the AI PM's involvement, from basic expectations to additional tasks and capabilities you can bring to the team. These six stages can be mapped to any of the technical lifecycles you saw earlier.

STAGE 1: IDEATION AND PROBLEM DEFINITION

This stage is the very beginning of your AI implementation. It is part of the exploration phase of the EMED methodology introduced in Chapter 4, as it starts before the project actually becomes a project. As we already mentioned, this part of the project is that gray area where roles and responsibilities are still not confirmed. As an AI PM, you know your role at this stage is to minimize potential risks by making sure your projects make sense from both a technical and a business perspective and are realistic in the context of your organization and team.

Here are the main elements you need to keep in mind.

Use case discovery

As an AI PM, you have a role as both a facilitator and a decision maker in choosing an AI use case that will be successful for your organization, your team, and your own career. You will want to undertake projects with relevant outcomes that will be successfully completed, as these will build your team's reputation and lead to more projects and investment.

During the discovery exercise, it's important to keep things simple. First, you will be discussing potential use cases with professionals with very different backgrounds, including executives from your own organization or your clients and other professionals with varying levels of AI knowledge. For this reason, you need to orchestrate discussions so that misguided ideas are discarded on the basis of reasoning that all stakeholders understand and support. Moreover, it is helpful to facilitate discovery by using simple visual references that leave out any unnecessary complexity. Remember, people who are less familiar with AI are often afraid of being exposed as less knowledgeable or of making poor decisions based on a lack of knowledge, and discussions can quickly get too complex if not properly managed.

Table 5-1 shows the simple structure we use during our use case discovery workshops. A basic spreadsheet can help you organize the discussion case by case while allowing you to add information during the discussion. You'll want to note the what (use case name), the who (responsible team; whether the user is internal or an external customer), and the type of project.

The discussion in Chapter 2 will be important here, because if you are knowledgeable about the types of AI technologies, the related models, and trade-offs between performance and complexity, you will be well positioned to explain the potential AI approach for each use case. Especially if no technical folks are part of the discovery process, you will need to become the key resource who guides the other stakeholders.

Table 5-1. Use case discovery

#	Use case	Department	Internal/ external	Type of project (GenAI, ML, DL, NLP, etc.)
1	Support chatbot L1	Customer success	External	Generative AI, LLM + RAG
2	Numerical sales prediction	Sales	Internal	Machine learning, regression tasks
3	Social media score	Marketing	Internal	Natural language processing, sentiment analysis
4	Web bot	All	External	Generative AI
5	Customer segmentation	Marketing (VP)	Internal	Clustering ML
...				

The output of this step is a simple yet valuable catalog of use cases that can be evaluated for their potential impact and available resources.

Use case evaluation

The use case evaluation exercise collects high-level information about both business impact and technical feasibility, which will help during the prioritization exercise. Try to clarify for each use case whether the project's value stems from cost reduction, revenue generation, or product differentiation. Also, define the business KPIs that will track these value and impact hypotheses. Either during or immediately after that discussion, also note the technical, organizational, and human resources that the project needs (and if these resources may not be available). Table 5-2 shows an example of your notes from this step.

Table 5-2. Use case evaluation

#	Use case	Impact	KPIs	Available resources (talent, budget, sponsor, etc.)
1	Support chatbot L1	Cost saving for solving issues	Saved time per day	AI engineers, cloud infra, some internal knowledge base, sponsored by SVP customer success
2	Numerical sales prediction	Better planning		Partial data
3	Social media score	Increasing revenue by better targeting clients	Client score	No sponsor
4	Web bot	Cost saving for customer success, and increased user satisfaction	Time to solve an issue	
5	Customer segmentation	Better marketing	% of clicks	Infra for ML, data scientists with relevant clustering experience, and VP support. We have all the data required.
…				

By the end of this exercise, you will have a clear view of the potential use cases so you can begin to analyze data requirements and other resources in detail, allowing the organization to prioritize appropriately.

Data source availability and mapping

The next step is to analyze potential data sources and map them to specific use case needs. As you can see in Table 5-3, the first step is to create a catalog enumerating the main data sources that are available, including details related to the kind of data system, who manages it, and the collection method.

Table 5-3. Data sources catalog

#	Data source	System	Asset name	Key contact	Additional information (e.g., collection method)
a	Customer data	SQL	Database #7	DB admin (Adrian)	Access via DBMS
b	Market data	API $$$	...	Meta/Twitter, via backend dev	API
c	Q&As + technical documentation	Data lake	DL #2 (AWS S3)	Cloud admin (Malini)	API
...					

Keep in mind that data source discovery and cataloging may be a new exercise for the organization or a deep dive into existing data governance activities. If the latter, your team may already be using a platform like Atlan, Collibra, or Microsoft Purview, which likely contains the required data samples and metadata for the data sources you need.

Regardless of the current state of your organization, after the data catalog is created, you will have to lead a mapping exercise to confirm the availability of data sources in the context of the specific use cases that have been identified. The goal is to highlight those use cases that are most feasible from a data availability perspective.

As you can see in Table 5-4, this mapping is a simple yet intuitive way to represent data requirements and availability in a visual way.

Table 5-4. Data sources and use cases mapping

Use cases	UC 1	UC 2	UC 3	UC 4	... UC n
Data sources					
DS a	✓	✓	TBC[a]	✓	TBC
DS b	✓	✗	✗	✓	TBC
DS c	✓	✗	✗	✓	TBC
... DS n	✗	✗	✓	✓	TBC
[a] To be confirmed					

This visual simplicity is exactly what you need to help the team justify go/no-go decisions for each use case. In Table 5-4, you can see that the second use case is likely to be discarded right away due to a lack of required data. Decision making that is supported by clear rationales is necessary during your discussions with executives, clients, and even your technical team.

Premortem analysis

As part of your risk mitigation approach, you can use a premortem activity to analyze potential issues, engaging in a thought experiment about what *could* potentially go wrong. Instead of waiting for the traditional postmortem to learn what went wrong after the fact, this technique engages multidisciplinary teams in proactive troubleshooting. During the premortem, they will spot all sorts of technical, organizational, and business-related issues—and consider how to mitigate them. Table 5-5 illustrates a premortem exercise in which potential risks have been organized by whether they are contextual, business, or technical risks.

Table 5-5. Premortem table

Category	Risk	What could go wrong
Contextual	Regulation and compliance	Our tools are not ready for regulation X or standard Y.
	Proper usage	The new AI solution may be used poorly by user group Z.
	Internal concerns	...
Business	Wrong use cases discovery and prioritization	
	Lack of quantitative usage scenarios	
	Unexpected cost	
	Unclear business case	
	Innovation dilemma	
Technical	High complexity	
	Low performance	
	Lack of resources	
	Security concerns	

As you can imagine, the types of risks the team will surface depend on the use case and the specific context of your organization. Use this table as a template that you can adjust to fit your needs.

Prioritization and long-term planning

Finally, based on the information gathered in the use case descriptions, potential value analysis, technical and data considerations, and premortem risks, you should be able to guide the prioritization of the most valuable cases for your organization. You can use a 2 × 2 matrix (Figure 5-8) with "business value" and "technical feasibility" axes, placing your use cases in the appropriate quadrants. Those in the upper right quadrant are the most feasible and have the greatest potential impact, and these will be the priority use cases.

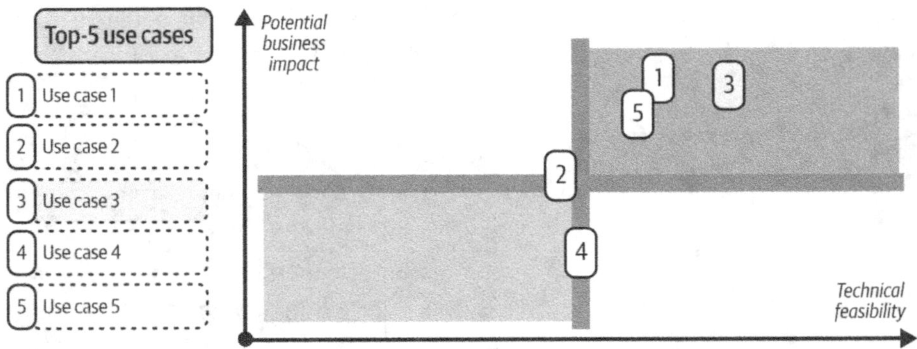

Figure 5-8. Classic 2 × 2 prioritization matrix

Assuming that you have identified at least one use case with good feasibility and impact, you can now move on to create a long-term, inter-use case roadmap like the one in Figure 5-9.

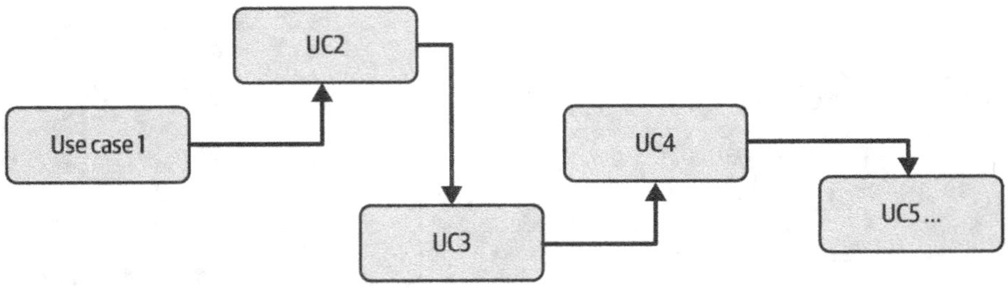

Figure 5-9. Inter-use case roadmap for long-term planning

As a project leader, you can leverage this visualization of your long-term plan to explain the increasing AI maturity that you and your team will develop project after project. This growth will positively affect your future projects as the team will leverage the skills, prepared data, and deployed infrastructure it has accumulated during past projects.

This collection of best practices, figures, and tables is an AI exploration toolkit that you can leverage to help guide your ideation and problem definition discussions during Stage 1. In this way, you will reduce the risk of AI failure even before starting your project. Then in the next stage, you will begin to make tangible progress in terms of access to data sources, preliminary data analysis, and initial validation.

STAGE 2: DATA COLLECTION AND PREPARATION

Let's assume you have already chosen your project and you are now in the mobilization phase of the EMED methodology. As an AI PM, your focus is on guaranteeing you will have the proper technical and human resources to be successful once the project starts. For many AI projects, data is critical. As you saw while exploring ML, DL, NLP, and GenAI models in Chapter 2, the importance of data for the end-to-end architecture and model training depends on the type of AI.

Here are a series of steps related to data science and data for AI activities. You can connect these activities to considerations for the shape of your project and data-centric risk assessments.

Exploratory data analysis

As you saw in Chapter 4, exploratory data analysis refers to the ability to explore and analyze data sources from both a statistical and a business point of view. Let's start by talking about the business side of EDA, always keeping in mind that the statistical and business aspects interact.

This process has an intuitive quality, as it focuses on analyzing the data to confirm business facts or to evaluate potential hypotheses. For example, you may want to confirm whether your data reflects what you think know about your business (e.g., trends, timetables). Or you may want to understand the cause-and-effect relationships between specific moments and changes in your business operations (e.g., whether a marketing investment yields significant changes in your client segments). As an AI PM working with both clients/users and technical teams, you can serve as a translator between their worlds and as a source of the questions and hypotheses that your data scientists will need to complete their analysis.

Turning now to statistical EDA, your ability to contribute will depend on your level of technical knowledge or the kind of tools you can leverage to analyze data (e.g., by coding in Python or SQL or by using AI tools with natural language prompts). EDA comprises several kinds of technical tasks:

Data profiling

This means generating a structured summary of the dataset you are analyzing. It includes information such as the numbers of rows and columns (for structured data), column names, data types, missing values, unique values, and basic statistics such as averages and ranges. Profiling gives a quick snapshot of the dataset's structure and quality, which is critical to confirm the technical feasibility of your AI project. It also relies on visual methods such as bar charts, line plots, and heatmaps to make trends and patterns easier to see and explain.

Data cleaning and preparation

After gaining an understanding of the dataset, your team needs to fix issues such as missing values, duplicates, and inconsistent formats. This includes solving heterogeneity issues in which multiple sources represent similar kinds of information in different formats (e.g., dates as YYYY-MM-DD versus MM-DD-YYYY, or using commas or points for decimals). This step ensures that the data is reliable and ready for deeper exploration, and it is a key requirement to be able to relate different data sources while keeping the statistical value of the data.

Data transformation

The idea here is to reshape the data into more useful forms, such as by converting text into numbers, normalizing values, or creating new columns from existing ones. Transformation makes the data easier to analyze.

Variable-level analysis

This includes conducting univariate analysis, in which each variable is studied individually using summary statistics (mean, median, mode), and using simple plots like histograms to understand the distribution and spread of single features. It also includes using multivariate analysis to analyze the relationships between two or more variables to uncover patterns and dependencies.

Outlier detection

You will want to pay special attention to unusual data points that don't follow general trends, as they can be caused either by data inconsistencies or by the special nature of an outlier. Training your models on data that includes statistical exceptions will make the models more representative and complete. Alternatively, outliers can be signals that your team needs to clean and filter the information to ensure that all the data used brings statistical value to the model. Outliers are identified using techniques like box plots or z-scores.

Feature importance

Measuring how much each feature contributes to predicting a target variable helps to identify which variables are most influential and which can be ignored. Determinations of feature importance are often used after building models to guide decisions about which features to keep or refine.

Feature engineering

By creating or transforming features, you can make the data more useful. For example, your data team can create new columns, built from existing ones, with normalized values and encoded data. The goal is to better represent the underlying patterns and facilitate later analysis or modeling. As an AI PM, you are aware that dedicating resources to these activities is key, as choosing proper features can make AI modeling easier.

Despite the technical nature of these tasks, your ability to collaborate with the data scientists and engineers who will work on them is important, because you will help guide the exploration of the data. You will also explain the data insights to relevant stakeholders, such as executives when you need additional support or clients if you need to justify the limits of the dataset and the impact on future AI project stages.

Data source evaluation

In parallel with (and after) the initial exploration and EDA, your team will start to get a sense of the quality of the data sources, as well as how useful they are for the purpose of your AI project. For example, you may have missing values or outliers that you need to handle before injecting the input dataset into your AI model. But the data quality exercise refers not only to the statistical completeness of your data but also to the factors that are specific to your AI use case and what you want to accomplish. In Figure 5-10, you can see an example of quality analysis by data source, based on the template we use for our AI projects.

Data source	Evaluation of quality factors from 1 (low) to 4 (high)						Recommended actions
	Volume	Joinability	Relevance	Consistency	Clarity	Timeliness	
Example 1 API	4	4	4	4	4	4	
Example 2 DB	4	3	4	4	4	1	Increase the data refresh every 30 min
Example 3 data lake	4	4	4	4	3	1	
Example 4 DB2	4	3	4	4	4	4	Transform data fields to map new structure
Example 5	4	4	3	4	4	4	
Example 6	3	4	3	4	4	2	
Example 7 Another DB	4	2	1	4	4	4	Keep the data as archive
...	4	4	4	4	4	2	
Example N	3	1	4	4	4	2	

Figure 5-10. Data quality factors and evaluation

By using this template, you can analyze how suitable a data source is for your AI project but also draft a series of recommendations that can help your team and other relevant departments (e.g., IT) improve the shape of those data assets, based on a set of factors:

Volume

The amount of data available from the source. A higher score means there's enough data to support reliable analysis and decision making.

Joinability

How easily the data can be connected with other datasets. For example, having consistent IDs or keys across sources makes it easier to combine information.

Relevance

How useful the data is for the intended business or analytical purpose. High relevance means the data directly supports the questions or goals being studied.

Consistency

Refers to whether the data values are uniform and follow the same rules across records and sources. Inconsistent data might show conflicting values for the same entity.

Clarity

How understandable the data is, including clear definitions, labels, and metadata. High clarity makes it easier for analysts to interpret the data correctly.

Timeliness

How up-to-date the data is relative to the needs of the analysis. Timely data reflects the current situation, while outdated data may have limited usefulness.

These quality factors are our own recommendations for what you need to keep in mind as you evaluate your data sources. There are also international organizations and standards for data management, such as the Data Management Capability Assessment Model (*https://oreil.ly/lkjS3*) and Data Management Association (*https://oreil.ly/IYHuu*), that offer their own sets of data quality factors and checklists.

Data transformation and pipeline documentation

After conducting data analysis and evaluation, your data engineers will likely work to prepare the pipelines that will carry, transform, and combine information from the original data sources in an automated way. These pipelines will generate the unified dataset that will serve as an input for your AI model training.

Your role includes understanding the logic of this transformation and enabling your team to invest time in documenting the entire process, a critical but often forgotten step. This documentation will be necessary later to replicate or modify the pipelines, especially if your data engineers move to other teams or even other organizations.

Data governance and compliance evaluation

Depending on the scope of your AI PM role, you may want to leverage your position to facilitate any preliminary data governance and compliance discussion. This will focus on the big picture of data management in the organization and its impact on programmatic access to the data sources. These discussions will also cover the relevant considerations in terms of data privacy and copyrights. For this exercise, you will rely on data and compliance resources, including legal officers and chief data officers, depending on your organization's internal structure. As an AI PM, you will be engaged at this step to forestall any potential risk during and after implementation.

Once you complete these steps, your team may still have some iterations to adjust details, improve the dataset, or even create multiple versions of the dataset and features to test data-centric approaches where different combinations may generate different levels of performance. Make sure you are part of the entire process so that later you can understand the related considerations at the modeling, architecture, evaluation, and solution stages. You can even pick up some of the technical tasks, perhaps leveraging tools like ChatGPT or Microsoft Copilot Analyst to analyze data assets.

STAGE 3: AI MODEL DEVELOPMENT AND EXPERIMENTATION

This stage focuses on the modeling activities, which may include training AI models from scratch or leveraging existing models and combining them with specific knowledge bases and instructions. Your ability to generalize from past examples and situations will be crucial here.

If you are starting your AI journey, pay attention to these steps and take notes in your "Chapter 5 Notebook" on page 220 so you can refer to them during your next AI project.

Modeling approach

Your team will likely decide on a modeling approach before the development phase begins. Key considerations include the type of approach and models you can potentially use. Here are the key considerations that you'll keep in mind as you facilitate technical discussions with your team:

Type of AI model

From reading Chapter 2, you should be able to determine if your new AI project requires a specific kind of AI model (e.g., ML, DL, NLP, LLM) or at least be able to identify any knowledge gap you may have so you can put the relevant questions to your team. At the end of the day, the main goal is to make sense of the mix of AI models available and make a decision together. Your choice will depend on factors such as fit with use cases, performance, cost, and availability. You will likely figure this out in collaboration with your data scientists and AI engineers, depending on the case.

Build versus leverage

Depending on your organization's and team's level of AI experience, you may have to facilitate discussions to decide if you will build your own models or leverage existing ones. The second option may include deploying open source models for free (instead of using your own infrastructure) or leveraging managed AI models via cloud providers. Regardless of the option your team chooses, the main consideration for you as the AI PM is to plan any financial investment required to acquire access to a model or infrastructure. Remember that the level of computing power needed will depend on the type of model and you will need to rely on your team's estimation of this resource (e.g., you may need virtual machines with a specific amount of processing and memory capability).

Role of human knowledge

In Chapter 2, you learned the meaning of supervised and unsupervised learning. In general, most of your projects will involve some human supervision in order to label past data samples. For example, past vendor invoices could be labeled as paid or unpaid so that your team can implement a binary ML classifier that predicts vendors who pose a potential risk of nonpayment. But the project could also involve a simple LLM that needs a few examples (i.e., a few-shot approach) to guide the model to provide better answers. Your main consideration is identifying the people who can bring the required knowledge to bear (e.g., a subject matter expert for financial operations) and when they will be needed, depending on the type of model and lifecycle.

Baseline (naive) versus best model

Whatever the problem you are trying to solve, there are always different AI modeling alternatives. One way to plan the modeling activities is to choose an easy baseline or "naive" approach to get quick results; these will then serve as a basis for comparison to other models that will take more time and resources. Comparing the baseline model to more sophisticated models is a way to measure the improvement in performance of the latter and gives you evidence to justify investing in more-advanced development.

Resource planning

The combination of modeling approach and organizational context will help you plan resources accordingly. For example, planning who to have on the project team is different for an ML project than for a GenAI project, you won't need the same skills for a cloud-first project as for an on-premises project, and your aggregated team skills won't be the same at an organization that builds custom models and an organization that uses model providers.

The same is true for infrastructure and tooling resources. As an AI PM, you can develop some intuition for what will be needed, but you will need to take a bottom-up approach, relying on your technical team members to explain which platforms you need, how many GPUs are required for a specific project, and, of course, the impact on overall project cost. And remember, the success of the resource-planning exercise depends on your ability to make accurate estimates for different stages (from pilot to production) and scenarios (e.g., based on the projected use of the AI tool).

Model information for compliance

The importance of compliance depends on the project's context, including the modeling approach, the involvement of third parties (such as technology providers), geographic specifics (for both the organization and the AI application's users), and the specific vertical industry. You will again be central to a risk-based approach in which your AI project management background is essential. You will be structuring a project workstream to collect all relevant information about model descriptions (usually by leveraging existing model cards and official documentation from providers), as well as any information generated during the experimentation and testing phases.

Regulations such as the EU AI Act or standards like ISO 42001 for AI management systems are good references you may want to review at this stage. Supporting compliance at this point in the process ties into the AI lifecycles you have learned about in this chapter, as a risk-based approach, in which you identify compliance requirements and risk mitigation measures, will be relevant at each stage of the lifecycle.

Access to models

Your role as an AI PM is key to retrieving any relevant information, including information beyond core technical aspects, that helps your project succeed. Part of the resource-planning exercise we mentioned earlier is doing a deep dive into cost estimation. The AI modeling approach will impact this estimate, so you'll need to understand these considerations that bear on whether you build or buy:

Purchasing modality

> This refers to how your team gets access to the required models. Your organization might pay only for compute capacity, paying based on the number of interactions with the models, or it might reserve instances of a specific model or service by leveraging monthly or yearly discounts. The latter arrangement is often used with cloud platforms such as Microsoft Azure, AWS, or Google Cloud. Understanding the purchasing modality will help you not only estimate costs for the AI models required for your projects but also plan the integration requirements for the technical team to leverage them.

Unitary cost

> Once you know how your team is acquiring the models, you will need to get into the details of costs. If you get a specific computing or reserve instance, then the goal is to see how much you can leverage the resource for a specific price, based on potential usage scenarios. This could be about choosing and optimizing virtual machines with enough GPUs or memory for regular or peak usage, or the team might just be sending requests to APIs where there is a specific cost per number of calls. In the case of GenAI, you may pay a set price based on the number of tokens consumed, keeping in mind that the number of tokens used per word will depend on the language (e.g., on average 75 tokens are used per 100 words in English). Some resources that may help are the official calculators from the cloud providers (e.g., Azure (*https://oreil.ly/RQbvS*), AWS (*https://calcula tor.aws*), GCP (*https://oreil.ly/OHDIO*), Oracle (*https://oreil.ly/M48ll*)) or even token calculators (*https://oreil.ly/XNtxH*) for GenAI projects.

Remember, access to models and the related costs depend directly on how your team approaches AI development. Try to use a bottom-up approach to aggregate all potential model costs based on various usage scenarios, then add these to other human and general project costs. If your company has some level of maturity in terms of cloud and AI usage, you may collaborate with FinOps (*https://www.finops.org*) (financial operations) professionals, who can help you plan to optimize cost strategies and increase the ROI of specific projects, tools, and AI product features.

Explaining results

The AI model development stage includes explaining your AI progress through different lenses, so any stakeholder or even early users can understand the outcome of the project—how it works and its preliminary results. As the AI PM, you may facilitate the technical-business translation of these topics:

Project-level progress
> You are the interface between the implementation team and all other stakeholders, so it will often fall to you to share the team's progress, challenges, and results during the AI model experimentation phase. Think of this phase as a set of sprints in which you will be sharing news, updates on completed iterations, and progress against target performance milestones.

AI model considerations
> Besides explaining the choice of model as needed (e.g., a client or an executive wants to understand the logic behind the AI implementation and how it works), you may need to discuss model considerations such as explainability (i.e., the thought process behind the model) and interpretability (the ability to understand the model's logic). Depending on the model, you will need to explain the trade-offs and advantages of certain approaches and the model's fit with specific use cases and needs. In Figure 5-11, you can see a visualization of model trade-offs between higher predictive performance and interpretability. You can use such a chart as a visual reference when you need to explain model choices or even to showcase differences between baseline (naive) and advanced options.

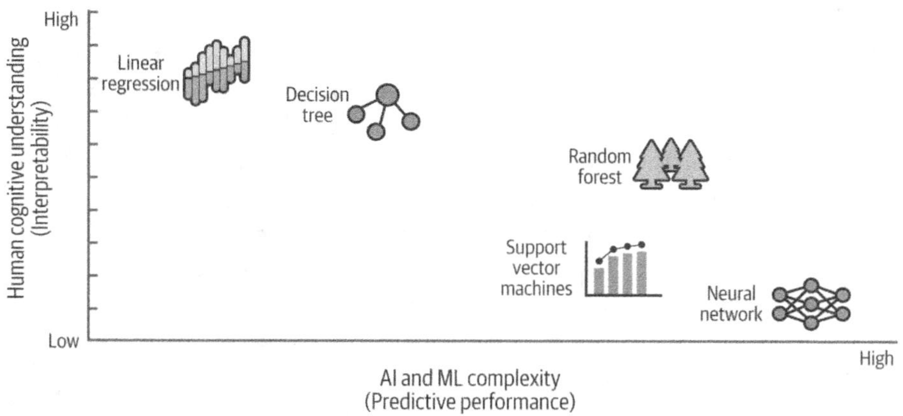

Figure 5-11. Trade-off between performance and interpretability for different models

Use case/application results

Regardless of your project's progress or model results, what will really matter in the end is the use case you are working on and its impact on the end application your team is trying to build. Depending on who the end client and users are, you may want to use the model development phase to get some early feedback from them and to discuss their potential role in the human-in-the-loop mechanisms that will allow them to supervise and validate AI outcomes. You can also leverage visual mockups or prototypes with tools like Figma, Lovable, or Balsamiq to illustrate future applications of the model or specific user interface steps.

These are just a few recommendations for you to think about so you can make the most of the model development and experimentation phase. Even if these seem like highly technical steps, as you reflect on your role, you will develop an understanding of their relevance to your job. Write them down in your "Chapter 5 Notebook" on page 220 for future reference. Let's now move on to the performance evaluation and validation phase.

STAGE 4: AI EVALUATION AND VALIDATION

This stage is deeply interconnected with Stage 3. Performance evaluation occurs after each model experiment iteration, while final validation takes into account the entire process to make an informed decision about what will be deployed.

Performance metrics

Between the first ideation stage and this evaluation and validation phase, you will start making sense of both the business and technical metrics that will be relevant for your use case and the related AI development. The first type of metrics is usually more intuitive for any PM: potential growth, increased revenue, generated savings, ROI, etc. These serve as metrics for any project and so are quite familiar, and they are the quantitative levers you can use to justify the business value of any initiative, including AI initiatives. On the other hand, you also have available a vast array of technical metrics that are directly related to the kind of AI you are planning to implement. Table 5-6 lists the types of models you learned about in Chapter 2 along with their main metrics.

Table 5-6. AI model metrics

AI model type	Metric	Range of values	Purpose
Classification	AUC-ROC (receiver operating characteristic–area under the curve)	Between 0 and 1 (higher is better)	Measures how well a model distinguishes between classes
	Precision	Between 0 and 1 (higher is better)	Measures the proportion of correctly identified positive results out of total predicted positives
	Recall	Between 0 and 1 (higher is better)	Measures the proportion of actual positives correctly identified
	F1 score (based on precision and recall)	Between 0 and 1 (higher is better)	Balances precision and recall for imbalanced datasets
	F2 score (based on precision and recall)	Between 0 and 1 (higher is better)	A weighted average of precision and recall, giving more importance to recall, to catch true positives

AI model type	Metric	Range of values	Purpose
Regression	MAE (mean absolute error)	0 to ∞ (lower is better)	Measures average absolute error between predicted and actual values
	MSE (mean squared error)	0 to ∞ (lower is better)	Penalizes larger errors more heavily than MAE
	R^2 score	-∞ to 1	Indicates how well the model explains variance in data
NLP	BLEU (bilingual evaluation understudy)	Between 0 and 1 (higher is better)	Compares generated text with reference translations
	ROUGE (Recall-oriented understudy for gisting evaluation)	Between 0 and 1 (higher is better)	Measures overlap between generated and reference summaries
	Perplexity	1 to ∞ (lower is better)	Measures how well a model predicts a sequence of words
GenAI	Groundedness	Between 0 and 1 (higher is better)	Measures factual accuracy of AI-generated content
	Relevance	Between 0 and 1 (higher is better)	Evaluates how contextually appropriate a response is
	Toxicity score	Between 0 and 1 (lower is better)	Measures presence of harmful, biased, or offensive language
	Diversity	Between 0 and 1 (higher is better)	Evaluates variety in generated content, reducing repetitiveness

AI model type	Metric	Range of values	Purpose
GenAI *cont.*	Coherence	Between 0 and 1 (higher is better)	Measures logical consistency and readability of AI-generated text
	Fluency	Between 0 and 1 (higher is better)	Assesses grammatical accuracy and natural flow of generated text
	Faithfulness	Between 0 and 1 (higher is better)	Ensures generated content accurately reflects given input prompts
	Style adherence	Between 0 and 1 (higher is better)	Evaluates whether generated content follows a specific writing or artistic style
	Informativeness	Between 0 and 1 (higher is better)	Measures how much useful information is provided in generated content

AI Model Performance Metrics

Precision

Precision measures the proportion of predicted positive results that are actually correct. Precision answers the question: When the model says something is positive, how often is it right? It's especially important in systems where false alarms create operational costs or user frustration. If a spam filter flags 100 emails as spam, and 90 are truly spam messages, the system has 90% precision. A spam filter with low precision may incorrectly block legitimate emails or trigger unnecessary manual reviews.

Recall

Recall measures the proportion of actual positive cases that the model successfully identifies. If there are 120 spam emails in an inbox and the filter detects 90 of them, the recall is 75%. Recall becomes critical when missing important cases carries a high cost, such as in disease-screening systems. While high recall reduces the risk of missed critical events, it often comes at the cost of more false positives.

F1 score

The F1 score combines precision and recall into a single metric that balances both. It penalizes models that perform well on one metric but poorly on the other, which is why it is useful when both types of errors matter. Here is how it is calculated:

$$F1 = 2 \times \frac{Precision \times Recall}{Precision + Recall}$$

Human evaluations for GenAI and LLMs

While precision and recall work well for classification models, GenAI systems often require human judgment to evaluate output quality. In this case, reviewers score model responses based on criteria, as described in Table 5-6. For GenAI systems, human evaluation often becomes the most important metric, because automated metrics may not capture usefulness or tone.

Choosing the right evaluation metric ensures that model optimization aligns with real business outcomes, not just technical benchmarks.

Instead of trying to memorize the technical details of each of these metrics, bookmark this page and use it as a reference anytime you discuss quantitative success criteria at a technical level with your team. Depending on the type of AI that your project leverages, you can ask your technical team (usually data scientists and AI engineers) about the logic behind it and which metric will make more sense for a given use case. For example, if you are working on a health care project where false negatives can be more important than false positives, the team is likely to use an F2 score instead of an F1 score. Or when a GenAI tool connects to an internal knowledge base, the team may suggest groundedness as a way to quantify how the new AI tool adheres to that baseline knowledge, avoiding hallucinations or inaccurate information.

Remember, your role is about facilitating discussions and asking the proper questions to help the team develop a clear plan to quantify performance before, during, and after core modeling. This collaboration allows you to align the technical team and end clients on a "good enough" success threshold, ensuring expectations are clear and realistic. Since an AI system is never perfect, it is important to manage expectations and thereby avoid future disappointment. From an intra-project perspective, this is a great way to decide with your team what the target performance should be. You can also help them scope their experimentation sprints by deciding which metric will be relevant, what value they will try to achieve, what computing and human resources they will need, and how long each iteration will take. Scheduling this discussion before experimentation occurs will help you adjust your roadmap and limit endless cycles of iterations.

Safety testing evaluation

Besides the regular performance metrics, there are questions related to how safe and trustworthy the models (and therefore their applications) are. This kind of analysis includes several considerations:

AI content safety
> This refers to the ability to test and protect models against attacks that come directly via prompts, from user interfaces, and even hidden within images or emails. It is a new domain, mostly oriented to GenAI models that interact in a seamless way (i.e., via natural language) with general users and potential attackers. The term also refers to the ability to filter any potential results that include negative content, such as violence or an invitation to danger or harm. The goal is to reduce the risk of AI misbehavior by identifying specific scenarios in which the model could behave inappropriately.
>
> As the AI PM, you want to enable functional analysis of the AI models and applications so they can be tested from an ethical hacking and quality assurance perspective. To do this, you may leverage your own skills as well as those of a variety of AI and security professionals in your organization.

Ethical evaluations
> AI evaluation and validation can perform bias detection by evaluating negative AI model outcomes toward specific segments of people. It can conduct model fairness audits to analyze and correct such biased scenarios. Once again, this exercise may combine functional analysis and technical knowledge of specific responsible AI toolkits such as Microsoft's (*https://responsibleaitoolbox.ai*) and IBM's (*https://oreil.ly/xFomN*) RAI toolboxes. Your role

will consist of asking the appropriate questions and facilitating discussions to explore all potential ethical issues.

These topics tie back to the idea of the AI PM as a responsible AI champion for the project and organization. Increasing your profile in this area is a good way to increase your value to the AI team and become the interface between general AI governance programs and the reality of your AI project. Besides facilitating ethical-technical discussions, you can also enable the escalation system before and during the implementation phase, in which you will collectively spot specific risks, envision risk mitigation measures (e.g., technical guardrails, additional reviews), and share top concerns with the overall AI governance structure or committee, when applicable.

Documented results

Even if this is an obvious part of any project, documenting the entire process becomes even more necessary in the context of AI. All activities and outcomes from this and previous stages should be carefully documented, including the choice of data sources and transformations, as well as the AI-modeling iterations from experimentation to final validation, including potential A/B testing scenarios and user interviews. Make sure your backlog and story points include time for your team to work on this. Depending on the available time, you may plan knowledge transfer activities within your organization or with your clients if the project is for an external entity.

Now that you have completed the core development of your AI project, the last two stages will focus on the immediate deployment and integration activities at scale (Stage 5) and the ongoing maintenance and final, long-term decommission of the system (Stage 6).

STAGE 5: DEPLOYMENT AND AI SYSTEM INTEGRATION

In this stage, you convert your AI project into something that goes from a pilot to a production-level development. You'll guide your project and team to success by making sure that all the relevant pieces (e.g., technical blocks, architecture considerations) are in place.

Infrastructure considerations for AI at scale

The choice of infrastructure (e.g., cloud or on-premises environments) or technology providers reflects the need to balance scalability and flexibility on the one hand and control, compliance, or latency requirements on the other. For you, this means evaluating business priorities (e.g., projected AI usage), budget constraints and cost, and regulatory considerations. It also means coordinating with your technical teams to ensure that the chosen infrastructure aligns with both technical and organizational needs.

API development for AI model deployment

APIs serve as the bridge between AI models and business applications, defining how predictions, insights, or decisions are accessed and integrated into workflows. You will play a key role in ensuring that development teams follow clear documentation standards, version control practices, and security guidelines so that stakeholders can easily adopt and trust the deployed model. The same applies to new protocols such as MCP or A2A for GenAI, as they all enable interoperability with other technical building blocks and even external applications.

CI/CD and MLOps for AI model automation

Continuous integration and deployment pipelines, paired with MLOps practices, form the foundations of reliable AI delivery, ensuring that updates and improvements move smoothly from development to production. You need to make sure that your team thinks about how to resource these pipelines and how their monitoring and testing procedures meet both technical and business quality standards.

Model retraining pipelines and optimization strategies

Related to the previous point, retraining pipelines is important to keep models accurate over time. You can negotiate with your team (or with the team taking ownership of the new AI application) about the establishment of policies for when and how retraining will occur, help facilitate the discussions about balancing performance improvements with cost considerations, and ensure that technical teams have the right datasets and infrastructure to maintain model performance.

Scaling AI solutions for enterprise use

Enterprise-grade AI involves the design of systems that can accommodate growth, whether through larger data volumes, higher user demand, higher access to API calls for specific AI models, or distributed deployments across regions. A good option is to combine your AI project management background with an architecture mindset as you coordinate scaling strategies with stakeholders and ensure that systems are designed not only for immediate functionality but also for long-term sustainability and enterprise-wide integration.

General cybersecurity

Cybersecurity for AI deployments includes the protection of data, models, and integration points from vulnerabilities, covering areas like encryption, identity management, and ongoing monitoring. You can make sure that any cybersecurity requirements are embedded into AI project planning, serve as an interface with compliance and security teams, and maintain accountability for aligning AI deployment with organizational risk management policies. From the standpoint of your professional development journey, this is a good area in which to expand your knowledge and scope of activities, as data/AI and security departments are often not that well connected and synchronized. Use your transversal skills to address this opportunity.

STAGE 6: MAINTENANCE AND END OF AI LIFECYCLE

Now imagine that the actual AI project has been completed but you still have some involvement or you are collaborating with the unit or team in charge of maintaining the AI-enabled application. This is most likely to happen in the context of internal AI projects. For external projects with paid clients, you are likely to remain a relevant contact for them, but they will take care of the maintenance activities.

Here are the key aspects you'll need to keep in mind.

AI system and model versioning

Versioning ensures that every iteration of a model and its supporting system components can be traced, reproduced, and compared against previous states. As an AI PM, you will be involved in establishing governance over version control practices, ensuring that documentation is kept current and that stakeholders understand the implications of rolling back or deploying new versions. This activity ties into governance and compliance activities, as documenting system and model versions will enable you to collect all relevant information that may be required by stakeholders such as regulators and clients.

AI incidents management

Failures in deployed AI systems may arise from data anomalies, infrastructure issues, or unexpected model behavior. If you are still involved and leading this phase of the AI project, you may coordinate the creation of incident response plans, define escalation paths, and ensure that the maintenance team has the resources and protocols to resolve failures quickly while communicating transparently with stakeholders.

Real-time monitoring and AI model auditing

Monitoring and auditing provide visibility into how AI systems behave under production conditions, tracking performance, fairness, and compliance. You or the PM in charge of the maintenance phase will ensure that monitoring tools are integrated into operations, audit logs are available for internal or external review, and findings are systematically translated into corrective or preventive actions.

AI model drift detection and retraining strategies

Model drift describes the decline in performance that occurs over time as data patterns shift. Addressing this depends on the specific foundations your team has created in the previous deployment phase, and you may need to oversee the definition of drift detection thresholds, ensure that retraining schedules are in place, and balance the operational cost of retraining with the business need for accuracy and reliability.

Documented end of lifecycle

When the AI application reaches the end of its useful life, a structured retirement plan prevents disruption and safeguards organizational knowledge. The AI PM in charge is responsible for coordinating the decommissioning process, ensuring that data and models are archived appropriately and that a full record of the system's lifecycle is documented for compliance and future reference.

This part of the project will rely heavily on the delivery context. If you have already delivered your AI development to a different department or client, then you won't be leading this phase. However, remember that as an AI PM, you are likely to have a great deal of aggregated knowledge from the different development activities, and this knowledge can be very helpful to the people in charge of the final maintenance and decommissioning phases. Make yourself necessary and available. Also, you may want to revisit the entire project lifecycle and note specific assets and activities from each phase that you want to highlight as relevant for the postdelivery activities.

Not every AI PM will work for a model provider like OpenAI or Anthropic. However, even if you don't work for this kind of company, it can help to understand what the different training phases are and how your team can leverage existing models to adapt them to your specific project needs. Let's explore some considerations from the perspective of the GenAI model training lifecycle.

Lifecycle for Generative AI Model Training

While most AI project lifecycles follow a similar kind of training and inference model pattern, GenAI brings a new level of complexity. AI PMs working for AI model builders such as OpenAI, Anthropic, Google DeepMind, Microsoft AI, and other frontier labs need to adapt to a completely different pattern: pretraining, posttraining, and inference. The same is true for PMs who work for companies that leverage pretrained models from these labs and then decide to fine-tune them for advanced tasks, performance, or even security adjustments. Keep in mind that many AI projects nowadays leverage GenAI technologies, so you are likely to see this pattern during your career.

The training process relies on several stages related to the GenAI model lifecycle, which includes the steps from initial model conception and parametrization to the final customization and consumption. The specifics depend on the model version and provider. Figure 5-12 shows a general overview of techniques and steps for each stage.

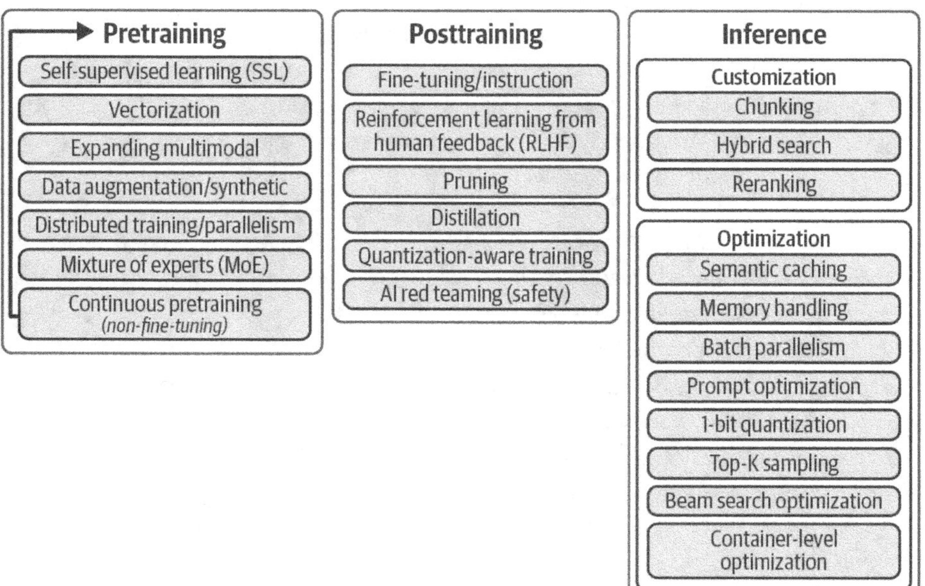

Figure 5-12. GenAI techniques from training to inference

These stages and steps are critical because they are part of an area of knowledge that is still unfamiliar to many: training and customization techniques that determine the overall scope of knowledge and performance of the models you will use for your GenAI projects.

PRETRAINING

In this foundational phase, the model learns from large-scale, unstructured datasets to develop a fundamental understanding of language, grammar, and contextual relationships. This phase is typically covered by the AI model provider.

Depending on the model and the training approach, the pretraining phase may include techniques such as these.

Self-supervised learning (SSL)

In this type of unsupervised learning, a model generates its own labels from the data rather than relying on human annotations. It allows language and multimodal models to learn representations autonomously from text, images, or other content. Unlike supervised learning, where labeled data is required, SSL leverages inherent structures in the data. The model is trained to predict missing or occluded parts of its input (e.g., predicting masked words in a sentence). This approach brings efficiency gains and reduced reliance on human labeling, resulting in lower operational costs and faster model iteration cycles.

The SSL process relies on infrastructure and computing power via GPUs. The compute requirements depend mostly on the amount of information, training iterations, and intended model size, among other factors.

Vectorization

This technique converts raw text into numerical representations (known as *embeddings*) that a model can process. Compared to regular one-hot encoding that treats words as discrete, independent symbols, the goal of embeddings is to encode the semantics and relationships between words efficiently. This means that words, sentences, or documents are transformed into multidimensional vectors, where similar words are closer in vector space. These models are used for text similarity, semantic search, and RAG use cases. There are different embeddings techniques, depending on the vectorization scope:

Word embeddings

Word2Vec, GloVe, and FastText generate static word representations. These embeddings are dense vector representations of words that encode both semantic meaning and relationships in a continuous, high-dimensional space. They capture contextual similarities, allowing models to understand relationships such as synonymy, analogy, and context awareness.

Sentence embeddings

Models like Sentence-BERT (SBERT) and Universal Sentence Encoder provide vectorized sentence representations, which are numerical embeddings that capture the semantic meaning of entire sentences rather than individual words. Unlike traditional word embeddings, which provide static representations of words, sentence embeddings take context into account and provide a more holistic understanding of the input text.

Contextual embeddings

These embeddings dynamically change based on surrounding words. They are generated using deep neural networks, particularly transformer-like algorithms, and can handle highly changing contexts, polysemy (words with different meanings), and higher dimensionality to include more features to represent information in vector spaces.

Expanding multimodal

Traditional LLMs process only text, but multimodal models integrate multiple types of data, such as images, video, and audio. In pretraining, the model can learn joint representations across different modalities, allowing it to first understand and then generate diverse types of content. The main advantage comes from doing so in a native way, instead of combining multiple models during the integration and inference tasks. However, this requires a large-scale dataset covering multiple modalities, and aligning different data types effectively is computationally expensive. Also, multimodality brings new challenges during the inference stage, such as the increased inference latency due to the need to process multiple high-dimensional inputs.

Data augmentation

Data augmentation is a data-centric way to enhance model performance by artificially expanding the training dataset through various transformations. This may include techniques such as:

Synthetic data

This approach involves creating artificial text datasets to enhance training, fine-tuning, and alignment. It helps overcome data scarcity, reduce biases, and generate domain-specific content efficiently. Like regular datasets, it requires techniques such as data quality control and bias reinforcement.

Back-translation

This involves translating a sentence into another language and then back to generate diverse paraphrases.

Synonym replacement

This technique maintains the original meaning while altering sentence structure to create multiple versions.

Noise injection

This technique introduces minor perturbations to the text to enhance robustness against typos.

These and other data generation and augmentation techniques help reduce overfitting and make models more generalizable, and they are especially useful for minority languages where limited labeled data exists.

Distributed training

Training large-scale LLMs requires distributed computing across multiple GPUs to handle massive datasets efficiently. These GPUs are easily accessible via cloud AI infrastructure, but they rely on distributed training building blocks for large-scale training. The value of this approach is clear, but it also brings potential network latency challenges that are usually solved with clear network topologies and interconnected requirements. You can implement distributed training by using different parallelization strategies, including data-, model-, or pipeline-level mechanisms:

Data parallelism

This means that the entire model is replicated across multiple GPUs, with each GPU processing a different mini-batch of data. During training, each replica computes gradients independently, and these are then averaged and synchronized across GPUs before updating the model parameters. This approach is effective when the model fits within a single GPU's memory but requires large-scale data processing, so it is more suitable for highly efficient small language models (SLMs).

Model parallelism

This requires splitting different parts of the model across GPUs to distribute computation. The model itself is split across multiple GPUs, with each GPU handling the different parts. This approach is useful when the model is too large to fit into a single GPU, as it is the case for most of the LLMs. That said, this approach introduces communication overhead.

Pipeline parallelism

In this case, training is split into sequential stages across multiple processors. Fine-tuning is a key part of the posttraining stage, as it modifies pre-trained models for specific tasks by updating their weights using task-specific datasets. There are different stages instead of parts, with each stage assigned to a different GPU, forming a sequential pipeline. The batches are processed in stages, passing intermediate information across GPUs. This method is commonly used in transformer-based models where training large-scale networks requires optimizing both memory and computational efficiency.

Mixture of experts

In Mixture of experts (MoE), the model is based on multiple "expert" subnetworks, where each expert specializes in learning different aspects of the data. During the pretraining, the model dynamically selects a subset of these experts for each input (this is based on the idea of sparse activation patterns), allowing the model to leverage different experts' specialized knowledge for different types of tasks or input features. This approach is designed to make the model more efficient by activating only a subset of the available experts at any given time, reducing computational costs and memory usage compared to using all experts simultaneously.

Pretraining techniques are not widely known by most GenAI adopters, but this section lists a good selection of them. Keep in mind that, unless you are directly involved in training new models, this stage will be mostly covered by the AI model provider. However, you will need to be mindful of the posttraining phase, as your AI team may leverage some of these techniques to adjust preexisting models during AI project implementation.

POSTTRAINING

Once pretraining is complete, models require additional refinement through posttraining techniques to improve efficiency, alignment, performance, and adaptation to certain kinds of tasks. Here are some of the techniques you may hear about.

Fine-tuning

This is the key part of the posttraining stage, as it modifies pretrained models for specific tasks by updating their weights using task-specific datasets. You need to know that *model weights* are the numerical parameters that a model learns during training, which determine how the model processes inputs to make predictions. During the fine-tuning process, the goal is to take the pretrained model and further train it on a smaller, task-specific dataset to adapt it for a particular application. This is effective because fine-tuning adjusts model weights while retaining general knowledge, making it more efficient and flexible in terms of knowledge. There are different ways to perform fine-tuning:

Regular, full fine-tuning
> In this case, all model parameters are updated, requiring extensive computational resources but leading to high task performance.

PEFT fine-tuning
> Based on parameter-efficient fine-tuning (PEFT) techniques, technologies like low-rank adaptation provide an optimized approach that freezes the base weights and updates only the low-rank adapter parameters' weights (instead of all parameters), significantly reducing memory usage.

Fine-tuning includes the notion of *model instruction*. When an LLM is instructed, the model is specifically trained to understand and respond to conversational prompts, where the focus is on aligning its behavior with user instructions. This means the model is designed to follow user commands or queries more accurately, ensuring that its responses match the expected tone, format, or context of the conversation. The model can handle more complex instructions, provide precise answers, and adapt its responses based on the specific guidance given by the user.

From a chat capability perspective, a *non-instructed LLM* could still engage in conversation and generate responses, but it might not always interpret specific user requests properly, which could lead to the generation of more general or less targeted answers or require the user to provide more context. However, most of the non-instructed LLMs are made available for subsequent fine-tuning and not for direct use.

Reinforcement learning from human feedback

RLHF is a method used to fine-tune ML models, particularly LLMs, by integrating human feedback into the training process. After the initial pretraining process, the model is deployed in a controlled environment where it interacts with humans. Human evaluators act as SMEs for specific domains of knowledge and industries and provide feedback on the model's outputs, rating them based on factors like accuracy, relevance, and ethical considerations. This feedback is used to create a reward model, which assigns numerical values to the outputs based on their quality. The model is then optimized using RL techniques so it can learn to adjust its responses and maximize these rewards over time. This process allows the model to align its behavior with human preferences, improving its performance and reducing undesirable outputs.

Pruning

Pruning is a posttraining technique used to reduce the size and complexity of a pretrained model by removing less important or redundant parts, such as weights, neurons, or entire layers. The goal of pruning is to make the model more efficient, improving memory usage and computational speed and reducing inference time while striving to maintain performance. This process is especially useful for deploying large models in resource-constrained environments, like mobile devices or edge computing, where hardware limitations make running full-scale models challenging. You need to keep in mind that there is a trade-off between compression ratio and model accuracy, but pruning is certainly a good option to reach higher efficiencies. Here is the general process:

Step 1

The process of pruning starts with identifying which parts of the model are unnecessary or contribute minimally to its output. This can be done by examining the magnitude of weights, where small weights are considered less important, or using more advanced methods such as sparsity-based pruning, where certain connections between neurons are set to zero or removed entirely. In addition to pruning individual weights, entire neurons or even layers of the model can be pruned if they don't significantly affect the model's performance. For example, some parts of a transformer model, like attention heads, can be pruned without severely impacting accuracy.

Step 2

After pruning, the model typically undergoes fine-tuning to recover any lost performance due to the removal of weights or neurons. This new fine-tuning process allows the model to adapt to its reduced structure while retaining most of its learning and generalization abilities. In this case, post-pruning fine-tuning is essential because pruning can sometimes introduce a loss of accuracy; the fine-tuning helps to restore the model's effectiveness by reoptimizing the remaining parameters.

Steps 3+

Pruning is often performed incrementally, meaning that parts of the model are pruned step-by-step, with performance being evaluated and reoptimized (via iterative fine-tuning) after each step. This helps mitigate the risk of overly degrading the model's capabilities. If too many important components are removed at once, the model could lose its ability to generalize, leading to a significant drop in performance, especially in complex tasks requiring deeper reasoning.

In general, LLM pruning optimizes LLMs by eliminating unnecessary components, making them more manageable for real-world applications and reducing the compute requirements for deployment.

Distillation

This technique trains a smaller model (e.g., an SLM) to replicate LLM behavior, allowing efficient deployment for specific topics and tasks. Distillation helps create more efficient "student" models from larger "teacher" models without sacrificing performance. The goal of distillation is to reduce the size and computational requirements of a model while maintaining a similar level of accuracy, making it easier to deploy in resource-constrained environments with limited processing power. There are two main challenges:

- Performance can be a challenge when distillation does not work for highly specialized teacher models.
- A balance must be negotiated between model size compression and performance.

That said, distillation is a great option for creating smaller language models based on task- or domain-specific scenarios and to deploy on edge devices or even to serve at scale.

Quantization

This technique can serve both training and inference purposes. Quantization-aware training (QAT) is a technique that helps reduce memory and compute requirements of GenAI models by representing their weights and activations with lower precision, preparing them during the training phase for efficient inference. In general terms, this process involves mapping model parameters such as weights to lower-bit representations (there are different levels based on geometric progression values like 1, 2, 4, 8, 16, or 32 bits) to make models more efficient for deployment on hardware with limited resources—like mobile devices, edge devices, and embedded systems—without significantly sacrificing performance. After the initial quantization, the model can be fine-tuned using the quantized parameters to compensate for any loss in accuracy caused by the reduced precision. Keep in mind that most of the current models follow 8- or 16-bit patterns, such as INT8 (integer) or FP16 (half precision).

AI red teaming (AI safety)

These are safety and security techniques that are applied at different times in the model lifecycle. They are applied posttraining to ensure that the model behaves properly, and continuous red-teaming activities are done to challenge and evaluate the model in different test scenarios. Please note that AI red-teaming practices are evolving quickly, and they can now be applied earlier, during pretraining, and later, during the inference and customization steps.

This overall training process includes multiple steps that collectively support obtaining something between good and superlative GenAI models. Even if the pretraining activities will be covered by the technology provider, you may need to explore some posttraining techniques with your data scientists and AI engineers, either to achieve a higher level of model performance or to adapt existing models to specific tasks and contexts.

INFERENCE

This topic refers to the process of using a GenAI model to generate outputs or predictions based on new, unseen input data. During *inference*, the model takes an input prompt and processes it to produce a response, leveraging the patterns and knowledge it has learned during its pre- and posttraining phases. This process is distinct from end-to-end training, as the model does not update its parameters during inference but instead simply applies the learned knowledge to make predictions.

Customization

After the initial training stages, the customization phase adapts the model for real-world applications. Some techniques used for customized inference are:

Chunking

This technique involves breaking long documents or datasets into smaller, more manageable segments, or "chunks," to improve information retrieval before processing inference queries. Since LLMs have a limited *context window* (i.e., they can only process a certain number of tokens at a time), chunking is a way to handle long documents. This technique improves retrieval efficiency in RAG systems and enhances performance in tasks like summarization, question answering, and document search by complementing models with specific knowledge bases.

Hybrid search

This approach combines keyword-based (lexical) search and semantic, embeddings-based search to improve information retrieval. Keyword-based methods rely on exact word matches, making them precise but limited when queries use synonyms or paraphrasing, while semantic search uses vector embeddings and retrieves results based on meaning rather than exact word matches. Semantic search improves recall but sometimes returns less precise results. By combining both methods, hybrid search ensures more accurate and comprehensive retrieval, making it ideal for assistants, search engines, and document retrieval in RAG systems.

Reranking

After retrieving an initial set of results, reranking applies a re-ranker model to reorder the results based on deep contextual relevance. Unlike traditional ranking methods that rely on precomputed scores, these re-rankers dynamically compare the query with each document, leading to more accurate rankings, especially for complex queries. While reranking significantly enhances precision in retrieval systems, it comes with higher computational costs, so it is typically used in a two-stage pipeline where hybrid search selects candidate documents first and reranking optimizes their order.

Optimization

During the inference phase, there are various optimizations that help improve response quality, efficiency, and speed for real-word applications. They are all complementary to each other. The list includes:

Semantic caching

This is the practice of storing and reusing the results of previous GenAI model queries based on their underlying meaning or semantic content. Instead of recomputing the entire output for every request, the system caches results for queries with similar meanings or contexts, allowing for faster responses by retrieving cached outputs for similar inputs. This is particularly useful in scenarios where identical or similar prompts are frequently requested, as it reduces the computational load and improves efficiency. Semantic caching relies on understanding the content and context of the inputs, enabling intelligent reuse of past results without requiring full model inference for every new query.

Memory handling

Efficient memory handling in LLMs combines several innovative approaches to optimize memory usage and improve model performance. These techniques dynamically allocate memory resources, manage large key-value caches, and reduce fragmentation to ensure that memory is used effectively during inference. By separating memory encoding and retrieval processes, some methods enable the model to store and access long-term contextual information, enhancing its ability to handle tasks involving long-form content. Additionally, models are equipped with the ability to explicitly store and retrieve knowledge in structured formats, improving their capacity for reasoning and handling complex, knowledge-intensive tasks. Temporal memory management further ensures that the model can adapt and update its knowledge over time, leading to better performance in tasks that require long-term understanding and context. Together, these strategies improve memory efficiency, scalability, and responsiveness across a wide range of applications.

Batch parallelism

With this technique, you can process multiple requests simultaneously for scalability. It involves processing multiple input prompts simultaneously in a single batch rather than sequentially. This approach allows GenAI models to generate multiple pieces of content (e.g., text or images) at once, leveraging the parallel processing power of hardware accelerators like GPUs. By processing inputs in parallel, batch parallelism reduces inference time, improves hardware utilization, and increases throughput, making it ideal for high-demand, large-scale applications. However, it may introduce some latency for individual requests and require more memory, especially for complex tasks or large batches.

Prompt optimization

Prompts can be optimized by carefully designing them to improve model responses and compressing them to speed up LLM inference. Prompt optimization can also focus on analyzing and improving the provided prompt based on advanced techniques that retrofeed the original prompt request to obtain better results.

1-bit quantization

You learned about quantization in the discussion of the posttraining stage. Microsoft BitNet (*https://oreil.ly/hoxoa*), released in 2024 by the Microsoft Research team, is a framework that performs a specific type of quantization that enables highly efficient inference of 1-bit quantized LLMs on CPUs instead of GPUs, significantly reducing memory usage and computational requirements.

Top-K sampling

This technique injects randomness into the inference process of LLMs while ensuring that the model only selects tokens from the top K most probable ones. The idea is to control text generation randomness to obtain coherent responses. When generating text, an LLM predicts the next word (or token) based on its current context. Instead of always picking the token with the highest probability, top-K sampling limits the pool of candidate tokens to the top K most likely options. From this restricted set, the model randomly selects a token, introducing variability into the generated text. This randomness helps the model avoid deterministic outputs while allowing diverse and creative responses.

Beam search optimization

Compared to top-K sampling, beam search optimization is a more systematic, deterministic approach, aimed at optimizing the overall sequence of tokens rather than individual token choices. During inference, LLMs use this technique to explore multiple potential sequences of words at each step and select the sequence that maximizes the overall probability of the entire sequence. Instead of selecting just the most likely next word, beam search keeps track of the top N sequences at each generation step, expanding each sequence with the most probable tokens. This allows the model to explore multiple "paths" in parallel, leading to more coherent and contextually accurate outputs, especially in complex or long-form generation tasks.

Container-level optimization

These techniques offer significant advantages for LLM inference by automating GPU node provisioning, optimizing resource utilization, and reducing operational costs through the use of lower-end GPUs for distributed workloads. Additionally, there are tools that provide fine-grained control over model configurations, data security, and fine-tuning parameters, allowing for tailored deployments while maintaining privacy and security. These features collectively streamline LLM inference, making it more efficient, cost-effective, and flexible for various AI applications.

This section has discussed various complex training cycles and techniques, along with common considerations during the inference phase. The AI project management lifecycle is a highly evolving area, with new techniques and libraries emerging continually, that nonetheless is starting to see some degree of standardization at the industry level. You, as a modern AI PM, will decide how much of your professional development you want to devote to learning the technical details so you can better guide discussions with your data and AI teams.

Conclusion

As you have seen in this chapter, there is no limit to how much you can expand your knowledge. Getting more specialized and technical will always help you be more relevant and facilitate more productive discussions with your technical teams. Regardless of the kind of AI you use for your projects, you have learned about the relevant lifecycle considerations. At this point, you should be able to identify your role and activities from end to end. That was this chapter's goal: to equip you with knowledge and a holistic overview of projects and lifecycles so you can adapt your AI project management toolkit and approach appropriately.

Chapter 5 Notebook

Tools for Managing AI Projects

The previous five chapters have explored topics such as core AI technologies, project lifecycles, AI project management approaches, and your evolving role as a modern AI project manager. This will all be useful as you seek to embrace the AI project management mindset, but you also need tools that let you implement your own approach.

In this chapter, you'll find information about all the tools and platforms used to manage (and participate in) AI projects, at both the managerial and technical levels. You can use these pages as the initial blueprint for building your own AI project toolkit, a curated set of systems that will help you facilitate your AI management tasks.

We will cover three categories of tools that you need to be familiar with, as shown in Figure 6-1.

Figure 6-1. Categories of tools for managing AI projects

These three categories represent the key tooling elements that you need in your pocket to manage AI projects end to end. They will help you handle everything from strategic planning to model deployment, giving you visibility across the AI lifecycle and a structured foundation for collaboration between business and technical stakeholders.

While some examples in this chapter will mention well-known vendor tools, the intention is not to recommend specific products or brands but to outline tool categories and their practical purposes for your AI journey. You'll then be able to design your toolkit based on your organization's maturity, budget, and preferred stack and tools. Please use the "Chapter 6 Notebook" on page 249 to jot down existing and potential tools, including those you may need to explore further because they are entirely new to you.

Now, let's get started with the core project management tools that will enable you to manage your AI initiatives, including the types of platforms you need in order to keep track of, document, and implement them. They are not exclusive to AI projects, but they will certainly remove roadblocks in and reduce the complexity of your AI initiatives.

The AI Project Management Tool Trifecta

Managing AI projects effectively requires a combination of visibility, structure, and traceability across several domains, including data, models, code, and collaboration. These three pillars form what we call the *AI project management tool trifecta.*

AI project tracking

These are the classic PM tools that ensure visibility into progress, dependencies, and deliverables. Boards and backlogs will help you keep track of your team's progress and the remaining activities to complete your project. This functionality is especially relevant for you as an AI PM, as AI projects will certainly involve multiple parallel workstreams. Robust tracking tools will help you synchronize these complex tasks, manage iterative experimentation cycles, and maintain transparency across data scientists, engineers, and business stakeholders.

Knowledge documentation

Documentation and knowledge management tools will help you capture and share technical AI knowledge at the team and company level, keeping in mind that any AI project builds new intellectual property and learnings for your organization. This is essential for your AI PM journey because AI initiatives rely heavily on reproducibility and shared understanding, from dataset preparation techniques to model assumptions and tuning experiments. Proper documentation will help prevent knowledge loss, enable model auditability, and ensure project continuity as teams or technologies evolve. A robust documentation habit will also help you maintain and secure your own knowledge and experience, allowing you to increasingly generalize your knowledge and apply it intelligently to new AI projects.

Technical management

Also known as *code management tools* or *repositories*, technical management systems ensure smooth workflows across data, models, and deployment, as well as automation of the entire AI lifecycle. Remember, managing repositories effectively is crucial to coordinating code, data pipelines, and model versions, ensuring consistent and traceable development. Technical oversight also supports risk management, regulatory compliance, and the seamless integration of AI systems into production environments.

Together, these tools create the operating system of your AI projects, keeping all contributors aligned and your work auditable, repeatable, and explainable. Let's explore some examples of each of these three categories.

PROJECT MANAGEMENT AND BOARD TOOLS FOR PROGRESS TRACKING

You can't manage what you can't visualize. This is especially true for AI projects that involve multidisciplinary teams with many different roles, such as data scientists, ML engineers, analysts, product owners, and compliance experts, each with different skill sets and mindsets, working on multiple tasks that are often interconnected. This kind of complex project scenario operates with different rhythms and deliverables, often asynchronously. So your job is not only about visualizing the activities but also about making sense of their entire extent, one sprint at a time.

Without the right tracking and coordination tools, it's easy for priorities to diverge or dependencies (e.g., an output from data engineers that becomes input for data scientists) to be missed. Modern project-tracking tools like Jira, Azure DevOps, Trello, Asana, and Notion go beyond basic task lists. They provide dashboards for burndown rates, team velocity, sprint analytics, and even predictive workload estimation.

For AI projects, these tools should help you include detailed milestones related to dataset curation and validation completion, model experimentation and testing checkpoints, ethical and compliance review stages, and model deployment readiness levels. From an experimentation point of view, these tools will help you scope mini experimentation sprints, allowing you to plan and track experimentation cycles and iterations with your team.

Keep in mind that AI projects are already very complex, so you want to remove any unnecessary complexity. By integrating these checkpoints, you will move beyond traditional software management to AI lifecycle visibility, where progress is measured by data work and model performance, not just lines of code or complex tasks. And to do so, you need tools that will make your life a bit simpler. Table 6-1 shows a representative selection of project-tracking tools you can use as a baseline for your own exploration.

Table 6-1. Summary of project management and board tools

Tool	Primary use	Example use cases
Jira/ Linear/ Azure DevOps	Agile sprint tracking, backlog management, burndown charts	Tracking data-labeling progress and ML model development sprints
Trello/ Asana	Lightweight Kanban workflows for small or hybrid teams	Managing proof-of-concept experiments or pilot AI initiatives
Notion	Combined task tracking, documentation, and dashboards	Linking sprints with dataset quality scores or experiment results
ClickUp	Integrated PM and time tracking with AI summaries	Predicting delivery bottlenecks and assigning resources dynamically

These are just a few examples of modern project management tools. Explore other tools and determine which one would be the best fit, not only for you but also for your data and AI team members, who need to feel comfortable interacting with the tool day-to-day. Based on our experience, you will probably need to prioritize their preferences and adapt to whatever tool works for the project and the team, rather than choosing one based on your own PM criteria and hoping they will adopt it.

DOCUMENTATION AND TRACKING TOOLS FOR AI KNOWLEDGE MANAGEMENT

As you already know, AI projects are knowledge-heavy and iterative. They evolve through cycles of experimentation, evaluation, and refinement, all of which must (or should) be documented for knowledge management, decision traceability, and AI assets reuse. In this case, documentation isn't just about general descriptions, meeting notes, or requirement sheets; it's about capturing the reasoning behind decisions. Why was a particular dataset selected? Why did one model outperform another? How did the team configure those models? And what trade-offs were made during deployment?

In this case, modern documentation platforms such as your internal wikis, Confluence, Notion, GitBook, or Read the Docs provide a structured approach to organizing these insights. At the same time, technical tools such as MLflow, Unity Catalog, or Weights & Biases serve as living repositories of model and parameter history, effectively bridging project documentation and experiment tracking.

If your organization and team are mature enough, you should treat documentation as an important "knowledge product," something that grows over time and gets reused in future AI initiatives. Teams that document well can accelerate future onboarding processes (very relevant for data and AI teams with high levels of rotation), improve reproducibility, and build long-term intellectual capital.

In terms of AI project management, documentation tools can influence two aspects of your own approach. First, you will increase the team's operational discipline, as documentation requires continuous awareness and internal organization to ensure no details are being lost. Second, you can create a dedicated workstream in your backlog for documentation tasks (alternatively, you can make sure that any technical task includes documentation as part of the acceptance criteria) to compensate for the time everyone will spend on this. Remember, most folks out there don't like to switch from their technical activities to "just" document things. Part of your role as an AI PM consists of finding a balanced approach to knowledge management, in which everyone recognizes the importance of proper documentation but it is done in a pragmatic enough way that team members feel they are using their time properly. And, of course, leveraging technical tracking tools will complement the knowledge exercise with automated insights about experiments, data stores, and other AI assets.

Use Table 6-2 as a source of inspiration for you and your team to choose your own documentation and tracking toolkit.

Table 6-2. Summary of documentation and tracking tools

Tool	Function	Example use cases
Confluence/Slab	Knowledge base and collaborative wikis	Recording architectural decisions, datasets used, and experiment notes
GitBook/Read the Docs	Structured documentation publishing	Hosting internal model cards, experiment logs, and decision records
Notion	Dynamic documentation with dashboards	Centralizing sprint updates, meeting notes, and retrospectives

Tool	Function	Example use cases
Weights & Biases	Experiment and model tracking	Recording hyperparameters, performance metrics, and training context
Obsidian/Roam Research	Linked-thought note-taking	Building a web of insights for cross-project learnings

Now that you have explored two-thirds of the tool trifecta, let's move on to technical, code-first management tools. Even if the AI PM does not usually choose these tools, the code repository choice and its connection with project backlog and documentation tools will set you and your team up for success, so pay close attention.

CODE REPOSITORY TOOLS FOR HOSTING AND DEPLOYMENT

Every AI project relies on a robust code management and version control strategy. But this isn't just about managing regular code; it also concerns model versions, data snapshots, and configuration files that must all evolve in sync. Platforms like GitHub, GitLab, and Bitbucket offer branching strategies to manage code at different stages of maturity. Depending on your organization and how you organize the code environments, these stages may include research, development, testing, production, and more. This structure must extend beyond general code to include AI models and data versioning, ensuring all three remain in sync across every environment. Make sure you understand your current code setup before you start any development effort.

Regarding data versioning, it is essential that you and your team keep track of the different datasets and feature stores. This is done using tools such as DVC or lakeFS, which will allow you to track datasets and their corresponding model results, ensuring reproducibility.

For open AI model collaboration, the Hugging Face Hub has become an industry reference, enabling developers and teams to share and reuse pretrained models, datasets, and evaluation benchmarks. Tools like MLflow are now widely used to track model versions.

A strong repository culture with proper organization and shared visibility reinforces transparency, auditability, and consistent workflows in your AI development, especially when your team integrates LLMOps or MLOps pipelines and CI/CD systems. For you as an AI PM, disciplined use of a repository tool is a good way to understand your team's AI model development and the code in general. Use access to these repositories for continuous upskilling, and leverage your team members to help you understand as many details as you can. Table 6-3 shows a selection of tools that will help your team manage code, datasets, and pretrained models.

Table 6-3. Summary of code repository and other tools

Tool	Function	Example use cases
GitHub/ GitLab/ Bitbucket	Code, model, and workflow management	Storing and versioning ML pipelines or model codebases
DVC/lakeFS	Dataset and experiment versioning	Tracking datasets used in specific training runs
Hugging Face Hub	Pretrained model and dataset sharing	Publishing and benchmarking NLP or vision models

Now that you have explored the three project, documentation, and code elements of your AI project management toolkit, let's analyze how AI can enable your PM journey. While "AI project management" is the main topic of this book, we are going to explore "AI for project management" for a bit.

Your AI-Enabled Tools for PM Productivity

At this point, you already know that the role and scope of the AI PM is changing fast, and the job includes all sorts of technical and PM factors that will impact the way you lead your projects. In order to remove complexity and free up time for you to upskill while managing your projects beyond regular coordination and reporting, you will need to rely on AI-augmented productivity tools that amplify your analytical, managerial, and creative capabilities. You are probably using general tools like ChatGPT or Copilot, but there are specific AI tools and features that will directly impact your project management work.

As you explore AI tools, remember: they don't replace your role and certainly not your own judgment. In fact, they actually enhance your focus and efficiency by automating repetitive work and summarizing complex updates. From a daily AI PM bandwidth perspective, adoption of these tools is a really important way to supercharge and scale up.

AUGMENTED TASK MANAGEMENT

AI-powered task management tools now include predictive features that can help you estimate effort, flag bottlenecks, and even summarize sprint retrospectives. Here are some of these tools:

- Jira, ClickUp, and Motion use AI for autoprioritization, which is a great option when your documentation and task description are high quality.

- Microsoft's Copilot for Planner can summarize project progress and assign tasks based on context, once again relying on existing text-based descriptions and an understanding of the project and team details.

- ChatGPT and Claude Cowork can be used to draft requirement documents, user stories, and use case outlines.

You can use the insights from these tools to optimize workload distribution across the technical and nontechnical team members on your AI project teams, especially when managing hybrid teams. But remember that you are the human-in-the-loop factor, and it's important that any AI outcome be reviewed through the lens of your human expertise and specific knowledge of your company, project, and team members.

DISCUSSIONS AND PROJECT KNOWLEDGE COLLECTION

As an extension of general documentation activities, team communication in AI projects often involves complex technical discussions, and losing those insights in chat threads or endless emails is a common risk. Modern communication tools now offer AI summarization, contextual tagging, and semantic search capabilities. For example, you can use functionality in Slack, Fireflies.ai, Otter.ai, or Microsoft Teams with Copilot to summarize meeting transcripts, surface decisions, or even automate task creation via integrations with the project backlog.

You can store those AI-generated summaries in your general documentation hub, as they often contain valuable information about design decisions or anticipated risks. Reviewing those notes can be a valuable source of knowledge for your own upskilling journey, and they may even help you spot new activities that you need to add to the project backlog.

ACCELERATED IDEATION AND PROTOTYPING

With generative AI tools becoming ever more powerful, ideation for AI projects is evolving rapidly. You can now brainstorm, visualize, and prototype faster than ever. Think about the possibilities from your perspective as an AI PM. You can expand the scope of your activities to become even more relevant to different aspects of the AI project exploration phase. Indeed, these tools are the superpowers that can help you close any technical gap you may have. Here are some tools you may want to try out:

- Miro or Figma with FigJam AI for collaborative brainstorming with technical and business stakeholders
- Runway, Midjourney, or Gamma for generating presentations from prompts
- Tools like Balsamiq (this one has no AI features, but it is simple and powerful) and Figma for application mock-ups
- Replit and Lovable for application and website prototyping, one of the most exciting areas of generative AI innovation
- GitHub Copilot, Claude, or Gemini via Google Colab to create data visualizations

Treat these generative AI tools as accelerators. They will help you translate early-stage ideas and existing pieces of information into tangible visual or textual artifacts quickly, not only making your AI PM life a bit easier but also enhancing how your value is perceived by the rest of your team and stakeholders. Table 6-4 provides a summary of categories and tools that you may want to review when you turn your attention to testing new tools.

Table 6-4. Summary of AI tools for PM productivity

Category	Tool	Example use cases
Task management	ClickUp, Motion, ChatGPT, Claude, MS Planner with Copilot	Autoprioritizing backlog tasks and predicting delivery risks
Discussions & notes	Slack AI, Fireflies.ai, Otter.ai	Capturing and summarizing model review meetings
Ideation & prototyping	Figma, ChatGPT, Runway, Gamma, Claude, Lovable, Replit	Creating wireframes, presentation drafts, and web prototypes for stakeholders

Remember: AI tools in this category are evolving literally every month, with new startups creating new kinds of solutions that expand on prior capabilities.

The superpowers you can develop with these tools are ever growing, so please make sure to keep track of new AI product announcements, names of startups that come up in team discussions, and new trials of nascent but promising tools.

Let's now focus on the core types of tools we use to enable AI developments. The next section deals with the full technology stack, with all the hardware and software elements that help data and AI professionals implement their AI projects.

The Technology Stack for AI Projects

The notion of a *technology stack* refers to a set of technologies used to build and run specific kinds of applications or tools, and the term *stack* describes how these different components are layered on top of each other to form a cohesive system. The baseline layers are usually required for the others to work (e.g., you need compute infrastructure to run the models on top, and you need them all together to build an application). Figure 6-2 will help you visualize the types of tools you will learn about in this section.

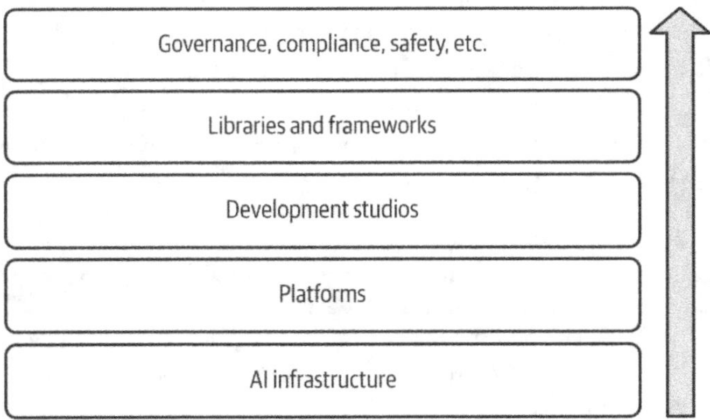

Figure 6-2. AI technology stack

This technical piece of your AI toolkit supports experimentation, model development, deployment, and governance. Even if you're not the primary user, understanding these components helps you manage technical dependencies and evaluate trade-offs. Even more important, from a PM perspective, it is critical to know the types of tools your team will be using, as sometimes you will contribute to the tool testing and procurement discussion. In that case, you want to find suitable tools for the level of technical knowledge within the team and for the type of project and ambitions of your organization.

AI INFRASTRUCTURE

The term *base infrastructure* refers to the mix of core services, IT networking, and interconnections between the services, computing capacity, and other resources (e.g., storage and memory) that are required to enable any application.

There are some technical assets you need to understand to manage your AI projects adequately. As you review these, keep in mind the difference between training a model and consuming it and the implications of using different types of models for your AI projects (e.g., ML processes less data and parameters than DL or LLMs and therefore requires less compute power).

CPUs and GPUs

CPUs and GPUs are the holy grail of technical implementations, representing the compute capacities that enable any AI project. Recall the types of models from the deep dive into technology in Chapter 2 and the lifecycle steps from Chapter 5. Each model has different capacities and trade-offs, and different levels of performance are required at different stages of the lifecycle. In simplest form, a model encapsulates a series of mathematical and statistical operations that require a machine that can crunch numbers at a proper pace, depending on the scale of the model.

While CPUs have been a commodity since the advent of personal computers (e.g., microprocessors from companies like Intel or AMD), GPUs have become the norm. GPUs have evolved from being just graphics cards for video games to being the engines that support the computing power required to run most modern AI models. Companies like NVIDIA saw an opportunity to create specialized hardware that optimizes all the operations required for AI-modeling activities.

In your AI projects, with the details depending on your organization's context, you will encounter technical environments that access those capabilities in very different ways. For example, if your organization has acquired hardware in the form of big servers, then there will be a specific amount of resources that your team can access, perhaps by asking your IT department for a GPU quota. The total amount of available resources will be limited by the earlier hardware acquisition decision, which was based on the organization's capital expenses (CAPEX) investment. CAPEX can evolve over time if your organization decides to buy more hardware. As you manage AI projects, keep in mind that this setup can lead to technical barriers if the resources are not estimated in advance during the exploration and mobilization phases. Moreover, finite resources can lead to competing priorities among different organizational stakeholders if multiple initiatives and projects rely on this type of asset.

Again, the key for you to avoid any issue will be to specify the type and amount of GPUs required for your project, and for that, you can only rely on the technical guidance from your team members. With enough level of detail, you can define not only "what" and "how much" but also "when," enabling your organization to allocate more or less resources dynamically to your project, freeing up some capacity once your team has completed the most compute-intensive activities.

Alternatively, if your company doesn't own the infrastructure, you may have a cloud-first context. This means that your organization rents capacity (i.e., operational expenses, or OPEX, investment) from cloud providers such as AWS, Microsoft Azure, Google Cloud Platform, IBM, Oracle, CoreWeave, OVHcloud, Crusoe, or others. In this scenario, the exercise is similar but slightly different. While you still need to quantify resources and plan in advance, accessing more CPUs or GPUs is accomplished via a few clicks by the cloud administrator, by providing access to virtual environments such as virtual machines (VMs). In this case, there is less likely to be competition for compute resources, as you can get as many VMs as you need. The key will be to work with your technical team members to understand how much capacity you will need, which usually translates into what kind of VM series you need. You can get GPU-optimized VMs for AI training purposes, others that are memory-optimized for processing and transforming data, and so forth. The technical mix and level of investment will depend on the nature of your end-to-end AI architectures.

From a cost perspective, CAPEX and OPEX scenarios are similar. As an AI PM, you will help your team define the required resources, and those resources have a direct cost associated with them. That cost impacts the ROI calculation that is always necessary to justify the value of your AI projects and that supports the prioritization that occurs during the first exploration phase.

Also, keep in mind that sometimes you will face hybrid scenarios. For example, your organization may decide to train the models with local infrastructure but then deploy the new model via cloud infrastructure.

Other computing units

AI infrastructure has evolved over the years, not only developing increased capacity to handle bigger models but also adding new ways to consume it. There are even new technologies that bring the promise of more efficient computing.

As you consider the implications of infrastructure for your AI projects, keep in mind two concepts: provisioned throughput units (PTUs) and Tensor Processing Units (TPUs) (*https://oreil.ly/LpFcp*). They sound similar, but they aren't the same. PTUs are a fixed-cost kind of capacity that big cloud providers sell as a reserved instance to get access to a specific number of interactions (tokens per minute) to run LLMs such as GPT-5 or Claude and build applications at scale. TPUs are an AI-first kind of infrastructure from Google that provides high computing capacity with a good performance-to-cost ratio.

The nature of your projects and organizational context will dictate whether these two elements are relevant for your AI implementations, but make sure to bookmark them in your browser and understand pricing and capacity in case you ever want to use them.

Now that you understand the base infrastructure layer, let's explore the platforms that sustain innovation on top of the AI infrastructure.

PLATFORMS

The platform level is the entryway to technical capabilities, as it helps create new deployments and architectures that sustain your AI projects. It is the foundation for model inference, connection to data sources, and application development. It leverages the baseline infrastructure with compute resources, storage environments, networking elements, and orchestration platforms.

AI cloud studios

This category includes tools that your team can use, like Amazon SageMaker AI and Amazon Bedrock, Microsoft Foundry, or Google's Vertex AI. These kinds of studios are visual interfaces that facilitate access to specific resources such as prebuilt models (often accessible via agnostic model catalogs and API endpoints), make it possible to build or adjust other models, and provide the resources necessary to connect those models with specific data sources and other monitoring, security, and compliance mechanisms.

If your organization is already leveraging these tools, that's a good sign for your work as an AI PM, as your team won't need to build everything from scratch. If the AI infrastructure is already provided and the platform studio is accessible to your technical team members, you can potentially implement an applied AI approach that focuses on building value rather than using one or two sprints just to prepare the setup.

Development and deployments

Based on standardized technologies like Docker (for containerization) and Kubernetes (for container orchestration), most platforms (whether cloud or not) include the ability to containerize developments that can then be replicated and redeployed to scale up implementations. This capability accelerates deployment at scale for larger AI initiatives, reaching more end users. It will be important for you as an AI PM to understand how implementations can be scaled up.

Underlying data layer

Tools like Databricks, Snowflake, BigQuery, and Microsoft Fabric are important, as they support the creation of *data lakehouse* architectures. This provides a unified data layer that is simple to build, scales cost-effectively without sacrificing performance, and allows you to train and connect with AI models. Which technology is chosen has implications for the eventual AI implementation, so you will want to be aware of the advantages and constraints involved with each of these platforms.

Summarizing, platforms include multiple capabilities. Usually, organizations have already adopted one or several platforms. But if you arrive at an organization in which this part of the technology stack is not consolidated, you will need to help your team consider cost and scalability based on different usage scenarios (e.g., from pilot to production), as both directly impact the project's ROI. Table 6-5 provides a summary of these infrastructure tools with examples and typical use cases.

Table 6-5. Summary of AI infrastructure tools

Tool	Function	Example use cases
Amazon SageMaker AI/Google's Vertex AI/Microsoft Foundry	Managed AI development and deployment	End-to-end workflow from data to production
Kubernetes/Docker	Container orchestration	Deploying reproducible ML services
Databricks/ Snowflake	Data lakehouse and pipeline management	Combining analytics and ML training at scale

Now that you have learned about AI infrastructure and the underlying platforms, let's go to the next layer, where we find the code development environments. Those environments can be an extension of the platforms, or they can be separate applications that consume resources from the AI infrastructure.

DEVELOPMENT SUITES

AI development environments centralize data and code-based activities. They're the "workbenches" for your software developers, data scientists, and ML engineers. Your teams are probably already using some of these tools, some of them connected to the code repository platforms you saw earlier in this chapter.

In general terms, they are either notebooks or full integrated development environments (IDEs). Examples include JupyterLab (a classic among data scientists and engineers for any AI implementation with coding languages like Python), Spyder, and Visual Studio (VS) Code for local or cloud-based coding.

Once again, ensure that your chosen studio integrates with your company's CI/CD pipelines and repositories. Disconnected tools are a common friction point and a potential source of inefficiencies for your AI projects. This is unlikely to happen in smaller organizations or with a leadership team of digital natives, but it could occur in larger or more traditional organizations.

Once you enter this code path, you can go as far as you want, exploring different libraries and toolkits. These assets are fundamental to your AI team's success, as they are packetized pieces of capabilities. You don't need to become an expert on these, but at least be familiar with their existence and recognize their names.

Code assistants and prototyping tools with generative AI

Code assistants are AI-powered engines that are either available as online platforms or are embedded directly into development environments. They help AI team members write, refactor, debug, document, and test code more efficiently. Rather than replacing IDEs, they integrate into them and operate within real repositories and production workflows. Examples include:

- GitHub Copilot, which integrates deeply into tools like VS Code and provides inline suggestions and chat-based support

- OpenAI's Codex, which generates functions and scripts from natural language

- Claude Code from Anthropic, which is particularly strong at reasoning across large codebases and supporting complex refactoring

- Cursor, an AI-native code editor built around conversational collaboration with the codebase

These tools are designed for structured, professional software development and support practices like version control, CI/CD pipelines, and formal code reviews.

As an AI PM, you are primarily interested in these assistants because they improve engineering productivity. They reduce boilerplate work, accelerate feature development, help onboard new developers, and increase test and documentation coverage. However, they require governance. It is important to define policies around code review, data privacy, proprietary repository access, and acceptable usage. They are accelerators, but they don't replace science, engineering, and development knowledge.

It is important to differentiate these assistants from another category of AI-powered prototyping builders. Tools such as Lovable, Replit, Windsurf, Bolt, and Base44 focus on rapid application generation from prompts. Instead of assisting developers within an existing codebase, they allow users to describe an application and automatically generate a working prototype, often including frontend interfaces, backend logic, and basic database connections.

These tools are typically designed for speed and accessibility. They lower the technical barrier to creating MVPs and demos, making them attractive to AI PMs, designers, and any team members who want to validate ideas quickly. In many cases, they abstract away traditional development environments and infrastructure setup, making adoption and usage very easy for everyone.

Libraries for non-LLM models

These libraries remain the backbone of ML and DL development. The classic examples are Scikit-learn (sklearn) for traditional ML, TensorFlow and PyTorch for DL, XGBoost and LightGBM for tabular predictive models, and Gensim for NLP.

Even if you as the AI PM are not making decisions about the technical framework, try to influence the decision so that the framework choice aligns with your team's existing expertise, because switching frameworks mid-project adds hidden costs. In many cases, your data scientists and engineers will have a working knowledge of these libraries already, but confirm this before starting the project.

New toolkits for generative AI

GenAI brings to the table a rapidly evolving list of new frameworks and libraries for working with LLMs, multimodal models, and prompt orchestration. If you work with GenAI technologies in your projects, you will certainly learn about these tools. Here are some examples:

- LangChain, LlamaIndex, and Haystack for LLM orchestration
- Transformers from Hugging Face for fine-tuning and model management
- A new set of industry protocols including Model Context Protocol (MCP) from Anthropic, Agent2Agent from Google, and Microsoft Agent Framework

Let's review the two you want to have top of mind for now:

Model Context Protocol
This open protocol, introduced initially by Anthropic and widely adopted by the industry, standardizes how LLM applications connect to external tools, data sources, and systems. MCP allows models to securely access context (like databases, files, APIs, and enterprise systems) in a structured and consistent way, making integrations more modular, interoperable, and scalable across vendors.

Agent2Agent (A2A)
Introduced by Google, A2A enables AI agents to communicate and collaborate with each other. It defines how agents exchange messages, share tasks, coordinate workflows, and delegate responsibilities, allowing multiple specialized agents to work together as part of a larger system. It includes the novel idea of an *agent card*, which is a file with structured metadata that describes an AI agent's identity, capabilities, interfaces, and communication details so other agents can discover and interact with it.

Remember, if you want to learn more about these tools, you need to stay alert for mentions of new startups, libraries, and solutions in the news and in conversations with your team members. You can even bring value to the rest of the team by introducing new options and facilitating their own technical analyses.

GOVERNANCE AND COMPLIANCE

As AI systems scale, governance tools ensure that models remain transparent, fair, and compliant. They offer dashboards, model explainability, bias detection, and audit trails. On the other hand, responsible AI (RAI) frameworks combine technical tools and ethical guidelines to operationalize fairness, accountability, and transparency. Both tools and frameworks can converge to create end-to-end compliance and ethics processes.

Some common examples are:

- Microsoft Purview and IBM's watsonx.governance for enterprise data and model governance

- Fiddler AI or Arize AI for model monitoring and drift detection

- Google's Responsible Generative AI Toolkit, OpenAI's Model Spec, or Microsoft's Responsible AI Standard and other open source libraries such as Fairlearn, AI Fairness 360 toolkit (AIF360), and SHAP (SHapley Additive exPlanations) for bias detection and explainability

Remember: you need to integrate AI governance processes early, not as an afterthought at the end of deployment. These tools and RAI frameworks are living documents that assess project risks at every milestone, in a recurrent and iterative manner.

Tool and Vendor Templates

How you operationalize your toolkit will depend on your organization's current level of AI maturity. This section provides a tooling checklist and a vendor analysis template to assist.

GENERAL TOOLING CHECKLIST

Table 6-6 will help you create a catalog of all the tools you are using or prefer to use for your AI projects.

This extensive table can help you track all the tools available in your organization and even find potential duplication (i.e., two or more different tools used in different areas of the organization that are being used for the same purpose). You can add or remove rows depending on the types of tools in use in your organization.

Table 6-6. General tooling checklist

Kind of tool	Category	Tool type	Primary purpose	Using? ✓	Selected tool(s)
Project management	Project tracking	Agile/Kanban tracking tools	Visualize progress, dependencies, sprints, and AI lifecycle milestones	☐	*e.g., Trello*
		Backlog & sprint analytics	Track velocity, burndown, and experimentation cycles	☐	*e.g., Jira*
	Knowledge documentation	Knowledge bases & wikis	Capture decisions, datasets, assumptions, and learnings	☐	
		Structured documentation publishing	Maintain model cards, decision logs, and experiment records	☐	
		Dynamic documentation & dashboards	Centralize notes, retrospectives, and sprint insights	☐	
		Experiment tracking & metadata stores	Record parameters, metrics, and training context	☐	
		Linked knowledge systems	Cross-project learning and insight mapping	☐	

Kind of tool	Category	Tool type	Primary purpose	Using? ✓	Selected tool(s)
Project management *cont.*	Technical management	Code repositories	Version control for code, models, and pipelines	☐	
		Dataset versioning	Track dataset evolution and training inputs	☐	
		Model versioning	Ensure reproducibility and auditability	☐	
		Model & dataset sharing	Reuse and benchmark AI assets	☐	
Productivity (AI-enabled)	Task management	AI-augmented task planning	Autoprioritization, effort estimation, and risk detection	☐	
		AI-assisted content drafting	Draft requirements, user stories, and use cases	☐	
	Discussions & notes	AI meeting summarization	Capture decisions, risks, and action items	☐	
		Semantic search & context tagging	Retrieve historical project knowledge	☐	
	Ideation & brainstorming	AI-assisted whiteboarding	Collaborative idea exploration	☐	

Kind of tool	Category	Tool type	Primary purpose	Using? ✓	Selected tool(s)
Productivity (AI-enabled) *cont.*	Ideation & prototyping	Rapid design & mockups	Visualize early concepts quickly	☐	
		Generative content creation	Generate presentations and visuals	☐	
		Rapid app & web prototyping	Build demos and proofs of concept	☐	
Technology stack	AI infrastructure	CPU compute	General-purpose processing	☐	
		GPU compute	Accelerated model training and inference	☐	
		Specialized AI compute	High-efficiency AI-first processing	☐	
		Reserved/ provisioned capacity	Predictable large-scale model inference	☐	
		On-prem infrastructure	CAPEX-based compute environments	☐	
		Cloud infrastructure	OPEX-based scalable compute environments	☐	
		Hybrid infrastructure	Combined on-prem and cloud setups	☐	

Kind of tool	Category	Tool type	Primary purpose	Using? ✓	Selected tool(s)
Technology stack *cont.*	Platforms	Managed AI platforms	End-to-end AI development and deployment	☐	
		Containerization & orchestration	Scalable, reproducible deployments	☐	
		Data lakehouse platforms	Unified analytics and ML training layer	☐	
	Development suites	Notebook environments	Interactive experimentation and analysis	☐	
		Integrated development environments (IDEs)	Production-grade AI development	☐	
		Code assistants with GenAI	Accelerated pace of development	☐	
		Prototyping tools with GenAI	Simple and quick prototyping for nontechnical roles	☐	

Kind of tool	Category	Tool type	Primary purpose	Using? ✓	Selected tool(s)
Technology stack *cont.*	Libraries & frameworks	Traditional ML libraries	Classical ML development	☐	
		DL frameworks	Neural network and DL models	☐	
		Tabular modeling libraries	Structured data prediction	☐	
		Classical NLP libraries	Text processing and topic modeling	☐	
		GenAI frameworks	LLM orchestration and prompt workflows	☐	
		Model fine-tuning & management	Adapt and manage foundation models	☐	
		Agent & protocol frameworks	Multi-agent systems and context sharing	☐	
	Governance & compliance	Enterprise AI governance	Data lineage, compliance, and auditability	☐	
		Model monitoring & drift detection	Performance, bias, and drift tracking	☐	
		Responsible AI frameworks	Ethical, transparent, and safe AI practices	☐	
		Explainability & bias detection	Model interpretability and fairness analysis	☐	

TOOL ANALYSIS AND EVALUATION

When selecting a tool, you of course want to take into account whether the tool's features and performance align with your team's needs, and cost is an obvious consideration as well. Another important consideration is how well positioned the tool's vendor is in the industry and the strength of its balance sheet. After all, you want to be reasonably certain that the provider of the tool will continue to support it and continue to innovate to keep up or lead with the latest technologies. Here are a few things to look at when evaluating tools.

Vendor profile

Evaluate the vendor's background, including its industry expertise, years in business, and financial stability. Choosing a tool is also placing a bet on the supplier's ability to deliver new innovations in the near future and over the long term.

Reputation

Research customer reviews, case studies, and analyst reports to gauge the vendor's reliability, trustworthiness, and past performance. Sources like Gartner or Forrester, among others, are usually good high-level indicators.

Pace of innovation

Assess how frequently the vendor updates and improves its products. Does it stay competitive with industry advancements? Its industry partnerships with other AI companies may help you understand how well positioned it really is.

Geographic considerations

For example, if you are located in Canada, you may want to understand the implications of working with vendors from other areas, such as the United States, Europe, or China. There may be complications in terms of applicable regulations, data transfer, sovereignty, etc.

Tool scope

Take into account whether the AI tool covers a broad range of functions or is specialized for a specific task. Either may be appropriate depending on your organization's needs:

Environment

Is the tool hosted in the cloud or on-premises? These options have different advantages. If you choose a cloud-based tool for AI, you also need to understand the level of service (i.e., infra or IaaS, platform or PaaS, software or SaaS, model or MaaS) as this will impact the total cost of ownership (TCO). If you are not familiar with these service configurations, make sure to look them up so you understand the differences.

Features

Decide if the tool should provide only raw AI compute power or include additional capabilities like data preprocessing, model training, governance, compliance, or workflow automation.

Type of models

Does the tool support the AI models (e.g., ML, DL, GenAI) that fit your business requirements? You may want to analyze the type of model license to learn whether the tool leverages proprietary and/or open source models.

AI knowledge scope

You may need to choose between general-purpose AI models and AI solutions tailored for particular industries and use cases. The best option really depends on how you are planning to use the tools; there is no right or wrong choice here.

Compliance and security

Ensure that the AI tool meets the necessary industry compliance standards (e.g., EU AI Act, CCPA, Quebec's Law 25, GDPR, Health Insurance Portability and Accountability Act [HIPAA]) and includes robust security measures to protect data.

Usage considerations

Analyze your internal user profile, as well as how tool pricing/cost will scale with usage. You want to ensure that the tool can support your organization's or team's growth without becoming prohibitively expensive. Think about these factors:

Technical level

Consider whether the tool requires deep technical expertise or supports no-code/low-code interfaces for broader accessibility to members of your team.

Interoperability

Verify up front whether the AI tool integrates smoothly with your existing tech stack, including cloud platforms, databases, and third-party software. Integration could be via API integrations or specific industry connectors.

Customization

Evaluate how flexible the tool is in terms of customization, API integrations, and adapting to your specific business workflows.

Service level

Assess the vendor's support structure, including response times, dedicated account management, and availability of technical assistance.

Pricing model

Understand whether the AI tool vendor will charge you based on usage (pay as you go) or a fixed subscription model, and assess how this aligns with your budget. Make sure you get a proper estimation of current and future costs based on your expected volume and growth scenario. The vendor may provide cost calculator tools.

Treat the following list as a checklist and ask yourself each of these questions during your decision-making process:

Internal considerations

How well does this tool align with the organization's strategic goals, existing workflows, and team capabilities?

Contractual aspects

Are there any hidden costs, vendor lock-in risks, or unclear billing structures that could pose challenges down the line?

Cost-versus-value trade-off

Does the potential value of this tool (as measured in, for example, efficiency, automation, or innovation) justify its TCO?

Potential ROI

What measurable returns in terms of cost savings, productivity gains, or revenue growth can we realistically expect from adopting this tool?

Industry reputation

Is the tool and its vendor well positioned in industry-level assets such as the Gartner Magic Quadrant (*https://oreil.ly/a2-cf*), the Forrester Total Economic Impact reports (*https://oreil.ly/_Wizf*), or the Forrester Wave (*https://oreil.ly/vPbor*)? Is the vendor improving its position to become an industry leader, or are there indicators of decline?

If you are like us and prefer to see all the factors laid out in a table, here is our own tool assessment template. You and other relevant stakeholders can use this to assist in making purchase decisions.

Table 6-7. Tool analysis template

Category	Item	Comments	OK?
Vendor profile	Reputation		☑
	Pace of innovation		☒
	Geographic considerations		...
Tool scope	Environment		
	Features		
	Type of models		
	AI knowledge scope		
	Compliance and security		
Usage considerations	Technical level		
	Interoperability		
	Customization		
	Service level		
	Pricing model		
Key questions			
Internal considerations			
Contractual aspects			
Cost-versus-value trade-off			
Potential ROI			
Industry reputation			
Final recommendation			
Name/Signature			

Conclusion

Your AI projects can be as complex or as simple as you need them to be in terms of technologies and tools. While you don't need to be an expert who understands the details of all AI tools, you do need to be familiar with the main categories of AI project management and productivity tools, and you need knowledge of the technology stack that your teams will leverage for their projects.

Remember, keep a learn-it-all attitude and try to expand the number of tools you're familiar with. In addition, keep tabs on new tools that come on the market; read online news releases, reviews, and user discussions to determine whether a new tool is one you might want to onboard to your organization. As an AI project manager, you will add value by introducing new options to your teams when appropriate.

Don't forget to leverage the tables and checklists provided in this chapter. Develop a regular habit of doing so to reinforce a practice of thorough and rigorous evaluation of your tooling options. And, as always, leverage your "Chapter 6 Notebook" on page 249 to record your new tool discoveries.

Chapter 6 Notebook

Tales of AI Project Innovation

To conclude this journey on a practical note, this chapter offers a collection of insights, recommendations, and past experiences. It serves as a way to integrate the concepts discussed in the preceding chapters with each other and with your lived experience as an AI project manager. We hope these final reflections resonate with you as you embark on your own AI initiatives.

Learnings and Mistakes

Over the last 15 years, we have observed several human and organizational patterns that persist in AI regardless of the technology used. While more powerful infrastructure and advanced models have changed AI implementations in important ways, the fundamental patterns in Figure 7-1 remain the same and will likely continue in the foreseeable future.

You'll notice that these lessons are not about the technology of AI. Instead, they reflect the "soft" side of AI management, the cultural and strategic nuances that determine project success. To navigate these, focus on the following core principles:

Stakeholder education enables adoption

We have seen that educating project stakeholders (such as clients, top executives, and even end users) on AI fundamentals, capabilities, and limitations is essential for collaboration and long-term adoption. When stakeholders understand how AI works and what outcomes are realistic, discussions become more productive, expectations are better managed, and resistance to change is significantly reduced.

Executive sponsors must be informed

Executive support is essential for funding and continuity. However, executive sponsorship is most effective when leaders understand not just the rationale for the project but also the complex details of its implementation. Informed sponsors help remove organizational obstacles, secure resources, and make better strategic decisions, ensuring that AI projects remain supported throughout their lifecycle.

Early end user involvement improves relevance

We have often found that involving end users early in the design process leads to more practical, trusted, and usable AI solutions. Even nontechnical users can provide insights that validate assumptions and help you avoid building technically sound systems that fail to solve real-world problems.

Define "good enough" performance

We have learned the hard way that pursuing perfection is often less valuable than defining a "good enough" threshold. By setting realistic quality thresholds up front, you reduce complexity, control costs, and keep stakeholders focused on business value rather than marginal model improvements. In many cases, the stakeholder's perception of utility matters more than the raw technical metrics. Of course, this requires transparency about the metrics you've chosen and the typical benchmarks for your industry; for example, a health care application demands a different performance level than a marketing tool. It is crucial to explain that the effort and cost required to move from "excellent" to "near perfect" are often exponential and may not yield a proportional return on investment.

Balance automation with human-in-the-loop

We have discovered that, due to both technical and ethical issues, fully automated AI systems are not always the optimal solution. Incorporating human-in-the-loop mechanisms improves accuracy and accountability, especially in complex or high-risk scenarios where human judgment remains essential. And, of course, it helps gain users' trust.

Narrow use cases outperform broad ambitions

AI performs best when applied to focused, clearly scoped tasks. Instead of chasing unrealistic "lessons learned," we recommend analyzing an end-to-end process, breaking it into stages, and designing for specific AI use cases with unique metrics for each.

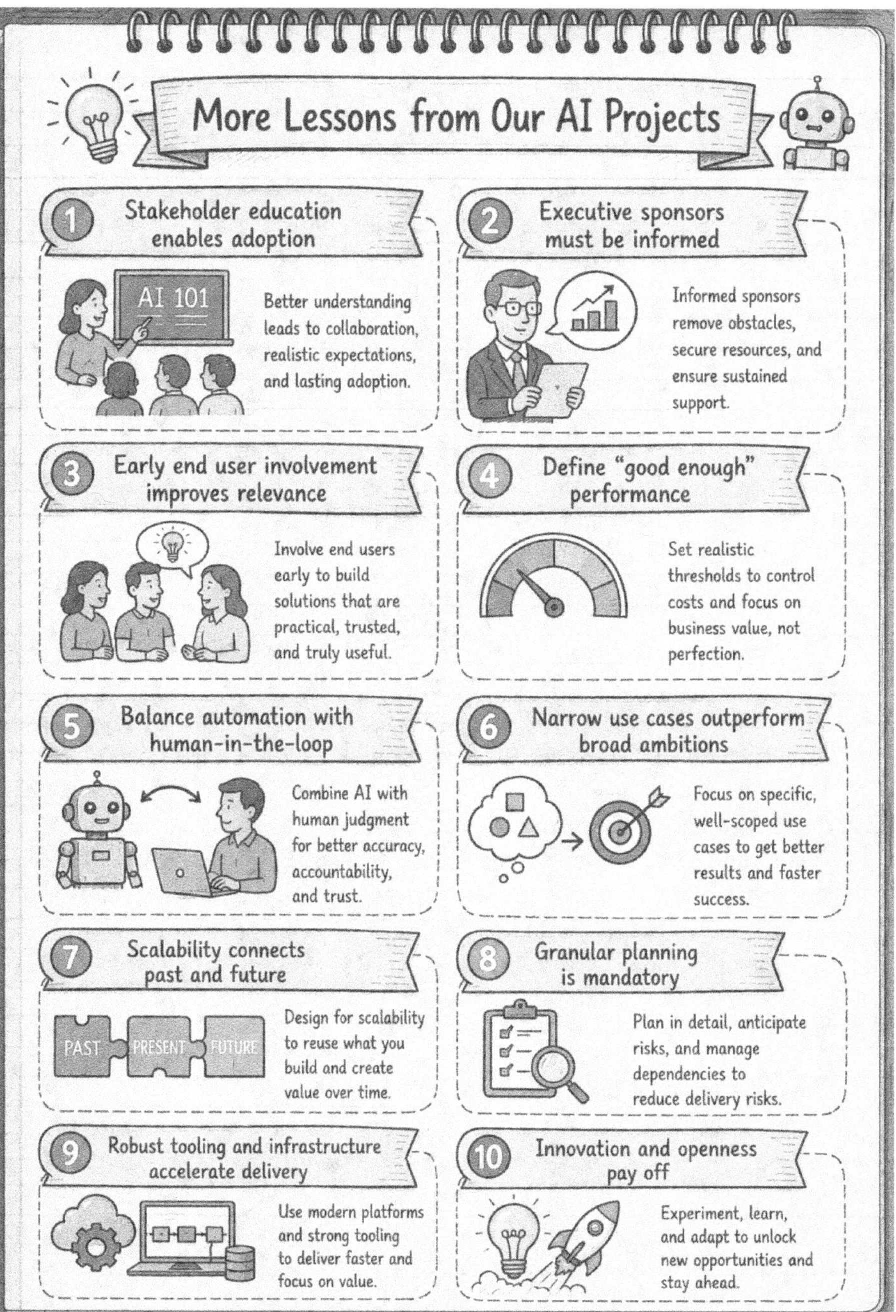

Figure 7-1. Lessons from our AI projects

Scalability connects past and future

Successful AI projects are rarely isolated efforts. By designing use cases with scalability in mind, you can reuse data, models, and infrastructure, building a coherent roadmap that connects previous lessons to future opportunities. This transferable use case strategy can create an optimal sequence for repurposing elements that require heavy investment. As an AI project manager, demonstrating this economy of scale across projects is a powerful way to secure stronger support from your sponsors.

Granular planning is mandatory

AI projects require more detailed planning than traditional software projects. Data quality, model uncertainty, regulatory concerns, and infrastructure dependencies must be anticipated and managed continuously to reduce delivery risks. Don't be afraid to plan the project end to end and then do a deep dive into the details. You'll do this with the help of your team, because they will bring the granular level of technical detail you need to build a highly actionable plan.

Robust tooling and infrastructure accelerate delivery

We have observed that robust AI platforms, tooling, and cloud infrastructure dramatically shorten implementation timelines. Standardized pipelines, reusable components, and mature MLOps practices allow us to focus less on technical setup and more on value creation. But even more important is the overall technology choice. We have seen large corporations reject cloud computing platforms without clear reasons to do so, leaving themselves to rebuild the wheel each time and failing due to a lack of proper human and technical resources. A word of advice: if an organization rejects modern cloud platforms or top-tier tools in favor of legacy infrastructure that doesn't support AI ambitions, proceed with caution.

Innovation and openness pay off

No one has ever made history by playing it safe. We have learned that organizations and teams that are willing to experiment, learn, and adapt consistently achieve better outcomes. Embracing innovation, even with calculated risk, enables faster learning cycles and positions the organization to take advantage of emerging AI capabilities. And with AI, that means some degree of belief—the willingness to take a leap of faith to start building maturity in the organization, step-by-step.

Keep these considerations in mind as you revisit your project lifecycle. Use the four stages of the EMED methodology to find opportunities to implement these best practices. Remember: as an AI project manager, you are the one leading the way in securing sponsorship, driving user adoption, and ensuring your team has the resources to succeed.

Leveraging the Power of Mission

It isn't every day that you find a mission-oriented AI project with a significant social good component, but when you do, the experience is transformative. We have encountered these projects a few times, often within contexts like health care or public safety. An example that stands out is a COVID-related project in Canada (*https://oreil.ly/C9D8G*) that we presented as a case study a few years ago.

That project was unique because it possessed every element of an ideal implementation. Originally, we planned an AI initiative to optimize shipping port logistics. When the pandemic hit in 2020, that project was put on standby; with port activity drastically reduced, there was little left to optimize. However, because we had already completed the exploration phase and a thorough exploratory data analysis, we deeply understood the data sources.

After a few days of thought, we pivoted. We proposed a new AI solution using the same data and team structure to prioritize critical cargo, such as masks and gloves. By using a mix of ML and NLP, we could find these items and predict the best physical setup for offloading while containers were still being prepared at the port of origin.

The concept seems pretty simple. To make it work, however, we needed a key resource: the willingness of executive stakeholders from both partner and competitor organizations to collaborate.

This is where having a sense of mission changed everything. Because of the urgent medical context, everyone was aligned. Roadblocks that would normally take months to clear vanished overnight as parties chose "co-opetition" over rivalry. With full access to human, data, and infrastructure resources, we built an ambitious roadmap that proved remarkably accurate as the project progressed.

Additionally, because everyone felt the weight of the mission, operations experts were heavily involved. Their daily insights were fundamental in creating an AI tool that integrated seamlessly into their morning workflows.

Ultimately, we learned that AI delivers the most value when it is mission-driven. While this project was centered on social good, it also demonstrates scalability for priority shipping and granular tracking, providing a clear ROI.

Remember, when you work on AI projects that start with a strong "why," you will find it easier to prioritize features, allocate resources effectively, and maintain alignment across technical and business teams. Such initiatives also motivate stakeholders to collaborate, avoid unnecessary blockers, focus on key value, and bring to bear all necessary resources.

Managing the Human Aspect

Managing AI projects requires a high level of human collaboration. Even more than traditional software development, AI projects bring together people with a diverse range of academic backgrounds, professional roles, and levels of AI literacy. This trend has been accentuated by the arrival of generative AI technologies, as more organizations and business-related professionals join the development lifecycle.

To succeed, therefore, you must navigate the needs of people with various distinct roles:

Data scientists (junior versus senior)
> AI projects often involve data scientists with very different levels of experience, from recent graduates to highly specialized senior researchers. You will need to adapt your communication style, the technical depth of the discussion, and performance expectations depending on the parties' levels of experience. More junior professionals may need clearer guidance, mentoring, and well-defined tasks, while senior data scientists often require more autonomy and strategic involvement to thrive. Task allocation must consider not only technical skill but also familiarity with the project's domain, data maturity, and tooling. Effective collaboration depends on aligning individual strengths with project needs, ensuring knowledge transfer, and avoiding gaps between theoretical expertise and production-oriented constraints.

Difficult clients
> Some clients or internal sponsors hold extremely high expectations regarding AI outcomes, often influenced by exposure to other organizations' success stories or marketing narratives. These stakeholders may be particularly demanding about deliverables such as slide decks (especially if they come from management consulting backgrounds), demos, or dashboards, sometimes prioritizing aesthetics or buzzwords over technical feasibility. Managing these relationships requires strong expectation setting,

clear communication about trade-offs, and continuous alignment between what is technically achievable and what is being promised. Translating complex AI concepts into compelling yet accurate narratives becomes essential to maintain trust while preventing overcommitment.

In addition, many stakeholders associate AI projects with trendy concepts such as LLMs, DL, or cutting-edge architectures when simpler approaches would better solve the problem. This creates a gap between the perceived value of a certain approach and what the business actually needs. Project leaders must actively guide stakeholders toward the right level of complexity, explaining why certain techniques are appropriate (or unnecessary) while keeping the focus on strategic goals. You will need to reframe discussions around outcomes, impact, and constraints rather than technologies and educate stakeholders without alienating them.

Professionals from diverse fields

AI projects increasingly involve professionals from business, legal, marketing, operations, and other nontechnical domains. While this diversity of perspectives is valuable, often missing is a strong understanding of AI concepts. For example, your nontechnical team members may confuse different technologies (e.g., rules-based systems versus ML versus generative AI). Such misunderstandings can lead to unrealistic assumptions, poor decision making, or misaligned requirements. Successful collaboration depends on building a shared vocabulary, simplifying explanations without oversimplifying reality, and creating feedback loops that ensure everyone understands what the system can and cannot do.

End users

End users are often the people most directly impacted by AI solutions, yet they may have limited visibility into how the system works or why it is being introduced. This can lead to fear of job displacement, resistance to adoption, or mistrust of AI-driven recommendations. In some cases, users may perceive the AI component as a "black box" that overrides their expertise rather than supporting it. Managing this dynamic requires early involvement of end users, transparent communication about the role of AI as an augmentation rather than a replacement, and practical training focused on day-to-day benefits. To ensure a project's acceptance and long-term success, it is just as important to address users' emotional and cultural concerns as to explain technical functionality.

You will undoubtedly encounter other individuals and groups where your soft skills will be your greatest asset. Remember the ADRIAN framework from Chapters 1 and 3; your ability to adapt your communication style based on the stakeholder and the project stage is what will ultimately drive the project to success. It's a challenging task, but one you are well-equipped to handle!

Dealing with AI Impostors

The AI domain presents a strange paradox. On one hand, even seasoned experts can experience impostor syndrome because the field evolves so rapidly that there is always a new tool or buzzword to master. On the other hand, there are a growing number of *AI impostors*, or individuals who speak with extreme confidence but possess little to no actual knowledge. Their influence can easily derail organizational decisions and jeopardize your projects.

To protect your team's productivity and the company's investment, you must monitor these key warning signals:

Dominating discussions without substance
> AI impostors often compensate for a lack of depth of knowledge by speaking frequently, interrupting structured discussions, or steering conversations toward vague, high-level statements. This behavior can derail productive technical or strategic exchanges, consume valuable meeting time, and discourage more knowledgeable contributors from speaking up. Over time, it creates decision fatigue and shifts focus away from concrete actions, deliverables, and evidence-based reasoning.

Relying on generic catchphrases
> Phrases such as "no data, no AI" or "AI won't replace you, but someone who uses AI will" are often used as conversation stoppers rather than as meaningful insights. While these statements may contain a grain of truth, they ignore nuance and context, such as data quality, problem framing, or the suitability of different AI approaches. Their repeated use can oversimplify complex trade-offs, reduce critical thinking, and replace informed debate with slogans.

Confusing technical fundamentals
> A major red flag is the tendency to confound structured and unstructured data, supervised learning and generative models, or real-time and batch constraints as if they were interchangeable. This lack of technical discrimi-

nation leads to unrealistic requirements, poor architectural choices, and misaligned expectations. It often manifests as proposing the same solution regardless of the problem, without understanding the specific data, performance, governance, or infrastructure needs of each AI approach.

Using risks to systematically block progress

Impostors frequently position themselves as "risk-aware" by repeatedly highlighting obstacles such as insufficient data maturity, lack of time, regulatory concerns, or organizational readiness without proposing concrete mitigation strategies. While these issues may be valid, the AI impostor will use them selectively to stall progress rather than to improve execution. This behavior creates inertia, discourages experimentation, and can prevent teams from delivering incremental value.

Reintroducing organizational politics

When technical arguments fail, impostors may shift the focus to internal power dynamics, such as ownership, hierarchy, or "territory." These arguments shift the focus away from user value and business outcomes and toward internal power dynamics. Over time, this erodes momentum and weakens accountability for results.

Defending legacy tools without evaluation

Resistance to change is framed as pragmatism or stability, but it often ignores evolving technical requirements, scalability constraints, or the limitations of legacy systems for modern AI workloads. Such rigidity can lock the organization into suboptimal solutions and prevent teams from adopting more appropriate or efficient technologies.

Invoking vague ethical arguments

AI impostors often invoke ethical concerns in a generic and superficial way, without understanding how these issues actually manifest in the use case, model type, or dataset at hand. Bias is treated as an abstract, universal risk rather than as a measurable, context-dependent phenomenon. Other topics, such as transparency and explainability, are often mixed up and misunderstood. These discussions rarely reference concrete metrics, protected attributes, data distributions, or regulatory requirements, and they often ignore whether the system is even making decisions that could produce discriminatory outcomes. While ethical considerations are critical, this kind of unfocused debate can create unnecessary fear, slow down delivery, and dilute genuinely important governance efforts by failing to distinguish real risks from irrelevant ones.

Your role as an AI project manager is to spot these situations and redirect the conversation toward evidence-based reasoning. AI is highly attractive, and many will try to become the most important voice in the room to further their personal interests. By filtering out this noise, you protect your team's focus and ensure the project stays aligned with its true objectives.

Spotting the Red Flags

One of the most frequent mistakes we have made is being overly optimistic when a project's context appears generally positive. We once managed a project that had everything: client alignment, ample funding, a top-tier technical team, and a rock-solid business case. The big surprise came at the end of the project, when the client demanded higher performance, insisting that any classification model with less than a 95% F1 score was a failure. Whether that threshold was realistic for the use case didn't matter to the client. The real red flag for the project was the lack of initial agreement on "good enough" performance. They didn't mention a target, and we never asked, an oversight that severely damaged the perceived value of the project.

Another example involved an AI initiative where the team was assigned during project mobilization. At the beginning of the execution phase, the company suddenly reallocated senior scientists and engineers to other projects. Internal politics were at play, with competing project leads vying for top talent through nontransparent processes. Instead of getting bogged down in politics, we pivoted to a data-driven approach: we presented an updated roadmap quantifying the pending workload and remaining bandwidth. By clearly showing that the project was not just delayed but at high risk of failure due to the talent gap, we prompted key stakeholders to step in and resolve the situation.

In a third case, we supported a fast-growing SaaS organization in the Europe, Middle East, and Africa region. While the organization's resources handled AI development, we managed the engineering and architecture enablement. The risk was clear up front: the company was expanding into regions where data center scalability would be limited. Even as its AI-enabled SaaS gained market traction, the underlying platform couldn't keep pace. We acted quickly, proposing a technical plan to use multiple regions within the same compliance scope (e.g., EU with GDPR) and dynamically rebalance computing requirements based on a pool of available resources. It took rigorous planning and technical persuasion to convince the client, but the proactive approach saved the platform from a future crash.

The conclusion is always the same: being proactive about monitoring for potential issues pays off. We have found that being direct and honest when sharing risks with clients is the fastest way to earn their trust. This transparency builds a solid foundation that drastically improves stakeholder dynamics throughout the project's execution.

Respecting the Profession

Whether you are an AI project manager or the person responsible for hiring one, you need to cultivate a healthy respect for this hybrid role's key skills. Keep in mind this trifecta of expertise: core role experience (e.g., project management), vertical domain expertise (e.g., health care, finance, supply chain), and technical AI know-how.

Regarding that last item, we are talking about more than just basic AI knowledge. An AI project manager must be able to understand and explain the key fundamentals covered in Chapter 2. Without this knowledge, it is impossible to bring value to a technical team or steer a project toward success.

We have seen many cases where hiring criteria focus heavily on just one axis, or perhaps two for senior roles that clearly require extensive vertical experience. However, hiring a PM without proper AI knowledge is a primary reason why many projects fail. AI initiatives are complex; they require deep, specialized expertise to navigate.

Whether you are building your own career or building a team, prioritize individuals with demonstrable knowledge of the subject matter. At the very least, make sure there is a rigorous upskilling plan in place to help them acquire advanced AI skills within their first 90 days. Respecting the technical depth of the profession is the first step toward project excellence.

Fear of Roadmapping

We've saved this tale for last, not because it is less relevant for your learning journey but because we want it to stay fresh in your mind: most people, regardless of their level of knowledge or experience, do not feel comfortable estimating and creating roadmaps.

This is probably true for most technology projects, but it is a definite reality for AI. The reason is simple: in certain environments, estimations are often accepted as fixed commitments. No one wants to commit when work involves high levels of uncertainty, complexity, or unproven technology.

While there is no magic formula, the following recommendations help you plan more effectively and, more importantly, empower your team to do the same:

Leverage spikes for research

In AI projects, uncertainty is not a failure of planning but a fundamental characteristic of the work. Spikes (time-boxed and well-justified research or exploration tasks) are a practical way to acknowledge this reality while still maintaining structure. They allow teams to test assumptions, assess data quality, benchmark models, validate tooling, or evaluate feasibility without prematurely committing to delivery timelines. Properly framed, spikes reduce long-term risk by transforming unknowns into informed decisions and by creating tangible outputs (findings, recommendations, prototypes) that feed more accurate estimations and roadmap updates.

Decompose work into estimable units

Large, vaguely defined tasks amplify fear of estimation because they hide complexity and ambiguity. Coaching team members to decompose work into smaller, well-scoped backlog items such as data acquisition, feature engineering experiments, model evaluation, or integration steps makes effort and risk more visible. Smaller tasks are easier to estimate, easier to reprioritize, and easier to adapt when assumptions change. This practice also encourages incremental delivery and learning, which is particularly valuable in AI projects where insights often emerge progressively rather than all at once.

Collaborate with technical experts

Estimation and roadmapping in AI projects should not be done in isolation or driven solely by AI project managers or business stakeholders. Data scientists, AI engineers, and data engineers possess critical hands-on experience with similar datasets, models, pipelines, and failure modes. Actively involving them in planning discussions helps surface hidden complexity, realistic dependencies, and practical constraints early on. Their past experiences provide valuable reference points for more accurate estimations. This collaborative approach also increases team ownership of the roadmap, reduces fear of commitment, and ensures that plans are grounded in technical reality rather than optimistic assumptions.

Manage uncertainty with realistic buffers

AI roadmaps should intentionally include buffers at both the task and project levels to account for experimentation, iteration, and rework. These buffers should be explicit and justified, not hidden or exaggerated to protect against unrealistic expectations. When done correctly, they provide flexibility to absorb surprises (e.g., data issues or model performance limitations) without constantly renegotiating timelines. Making uncertainty visible rather than implicit helps normalize it as part of the process and builds trust with stakeholders.

Evangelize the nature of AI roadmaps and estimations

One of the most effective ways to reduce fear of roadmapping is education. Teams and stakeholders must understand that an AI roadmap is a directional planning tool, not a fixed contract. It represents current assumptions, known risks, and prioritized objectives, all of which may evolve as new information emerges. Actively explaining trade-offs, potential pivots, and why estimations are probabilistic rather than absolute helps reset expectations. Over time, this transparency encourages healthier conversations about progress, value, and learning rather than rigid adherence to initial estimates that no longer reflect reality.

As AI maturity grows and patterns become more repetitive, estimation may become easier. For now, uncertainty is part of the territory. Your goal is to make everyone comfortable with the idea of estimating and help them accept that accuracy won't be perfect. Gather as many data points as possible, using sources from expert chats to industry benchmarks, to reassure your stakeholders while protecting your team's ability to innovate.

In Closing

Throughout this book, we have approached AI project management as a craft that sits between ambition and execution—not as hype or theory but as a structured way to move an AI initiative from idea to measurable value. You will do this by leveraging tools like the EMED methodology as well as other PM approaches and AI lifecycles.

One of the central lessons is that AI projects cannot be managed like traditional projects. They look similar on the surface because there are backlogs, sprints, roadmaps, and budgets, but the mechanics are different underneath. Outcomes are uncertain, experimentation is not optional, data quality can redefine scope overnight, and model performance becomes a moving target rather than a fixed acceptance criterion. Treating AI work as predictable feature delivery is often the first mistake organizations make. The AI project manager's job is to introduce structure without killing experimentation and to protect delivery without pretending certainty exists.

You have seen how AI management operates across strategic, tactical, and technical layers. At the strategic level, AI must be anchored to business objectives, governance frameworks, and long-term capability building. At the technical level, it depends on architectures, pipelines, MLOps or LLMOps practices, and disciplined performance monitoring. Your role sits primarily in the tactical layer, but you will only be successful if you understand the other two. You translate strategic intent into scoped initiatives, and you translate technical complexity into business language. The ability to translate in both directions is not an optional skill; it is a structural requirement for AI success.

A recurring theme across the chapters has been intentionality. Intentional use case selection. Intentional scoping. Intentional model choice. Not every problem requires deep learning, and not every workflow needs an LLM. Sometimes a well-structured ML model is more cost-effective, explainable, and operationally sustainable than a cutting-edge generative solution. As an AI project manager, you are responsible for facilitating those trade-off conversations early, before architecture decisions become sunk costs.

We also spent time clarifying what "technical enough" means for you. You will not be expected to train models, but you will be expected to understand the difference between, for example, regression and classification, supervised and unsupervised learning, pretraining and fine-tuning, and model accuracy and business impact. You must be comfortable discussing data pipelines, validation strategies, drift, retraining cycles, and infrastructure implications. This level of literacy allows you to make realistic plans, allocate the right resources, and challenge assumptions when necessary.

The lifecycle perspective is another core takeaway. AI projects do not end at deployment. Model monitoring, feedback loops, retraining, governance checks, and performance tracking are real parts of delivery. If you only manage experimentation and ignore operationalization, you risk falling into proof-of-concept cycles that never scale. If you only focus on production and ignore experimentation discipline, you risk shipping underperforming systems. Effective AI project management holds both phases together and defines clear transition criteria between them.

The ADRIAN framework we introduced is not meant as a slogan but as a practical structure. Analyze before committing. Define scope and success criteria clearly. Resource with realism, acknowledging skill gaps and infrastructure needs. Involve stakeholders continuously, not just at milestones. Agree formally on trade-offs and expectations. Navigate the project actively, nurturing both performance and team capability. When applied consistently, this structure reduces chaos without eliminating necessary iteration.

Another important lesson is that AI project management is as much about expectation management as it is about task management. There is a lot of hype around AI. Executives may expect breakthrough accuracy within fixed timelines. Clients may assume generative AI can replace complex workflows immediately. Engineers may underestimate the organizational friction of deployment. Your role is to ground the conversation in metrics, constraints, risk, and staged delivery. Clear communication of uncertainty is not weakness; it is leadership.

We also emphasized governance and responsibility. AI systems operate in environments shaped by regulation, privacy requirements, ethical considerations, and reputational risk. Transparency, explainability, and compliance are not external add-ons; they influence design decisions, documentation practices, and deployment timelines. The AI project manager often becomes the integrator between compliance, legal, data, and engineering teams. That integration prevents late-stage surprises that can derail entire initiatives.

Perhaps the most practical teaching across the book is this: AI project management is about continuously reconciling tension among three elements: experimentation versus delivery, innovation versus control, and technical ambition versus business value. There is no static formula that will serve, but there is a disciplined method for navigating those tensions.

As AI tooling continues to evolve, the barriers to building prototypes are lower than ever. But the discipline required to turn prototypes into reliable, governed, business-aligned systems remains high. That is the value you will bring as an AI project manager. Remember, successful AI initiatives are rarely the result of algorithms alone. They are the result of clear scoping, realistic planning, structured experimentation, responsible governance, and consistent stakeholder alignment. In other words, they are the result of strong AI project management.

As you reflect on all you have learned in these pages, we encourage you to note your key big-picture takeaways in the Notebook at the end of this chapter. These insights and those you have captured in the other chapters will form the foundation of your future development as an AI project manager.

The frameworks and concepts we covered are just tools; their impact comes from how you apply them. We'll be happy to accompany you on this journey. Feel free to reach out to us.

Malini Jain Runtasewee: *https://www.linkedin.com/in/jainmalini*

Adrián González Sánchez: *https://www.linkedin.com/in/adriangs86*

Chapter 7 Notebook

F

W

waiting, 163

waste types in Lean, 163

Waterfall methodology, 148-152

weekly summaries, 146

Weights & Biases, 96, 138, 225, 226

Williams, Ronald, 34

Windsurf, 236

word embeddings, 67, 208

Word2Vec, 67, 68, 208 

work agreements, 141

work in progress (WIP), 155

wrong project choices, 127

X

XGBoost, 46, 236

XP (see Extreme Programming)

About the Authors

Malini Jain Runtasewee is a senior cloud and data project manager at Toptal and a lecturer at IE University, Escuela de Organización Industrial, and EIP International Business School, where she teaches data and AI project management. She is also a coauthor of an AI fundamentals book published by ANAYA Multimedia. She has extensive experience leading the delivery of cloud and data initiatives across a diverse range of industries, working with organizations of varying sizes, from startups to large enterprises. Her international experience spans Canada, the United States, and Spain, where she has managed complex projects involving data platforms, artificial intelligence solutions, and digital transformation programs. Her work focuses on aligning business objectives with technological execution, enabling organizations to effectively operationalize data and AI capabilities in a scalable and sustainable manner.

Adrián González Sánchez is a product manager, AI & search at Microsoft AI, an academic director at IE University, and an author of multiple O'Reilly and Packt books and reports. He has previously worked for several AI companies in Europe and North America. He is part of a number of international initiatives, including the Spanish Observatory of Ethical and Social Impact of AI (OdiseIA) and The Linux Foundation, as well as the expert group for the EU AI Act Sandbox with the Spanish Government in Europe. He is a trainer for the École des Dirigeant(e)s at HEC Montréal and Concordia University in Canada, and he has released multiple online courses with O'Reilly Media, LinkedIn Learning, and The Linux Foundation. He also collaborates with 2U/GetSmarter as a tutor for MIT Sloan's AI executive courses. His areas of expertise include AI leadership and project management, responsible AI systems implementation, data and AI governance and compliance, and cloud computing.

Colophon

The cover art is by Susan Thompson. The series design is by Edie Freedman, Ellie Volckhausen, and Karen Montgomery. The cover fonts are Gilroy Semibold and Guardian Sans. The text fonts are Adobe Myriad Pro, Adobe Minion Pro, and Scala Pro, and the heading font is Benton Sans; the code font is Dalton Maag's Ubuntu Mono.

O'REILLY®

Learn from experts. Become one yourself.

60,000+ titles | Live events with experts
Role-based courses | Interactive learning
Certification preparation | Verifiable skills

Try the O'Reilly learning platform free for 10 days.